SALMAN RUS

Contemporary Critical Perspectives

Series Editors: Jeannette Baxter, Peter Childs, Sebastian Groes and Sean Matthews

Guides in the *Contemporary Critical Perspectives* series provide companions to reading and studying major contemporary authors. They include new critical essays combining textual readings, cultural analysis and discussion of key critical and theoretical issues in a clear, accessible style. Each guide also includes a preface by a major contemporary writer, a new interview with the author, discussion of film and TV adaptation and guidance on further reading.

Titles in the series include:

SALMAN RUSHDIE

Contemporary Critical Perspectives

Edited by
Robert Eaglestone and Martin McQuillan

B L O O M S B U R Y
LONDON · NEW DELHI · NEW YORK · SYDNEY

Bloomsbury Academic

An imprint of Bloomsbury Publishing Plc

50 Bedford Square	1385 Broadway
London	New York
WC1B 3DP	NY 10018
UK	USA

www.bloomsbury.com

First published 2013

British Library Cataloguing-in-Publication Data
A catalogue record for this book is available from the British Library.

ISBN: HB: 978-1-4411-3501-8
        PB: 978-1-4411-7345-4
     ePDF: 978-1-4411-4527-7
     ePub: 978-1-4411-9377-3

Library of Congress Cataloging-in-Publication Data
A catalog record for this book is available from the Library of Congress.

Typeset by Newgen Imaging Systems Pvt Ltd, Chennai, India
Printed and bound in Great Britain

Contents

Foreword

KENAN MALIK

When he was a child, Salman Rushdie recalls in his memoir *Joseph Anton*, his father read to him 'the great wonder tales of the East' – the stories of Scheherazade from the *Thousand and One Nights*, the animal fables of the ancient Indian *Panchatantra*, 'the marvels that poured like a waterfall from the *Kathasaritsagara*', the famous eleventh-century Sanskrit collection of myths, the 'tales of the mighty heroes collected in the *Hamzanama*', that tell of the legendary exploits of Amir Hamza, uncle to the Prophet Mohammed, and the ancient Persian classic *The Adventures of Hatim Tai*. Rushdie's father 'told them and retold them and remade them and reinvented them in his own way'. To grow up 'steeped in these tellings', Rushdie writes, 'was to learn two unforgettable lessons'. That 'stories were not true . . . but by being untrue they could make him feel and know truths that the truth could not tell him'. And that all stories 'belonged to him, just as they belonged to his father, Anis, and to everyone else' (Rushdie 2012: 12).

These were not just lessons that Rushdie learnt from his father. They are lessons that many of us learnt from Rushdie himself. Or, rather, they are ways of thinking about stories and truths and about what it is to be human that were embedded in Rushdie's own stories and that allowed those stories to speak to us in a new voice. Politicians, Rushdie once remarked on the BBC Radio programme *Desert Island Discs*, 'have got very good at inventing fictions which they tell us as the truth. It then becomes the job of the makers of fiction to start telling the real truth'. Few makers of fiction have wrestled more with the question of how their work can engage with the truth than Rushdie himself. Not the truth of facts, of course, or of science, but the truth of human experience, and in particular the experience of change and transformation, of dislocation and belongingness.

Rushdie always saw himself as a man inhabiting a world 'in-between' three cultures – those of India, Pakistan and England. What he wanted to discover through his fiction was how to 'connect the different worlds from which he had come', by exploring '*how the world joined up*, not only how the East flowed into the West and the West into the East, but how the past shaped the present while the present changed the understanding of the past, and how the imagined world, the location of dreams, art, invention and, yes, belief, leaked across the frontier that separated it from the everyday, "real" place in which human beings mistakenly believed they lived.' His writing was to 'explore the joining-ups and also disjointednesses of *here* and *there*, *then* and *now*, reality and dreams' (Rushdie 2012: 68–9).

The truth that emerges from Rushdie's writing is the truth of the experience of that in-between world, the world of migration and melange, a world in which the self became 'heterogenous rather homogenous, belonging to more than one place, multiple rather than singular, responding to more than one way of being, more than averagely mixed up'. 'How does newness enter the world?' (Rushdie 1988: 8), Rushdie asks in *The Satanic Verses*. The significance of Rushdie's great trilogy of the 1980s – *Midnight's Children*, *Shame* and *The Satanic Verses* – is that not only did he pose that question, but he also found a language through which to answer it. His novels interlaced reality, myth, dream and fantasy, turned history into fable and yet directly addressed highly charged contemporary political issues.

Like Rushdie, I was born in India but grew up in Britain. Like Rushdie, I was of a generation that did not think of itself as 'Muslim' or 'Hindu' or 'Sikh', or even as 'Asian' but rather as 'black', which for us was not an ethnic label but a political badge. Unlike our parents' generation, who had largely put up with discrimination, we were fierce in our opposition to racism. But we were equally fierce in our opposition to religion and to the traditions that often marked immigrant communities. We wanted to fashion a world in which we were neither defined by our differences nor denied the right to express them. And in the page of *Midnight's Children*, *Shame* and, especially, *The Satanic Verses,* I discovered, *we* discovered, such a world, a world in which we could think of 'difference' in a way that broke from the shackles both of racism and tradition, and yet did not deny the importance of belonging.

Much has been written in recent years by sociologists about the 'conflict of cultures' that immigrants supposedly face, especially when moving Third World to Western nations. Rushdie's writing helped transform the very notion of the conflict of cultures. Cultures, he insisted, are always conflictual because they are never authentic or fixed but ever churning and changing, forcing ideas, and memories, and thoughts and histories to clash with each other. Conflict was an inevitable part of facing up to the world. Rushdie was not, of course, alone in arguing this. But in forcing ideas, and memories, and thoughts and histories to clash with each other in the imagined worlds of his novels, he allowed the imagination to illuminate the real world too.

In reframing cultural conflict in this fashion, Rushdie spoke not just to the migrant experience but also to the experience of a world now becoming unstitched. The 1980s was a decade that saw the beginnings of the breakdown of traditional boundaries, physical, national, social and moral, and the creation of new social terrains for which there was as yet no map or compass. Rushdie's novels began to chart those terrains. The experience of a world unravelling, he suggested, was akin to the experience of migration and of the disruption and dislocation it created.

The breakdown of the old boundaries that Rushdie addressed in his novels created in many a sense of disorientation and a yearning for fixed points of reference. One expression of this was the growing significance of 'identity politics': the understanding of political attachments and collective interests in terms not of belief systems, programmatic manifestos, or party affiliation, but of distinct constituencies and communities defined in terms of much narrower, fixed identities, and, increasingly, the rooting of such identities in faith. As people began to cling ever more fiercely to particular cultural identities, so the symbols of such identities became ever more important and there developed inevitably resentment of, and hostility to, any attacks on such symbols. It is against this background that the 'Rushdie affair' emerged. If *The Satanic Verses* was a product of the breakdown of old boundaries so, too, was the campaign against the novel.

The roots of the campaign against *The Satanic Verses* are complex and as embedded in political strife as in religious belief: the roots, and consequences, of the Rushdie affair, are analysed in *From Fatwa to Jihad: The Rushdie Affair and Its Legacy* (2009). One way to understand it, however, is as the first great expression of fear of a mapless world, the first great contemporary confrontation over identity and the resources necessary for sustaining identity.

There had always been, of course, from the very beginnings of postwar immigration to Britain, social conflicts involving migrant communities. From the clashes at the Notting Hill Carnival to the Grunwick dispute, from the strike at Imperial Typewriters to the Broadwater Farm riot, such confrontations were in the main rooted in political conflicts, or emerged out of issues of discrimination or policing. They were conflicts of a kind familiar even prior to mass immigration. The Rushdie affair was different. It was the first major cultural confrontation, an encounter quite unlike anything that Britain had previously experienced. Muslim fury seemed to be driven not by questions of harassment or discrimination or poverty, but by a sense of hurt that Salman Rushdie's words had offended their deepest beliefs. Today, such conflicts are part of the cultural landscape. Not so in 1989.

Rushdie had long understood that stories embodied truths, and that they belonged to everyone. And because everyone had the right to refashion and retell every story, so the truths embodied in those stories could also be renewed. That understanding was woven into the fabric of his own stories. Yet those were the very ideas that the *fatwa* came to challenge. And those are the very ideas that, in the decades since the *fatwa*, have become increasingly contested.

There has been over the past three decades a growing insistence that stories do not belong to all; that many belong to particular cultures or communities or traditions. And those that do must be carefully curated to preserve their particular meaning and truth, and to ensure that such meaning and truth are safe from being questioned or challenged or ridiculed or defied. There has, at the same time, been growing scepticism about the idea that stories can express truths. Some insist that truths are embodied only in empirical facts, others that they are revealed only through a relationship with the divine.

Rushdie provides a direct challenge to all this. At the heart of his view of storytelling, indeed at the heart of his stories, lies the importance of the human, both as a storyteller and as a truthmaker. 'Man', as Rushdie puts it in *Joseph Anton*, is 'a storytelling animal, the only creature on earth that told itself stories to understand what kind of creature it was' (Rushdie 2012: 19). It is our ability to imagine that allows us to understand ourselves and the world as it is, and as it could be. Or, as Baal puts it in *The Satanic Verses*: 'A poet's work, to name tame the unnameable, to point at frauds, start arguments, shape the world and stop it from going to sleep' (Rushdie 1998: 97).

In an age in which the human is so often decried and the imagination so often denied, it is here that the real significance of Rushdie lies. It is for the insistence on the importance of the imagination to the human, and of the human to the imagination, that we should truly cherish Salman Rushdie.

Series Editors' Preface

The readership for contemporary fiction has never been greater. The explosion of reading groups and literary blogs, of university courses and school curricula, and even the apparent rude health of the literary marketplace, indicate an ever-growing appetite for new work, for writing which responds to the complex, changing and challenging times in which we live. At the same time, readers seem ever more eager to engage in conversations about their reading, to devour the review pages, to pack the sessions at literary festivals and author events. Reading is an increasingly social activity, as we seek to share and refine our experience of the book, to clarify and extend our understanding.

It is this tremendous enthusiasm for contemporary fiction to which the *Contemporary Critical Perspectives* series responds. Our ambition in these volumes is to offer readers of current fiction a comprehensive critical account of each author's work, presenting original, specially commissioned analyses of all aspects of their career, from a variety of different angles and approaches, as well as directions towards further reading and research. Our brief to the contributors was to be scholarly, to draw on the latest thinking about narrative, or philosophy, or psychology, indeed whatever seemed to them most significant in drawing out the meanings and force of the texts in question, but also to focus closely on the words on the page, the stories and scenarios and forms which all of us meet first when we open a book. We insisted that these essays be accessible to that mythical beast, the Common Reader, who might just as readily be spotted at the Lowdham Book Festival as in a college seminar. In this way, we hope to have presented critical assessments of our writers in such a way as to contribute something to both of those environments, and also to have done something to bring together the important qualities of each of them.

Jeannette Baxter, Peter Childs,
Sebastian Groes and Sean Matthews

Acknowledgements

The editors would like to thank their families and also colleagues at Royal Holloway, University of London and Kingston University for their support. We would also like to thank Jeannette Baxter, Sebastian Groes and Sean Matthews for their enthusiasm, and David Avital and Laura Murray, and all at Bloomsbury, for their work. Thanks, too, to Dr Nicole Edmondson who provided much for the further reading section.

Robert Eaglestone would especially like to thank the many students over many years who took his 'Salman Rushdie' course. I suspect I learned more about Rushdie from them than they learned from me.

Contributors

Eleanor Byrne is Senior Lecturer in English at Manchester Metropolitan University. Her publications include *Homi K. Bhabha* (2009) and *Deconstructing Disney* (2000) with Martin McQuillan. Her research interests include postcolonial literatures, theory and film, poststructuralism, deconstruction; literature and technology.

Marianne Corrigan teaches literature at Keele University, where she is a final year PhD candidate under the supervision of Dr Nick Bentley. Her research focuses on theories of globalization and cultural connectivity in the later novels of Salman Rushdie. She is a contributing author to the online journal of twenty-first-century fiction, 'Alluvium', and is particularly interested in the intersection of twenty-first-century literature and digital media.

Robert Eaglestone is Professor of Contemporary Literature and Thought at Royal Holloway, University of London. He works on contemporary literature and literary theory, contemporary philosophy and on Holocaust and Genocide studies. His publications include *Ethical Criticism: Reading after Levinas* (1997), *Doing English* (3rd ed., 2009) and *The Holocaust and the Postmodern* (2004) as author and *Teaching Holocaust Literature and Film* (Palgrave 2008), *Derrida's Legacies* (Routledge 2008), *J. M. Coetzee in Theory and Practice* (Continuum 2009) and Volume 2 of the *Blackwell Encyclopaedia of Literary and Cultural Theory* (2010) as editor. He is the Series Editor of *Routledge Critical Thinkers*. His work has been translated into five languages.

Kenan Malik is a writer, lecturer and broadcaster. His main academic interests are in the history of ideas, the history and philosophy of science, race, ethnicity and religion, and moral philosophy. His books include *From Fatwa to Jihad* (2009), shortlisted for the 2010 George Orwell Prize, *Strange Fruit: Why Both Sides Are Wrong in the Race Debate* (2008), *Man, Beast and Zombie: What Science Can and Cannot Tell Us about Human Nature* (2000) and *The Meaning of Race* (1996). His next book, on the history of moral thought, will be published in 2013.

Martin McQuillan is Professor of Literary Theory and Cultural Analysis at the London Graduate School and Dean of the Faculty of Arts and Social Sciences at Kingston University, London. His recent publications include *Deconstruction After 9/11*(2009), *Roland Barthes, or, The Profession of Cultural Studies* (2011) and *Deconstruction without Derrida* (2012). He is the editor of numerous volumes including *The Politics of Deconstruction:*

Jacques Derrida and the Other of Philosophy (2007), *Deconstruction Reading Politics* (2007), *The Origins of Deconstruction* (2008), *The Political Archive of Paul de Man: Sovereignty, Property and the Theotropic* (2012) and Paul de Man's *The Post-Romantic Predicament* (2012).

Anshuman A. Mondal is Reader in English at Brunel University and is currently an Arts and Humanities Research Council Research Fellow. He is the author of three books: *Nationalism and Post-Colonial Identity* (2003), *Amitav Ghosh* (2007) and *Young British Muslim Voices* (2008). He has published widely on Islam, politics and culture in the modern world, and is working on his next book, *After Rushdie: Muslims, Freedom of Expression and the Politics of Controversy*.

Stephen Morton is Senior Lecturer in Anglophone Literature at the University of Southampton. His publications include *Gayatri Spivak: Ethics, Subalternity and the Critique of Postcolonial Reason* (2007), *Salman Rushdie: Fictions of Postcolonial Modernity* (2007) and *Gayatri Chakravorty Spivak* (2002) and, as editor, *Foucault in an Age of Terror* (2008) and *Terror and the Postcolonial* (2009). His research interests include colonial states of emergency, Anglophone literatures from Canada and South Asia, postcolonial theory, critical theory, poetics and politics and visual culture.

Ankhi Mukherjee is Lecturer in English at the University of Oxford and Fellow of Wadham College. She is the author of *Aesthetic Hysteria: The Great Neurosis in Victorian Melodrama and Contemporary Fiction* (2007), *What Is a Classic?: Postcolonial Rewriting, Repetition, and Invention of the Canon* (2012) and editor of *A Companion to Psychoanalysis and Literature* (2010). She has also published widely on critical and cultural theory, intellectual history, postcolonial studies, Victorian literature and culture and contemporary British and South Asian Anglophone fiction.

Daniel O'Gorman is completing a PhD in post-9/11 fiction and critical theory in the Department of English at Royal Holloway, University of London, and has taught English Literature, Creative Writing, and Visual and Material Culture at Buckinghamshire New University. He has recently published a book chapter on Rushdie's *The Enchantress of Florence*, and has one on *Shalimar the Clown* currently in press. Daniel is also a co-convenor of the Literary and Critical Theory Seminar at the Institute of English Studies, University of London.

Andrew Teverson is Associate Dean in the Faculty of Arts and Social Sciences at Kingston University. His publications include *Salman Rushdie* (2007), and *Postcolonial Spaces: The Politics of Place in Contemporary Culture* (2012, co-edited with Sara Upstone). He has recently completed a book on fairy tale for the Routledge New Critical Idiom series (2013), and is currently editing a selection of Andrew Lang's essays on folklore for Pickering and Chatto (due for publication in 2013). Andrew has a PhD from Goldsmiths College, University of London, and a BA and MA from Durham University, UK.

Chronology of Salman Rushdie's Life

1947	Born 19 June, Bombay, India.
1954	Educated at Cathedral and John Connon School, Mumbai.
1961	Aged 14 sent to private education in England, at Rugby School.
1968	Graduates in History from King's College, University of Cambridge.
1968	Works briefly in Pakistan, but returns to London to work as an actor at the Oval House, in Kennington.
1969	Begins work as a copywriter.
1970	Copywriter for advertising agency Ogilvy & Mather until 1980 (penned the line 'That will do nicely' for American Express). Meets Clarissa Luard.
1974	Publication of novel *Grimus*. Travels to India for a long stay with Clarissa.
1976	Marries first wife Clarissa Luard (divorced 1987).
1979	Birth of son, Zafar.
1981	Publication of novel *Midnight's Children*. Wins Booker Prize for *Midnight's Children*. Shares James Tait Black Memorial Prize (*Midnight's Children*) with Paul Theroux (*Mosquito Coast*). English-Speaking Union Award, *Midnight's Children*.
1983	Publication of novel *Shame*.
1984	Awarded Prix du Meileur Livre Etranger (France) *Shame*.
1987	Publication of travel/political book *The Jaguar Smile: A Nicaraguan Journey*.
1988	Publication of novel *The Satanic Verses*. *The Satanic Verses* shortlisted for Booker Prize, wins Whitbread Prize. Marries second wife Marianne Wiggins (divorced 1993).
1989	14 February, Ayatollah Khomeini, Supreme Leader of Iran, issues *fatwa* against *The Satanic Verses*. Rushdie forced to live under police protection. 7 March, United Kingdom breaks off diplomatic relations with Iran. 3 June, Ayatollah Khomeini dies. 3 August, failed bomb attack in London, the bomb goes of prematurely killing the bomber and destroying two floors of the hotel where he was staying. Marianne Wiggins emerges from police protection to declare that their marriage of 13 months is over.
1990	Publication of children's book *Haroun and the Sea of Stories*. Release of Pakistani film *International Guerillas* portraying attack on Rushdie. British Board of Film Classification refuse it

a certificate on the grounds of criminal libel, Rushdie requests that the film be certified. It passes unnoticed at the UK box office. Under pressure, Rushdie issues statement that he has renewed his Islamic faith and will forbid future translations of his novel. Later withdraws statement describing himself as 'deranged' at the time.

1991   Japanese translator of *The Satanic Verses* killed; Italian translator attacked. December 12, gives address at Columbia University to mark two hundredth anniversary of the first amendment to the US Constitution, publicly retracts his conversion. Publication of essay collection *Imaginary Homelands: Essays and Criticism 1981–1991.*

1992   Publication of short story collection *Homeless by Choice* (with R. Jhabvala and V. S. Naipaul). Re-publication of essay collection *Imaginary Homelands* with the 'conversion' chapter replaced. Publication of *The Wizard of Oz* (BFI Film Classics). Awarded Writers' Guild Award (Best Children's Book) *Haroun and the Sea of Stories*. Awarded Kurt Tucholsky Prize (Sweden).

1993   Wins Booker of Booker (twenty-fifth anniversary) for *Midnight's Children*. Awarded Honorary Professorship at Massachusetts Institute of Technology (MIT does not award honorary degrees, only other previous honorary professor was Winston Churchill). William Nygaard, his Norwegian Publisher, shot. Awarded Prix Colette (Switzerland). 11 August, makes public appearance at U2 concert at Wembley Stadium. Publication of volume *For Rushdie* by 100 Arab and Muslim authors.

1994   Publication of short story collection *East, West.*

1995   Publication of novel *The Moor's Last Sigh*. Wins Whitbread Novel Award *The Moor's Last Sigh*

1996   Awarded European Union Aristeion Prize in Copenhagen for *The Moor's Last Sigh*. Named UK Author of the Year, Galaxy National Book Awards.

1997   Awarded Mantova Literary Prize (Italy). Marries third wife Elizabeth West (divorced 2004). Co-edited with Elizabeth West *Mirrorwork: 50 Years of Indian Writing, 1947–1997.*

1998   Awarded Budapest Grand Prize for Literature. 24 September, Iranian government of Mohammad Khatami gives public commitment to 'neither support nor hinder assassination operations on Rushdie' as a precondition of restoration of diplomatic relations with United Kingdom; Rushdie announces that he will now lead a public life.

1999   Publication of novel *The Ground Beneath Her Feet*. Awarded Freedom of the City, Mexico City. Awarded Commandeur de l'Orde des Arts et des Lettres (France). Publicly supports NATO bombing of Former Yugoslavia, condemned by Tariq Ali as part of the 'belligerati'. Birth of second son, Milan.

2000 Leaves London to live in New York.

2001 Publication of novel *Fury*. Cameo appearance in film version of *Bridget Jones' Diary*. 11 September, al-Qaeda attack on World Trade Centre, New York.

2002 Publication of collection *Step across This Line: Collected Nonfiction 1992–2002*.

2003 After evidencing support for US-led campaign to remove the Taliban in Afghanistan (2001), Rushdie condemns invasion of Iraq as 'unjustifiable'.

2004 Takes up role as president of PEN American Centre (until 2006). Marries fourth wife Padma Lakshmi (divorced 2007).

2005 Publication of novel *Shalimar the Clown*. Wins Whitbread Novel Award for second time. Declares his objection to UK government's 'Racial and Religious Hatred Act' in edited collection *Free Expression Is No Offence*. Ayatollah Ali Khamenei reaffirms original *fatwa*.

2006 Signs the manifesto 'Together Facing the New Totalitarianism' following the Danish Cartoons Affair.

2007 Knighted for his services to literature. Mass protests in Pakistan and Malaysia against knighthood. Al-Qaeda condemns knighthood and threatens response. Takes up five-year appointment as Distinguished Writer in Residence at Emory University. Appears as obstetrician-gynaecologist in *Then She Found Me*, directed by Helen Hunt.

2008 Publication of novel *The Enchantress of Florence*. Guest Editor, publication of *The Best American Short Stories*. Wins Best of the Booker (fortieth anniversary) by public vote for *Midnight's Children*. James Joyce Award (Dublin). Elected as Foreign Honorary Member of American Academy of Arts and Letters. Ron Evans, former police protection officer, publishes memoir of time with Rushdie, *On Her Majesty's Service*. Rushdie sues for libel over content of book. August 28, Rushdie receives an apology in the High Court in London from the book's authors and publishers.

2010 Publication of children's book *Luka and the Fire of Life*.

2012 Publication of *Joseph Anton: A Memoir*. Publishes short story 'In the South' exclusively on e-book format. Film version of *Midnight's Children*, directed by Deepa Mehta, screenplay by Rushdie. Appears on Twitter as @SalmanRushdie. Appearance at Jaipur Literature Festival cancelled due to death threats. Hari Kunzru and others sought by police for reading from *The Satanic Verses* (import of the book still banned in India, reading from an existing copy is not illegal).

2013 *The Next People*, US television series written by Rushdie for cable network Showtime, produced by Working Title

Salman Rushdie

ROBERT EAGLESTONE

A great writer does not merely live in a certain time but shapes the self-understanding of an age. This is true of Salman Rushdie. Marked out by his literary innovation in the novel, his role in global cultural politics and the form and content of his writing, he is clearly one of the most significant living writers in English today. More than this, his fiction leads us to comprehend more fully our histories, our dreams, our beliefs and fears – ourselves, in short – in the contemporary world.

Rushdie's Literary Impact

As a writer, Salman Rushdie has irrevocably changed the shape of the novel in English. This is not simply because of his success as a writer, not just because *Midnight's Children* (1981) won the Booker prize in 1981, and on the twenty-fifth and fortieth anniversaries of the Prize's establishment was judged both times to be the best Booker winner, not only because of his numerous international awards and literary knighthood. Literary prizes don't mean all that much. Rather, it is because his work has shaped two generations of writing and criticism and still continues to influence the novel's development. Indeed, it's not too strong to say that *Midnight's Children* inaugurated the 'contemporary' period of literature in English. Questions of 'periodization' in literature are always fraught. They are not just of academic interest, because how we put works into periods and categories reflects both how we understand the world and the role that literature has in shaping that world. Literary periods are not simply useful pigeonholes but are rather pointers to deeper and more important movements and historical moments. Usually, the dates of these periods – visible in the titles of books (say, 'British fiction from 1945') and in educational syllabi – are set by major historical events or major elections (in the United Kingdom, 1945, 1979, 1997). But this seems odd: surely literary periods should be set by watershed *literary* events which, while they reflect and, in retrospect, help shape the historical understanding of other sorts of historical events, are to some degree separate from them? The publication of *Midnights Children* in 1981 is such a watershed.

This watershed, and Rushdie's oeuvre more generally, shaped the texts that predated it into a tradition ('what happens when a new work of art is created is something that happens simultaneously to all the works of art which preceded it' (Eliot 1975: 38) as Eliot writes): Ankhi Mukerjee explores this in more detail in her essay in this book, 'The Rushdie Canon'. *Midnight's Children* stimulated a boom in contemporary writing. It is leaving a considerable literary legacy for the future.

Shaping the Past . . .

Midnights Children – and the novels that came after it, especially *The Satanic Verses* – represented an emergence into the dominant stream of literature in English of two different 'proto-traditions' of writing. First, the tradition of European anti-realism. In his memoir, *Joseph Anton*, Rushdie writes that the

> writers who has always spoken to him most clearly were members of what he thought of as a rival 'Great Tradition' to set against the Leavisite canon, writers who understood the unreality of 'reality' and the reality of the world's waking nightmare, the monstrous mutability of the everyday. (342)

These writers are symbolized most explicitly for Rushdie in Günter Grass. In his insightful and autobiographical essay on Grass he writes that there 'are books that open doors for their readers, doors in the head, doors whose existence they had not previously suspected' (Rushdie 1992: 276). Grass's *The Tin Drum* is such a book. Rushdie understands Grass as a migrant, a 'traveler across borders in the self, and in Time' (280), who has lost his roots, his society and even his language: his self-appointed task was to reinvent 'the German language . . . tearing it apart, ripping out the poisoned parts, and putting it back together' (279). Indeed, reading *The Tin Drum* illuminates much about Rushdie's work ('I have tried to learn the lessons of the midget drummer' (277) wrote Rushdie, referring to Grass's protagonist). And behind Grass is, for example, Bulgakov as well as a whole European tradition that aims at a sort of seriousness and political critique 'in dark times' which is unavailable to more conventional realism. This 'proto-tradition' too shares much of its DNA with the Latin American magical realism of Gabriel Garcia Marquez and Mario Vargas Llosa, whose novels also lie beneath much of Rushdie's work. (That said, however, Rushdie claims the film of *The Wizard of Oz* as his 'very first literary influence . . . it made a writer out of me'; Rushdie (2003: 3, 11); but the film, too, in its dreamy-fairytale anti-realism and its nascent political critique has more than a little in common with magical realism and with Grass's work. For example, the utopian yearning in the words of 'Somewhere over the rainbow' reflect the leftist beliefs of lyricist E. Y. Harburg, who was later blacklisted in Hollywood.)

The second tradition that Rushdie's work helped form in retrospect, certainly in the West, is, of course, that of Indian writing. Rushdie singles out as influences R. K. Narayan and his fictional town of Malgudi and, almost as Narayan's opposite, the wildly linguistically inventive G. V. Desani, who wrote *All about H. Hatterr*: reading this marvelous novel, too, illuminates Rushdie (as he freely admits: '[M]y own writing . . . learned a trick or two from him'; Rushdie 2003: 169). Rushdie's work shaped an understanding of both an Indian tradition of writing in English before his own and brought to the fore the European and Latin American traditions on which he drew.

It's the interplay of these influences – the Indian, the experimental European, the magical realist – which makes Rushdie's work something complex and unique and is part of the way in which it changed the scope of the novel in English. Put in this way, this confluence seems to suggest that the success of Rushdie's work was inevitable: but this literary critical judgment masks the huge aesthetic and intellectual effort which clearly channels these two streams into his two great novels of the 1980s, *Midnight's Children* and *The Satanic Verses*. This effort is clearly visible in the development between his first novel *Grimus* (1975) and *Midnight's Children* six years later. The latter discovers – and indeed revels in – the uses of history; the former, a quasi-allegorical science-fiction fantasy, seeks to escape history.

. . . Making the Future

The novel *Midnight's Children* was not only a huge international success – the first novel of the age of globalization, perhaps – but also represented the flourishing of new ways of writing about identity, nationhood, memory, personal and collective trauma, history, persecution, escape, evil, the interweaving of the personal and the political and writing itself which much contemporary fiction is still exploring. It made Rushdie an international celebrity. Writers from India, South Asia and the non-Western world found in it, and in its success, ways to represent non-Western subjects, and access to a flourishing global market, offering new representations of the non-Western world. Migrant writers from these regions, too, found that the novel also created a space, perhaps verbalizing for the first time on that scale the complexities of migration, the shifting visions and world views that mass-migration creates.

Midnight's Children was both castigated and praised for offering up a version of exotic India, for dealing with questions of migrancy: and these controversies perhaps show its power as a novel. Some critics diagnosed 'Rushdie-itis'" (Rushdie 2003: 166) but most writers in the 'post-Rushdie' wave developed clear, strong voices: Vikram Seth, Kiran Desai, Rohinton Mistry, Arundhati Roy, Gita Mehta. The wave continues: Jeet Thayil's

Narcopolis (2012) is set in Mumbai, and with its historical range, huge cast of characters and phantasmagoric events, it, too, follows currents set flowing by Rushdie. Zadie Smith's much-lauded first novel, *White Teeth* (2000) and Monica Ali's *Brick Lane* (2003) are also influenced by Rushdie's work. Rushdie's influence is seen further afield. It's visible in contemporary American writing. For example, Junot Diaz's sparkling novel *The Brief Wondrous Life of Oscar Wao* (2007), which won the Pulitzer Prize in 2008, is clearly influenced by Rushdie. Not only is about the migrant experience in the United States, it also concerns the relationship between the political and the personal (here, the Dominican dictator Rafael Trujillo and a family of his victims), wrapped in popular culture and written in a freewheeling, postmodern magical realist style, focussing on what the narrator calls 'Fukú', the 'Curse and the Doom of the New World', brought by 'screams of the enslaved' across the Atlantic. Like Rushide, too, the book is politically and morally serious, and yet witty and comic.

Rushdie as a global figure

But the importance of Rushdie and his work does not lie solely in the literary sphere. Like any very significant author, he is a global intellectual figure. Vassilena Parashkevova describes his 'cult status as a cultural commentator' (Parashkevova 2012: 2); in 'Rushdie's Non-fiction' Daniel O'Gorman examines his wider work and interventions. However, his fame stems also, of course, from the 'Rushdie affair', which, as Kenan Malik writes, raised 'some of the defining problems of the age': 'the nature of Islam, its relationship to the West, the meaning of multiculturalism, the limits of tolerance in a liberal society' (Malik 2009: xiii). As Malik's study *From Fatwa to Jihad* and other commentators have made clear, the actual content of *The Satanic Verses* was not really the issue: rather, Rushdie's novel became a lightening conductor for a number of long-brewing global social, political and cultural storms. Ironies abound here: while the questions the novel asks of Islam are serious ones (and echo those raised about Christianity by Dostoyevsky and one of the novel's 'greatest models' (Rushdie 1992: 404) Bulgakhov's *The Master and Margarita*), the 'blasphemies' of which it was accused are not linked to those questions. While the Ayatollah Khomeini, who issued the fatwa, is severely parodied in the novel, this was widely ignored. Worse, the novel was written in no small part for the people that the 'affair' so alienated: 'at the centre of the novel is a group of . . . British Muslims, struggling with . . . the problems of hybridisation and ghettoisation, or reconciling the old and the new' (Rushdie 1992: 394). This 'polarisation' ensured that the novel was less widely read among the people it concerned. Finally, the novel set out to celebrate

hybridity, impurity, intermingling, the transformation that comes of new
an unexpected combinations of human beings, cultures, ideas politics,
movies, songs. It rejoices in mongrelisation and fears the absolutism of the
Pure. Melange, hotchpotch, a bit of this and a bit of that is how newness
enters the world. It is the great possibility that mass migration gives to the
world, and I have tried to embrace it . . . It is a love song to our mongrel
selves. (394)

This beautiful quotation is perhaps the finest, most hopeful declaration
of the idea of multiculturalism that characterized much thinking in the
United Kingdom and elsewhere in the 1980s. Yet the 'affair' was, for
better or worse, to make clear very publicly precisely the limits of this
sort of multiculturalism and, again as Malik argues, its potentially dangerous unintended consequences. Stephen Morton explores the novel
further in his chapter on 'Postcolonial Secularism and Literary Form in
Salman Rushdie's Fiction'.

The 'affair' and Rushdie's role as both a lightening rod for anger
and weather vane for opinion (more than just a weather vane, a whole
steeple, in fact) continues. For example, the affair was reprised on a
smaller scale in January 2012, when he was forced to pull out of the
Jaipur Literary Festival, after a local politician, seeking re-election, had
inflamed popular feeling against Rushdie, and threats had been made
against the author's life. It was reprised yet again as this book was in
the final stages of preparation for publication over the hate-filled propa-
ganda 'film' *The Innocence of Muslims*. Anshuman Mondal explores the
continuing impact of the fatwa in his chapter 'Revisiting *The Satanic
Verses*: The *Fatwa* and Its Legacies'.

But Rushdie's work has always been visionary: in his novel *Fury*,
published 4 September 2001, for example, he invokes global terror and
destruction. His image of bombed skyscrapers at the conclusion of
The Moor's Last Sigh (1995) now makes uncanny reading: but his vision
stems not in foreseeing events but in a profounder sense of 'speaking
from outside'. The lesson he learnt from Grass ('Go for broke. Always
try to do too much. Dispense with safety nets'; Rushdie 1992: 277)
seems to have empowered Rushdie always to step beyond what is
conventional to challenge or question. Indeed, Rushdie sees this as his
role. In his 'Notes on Writing and the Nation', he writes that history

has become debateable. In the aftermath of Empire, in the age of super-power,
under the 'footprint' of the partisan simplifications beamed down to us from
satellites, we can no longer easily agree on *what is the case*, let alone what it
might mean. Literature steps into this ring. Historians, media moguls, politicians do not care for the intruder, but the intruder is a stubborn sort. In this
ambiguous atmosphere, upon this trampled earth, in these muddy waters,
there is work for him to do. (Rushdie 2003: 66–7)

The job of literature is to 'make' history, to make meaning in a public sphere. Perhaps the most significant role Rushdie sees himself playing here is defending free speech. This is not simply a *parti pris* matter for him nor a sign that he is unproblematically committed to a wider liberal agenda (he is not, and has expressed a range of views). For Rushdie, the relationship between freedom of speech and art links the micro and the macro scales. He writes that the

> creative process is rather like the processes of a free society. Many attitudes, many views of the world jostle and conflict within the artist, and from these frictions the spark, the work of art, is born. (Rushdie 2003: 232)

In his fiction and in his political activity, Rushdie seeks to defend the free interaction of views. But this is far from the only issue Rushdie sees as important. The range of his intellectual engagements as a global figure emerges from the 'thinking' of his fiction.

The 'Thinking' of Rushdie's Work

In his essay 'Damme, This Is the Oriental Scene for You!' Salman Rushide tells a story in part against himself. At a reading in Delhi, he is asked by a passionate reader 'fundamentally, what's your point?' (Rushdie 2003: 159): his authorial equivocations come to nothing.

> 'Please', I begged, 'do I have to have just one point?'
> 'Fundamentally', she said, with impressive firmness, 'yes'. (159)

Obviously the question is unilluminating. No novel has just one point. And yet . . . the charm and self-depreciation with which the anecdote is told, and the if-slightly-ridiculous-only-slightly nature of the 'impressive' questioner reveal something important about his work. Rushdie's novels do have points, they address issues. That there is not one point or that the issues are not clear cut is not to deny that that they are about something, that his novels *think*. A huge critical canon has grown up around Rushdie which focuses on exactly this. As we have suggested, the novels cover a huge swathe of issues and the chapters of this book address many of these. However, here, I am going to focus on three broad 'labels'. As with literary periods, these critical labels don't exist to simply shut away literary texts in boxes: rather they aim to draw attention to aspects of the texts.

Perhaps the most significant label applied to Rushdie is that of a 'postcolonial' author: indeed, he is not only taken almost as paradigmatic example of such but also helped the term become widely accepted. Rushdie's work 'thinks' about the 'postcolonial'. 'Postcolonial' literature describes the after effects of Empire and colonial power on the personal and on the political. This term looks very applicable to *Midnight's Children*, clearly a sort of national allegory (indeed, the critic Fredric Jameson, clearly with this novel in mind, once argued that all postcolonial fiction's were 'national allegories' because 'the story of the private individual destiny is always an allegory of the embattled situation of the public third world culture and society' (Jameson 1986: 69)). Much of Rushdie's work explicitly addresses Empire and its aftermath. Eleanor Byrne's chapter, 'Rushdie's Early Fiction and the Rise of Postcolonialism', addresses this in some detail. Yet even the name 'postcolonial' betrays a sort of a European and American 'post-imperial' idea. Surely, the experience of Empire was worldwide: if a contemporary novel drug addiction in Mumbai is 'post-colonial' and 'after Empire', so, surely is a contemporary novel about drug addiction in Birmingham. Perhaps now, Rushdie's work is better seen as global, as Marianne Corrigan argues in her chapter 'Rushdie as an International Writer'. But under whatever critical description, it is interested in the interaction of people and ideas in a globalized world.

The second term which is often used to describe Rushdie is 'postmodern'. Joe Brooker argues convincingly that Rushdie 'displayed a keen interest in contemporary ideas and . . . aligned his work with postmodernism' (Brooker 2010: 122). Postmodernism was not the dominant form of writing in the 1980s and 1990s but the dominant form of experimental writing from that period and can be seen to have several linked characteristics. Perhaps the most important of these here is its self-referentiality: in *Midnight's Children*, the novel is as much Salim's telling of the novel as the events it describes. Indeed, the critic Linda Hutcheon describes this as the move in the novel from mimesis of product to mimesis of process, from the representation of a finished world to the representation of the process of representation itself. 'Illuminated by a Ray of the Sun at Midnight: Storytelling and Sovereignty in Salman Rushdie's *The Enchantress of Florence*' by Martin McQuillan explores the often overlooked political ramifications of this. Postmodern fiction, too, often brings together high and low forms of culture, epic poetry and popular cinema, pop and classical music and so on with no difficulty. The first pages of *The Satanic Verses* refer to Christian, Hindu and Muslim teachings, *Paradise Lost*, Bollywood movies, Eastern and Western pop music, contemporary history and many other things in one bravura description of the fall of the two protagonists. Andrew Teverson analyses some aspects of this in his account of 'Salman Rushdie and the Post-Colonial Folk and Fairy Tale'. The term postmodern draws attention especially to the formal qualities of his fiction.

Finally, and often overlooked, is simply the paradoxical in Rushdie. We have cited his view that many 'attitudes, many views of the world jostle and conflict within the artist' and his fiction displays this, constantly setting one view against the other. The moral core of *Fury*, the

banker Balasubramanyam Venkataraghavan who saves the young protagonist from further abuse gives up his world to become a *sanyasi*,
seeking knowledge and peace in the approach to death. His then abandoned son Chandra spits: 'I hate knowledge! And Peace, too. I really hate
peace *a lot*' (*Fury* 81). And, while *Shalimar the Clown* ends, all readers will
agree that it does not conclude. There are no straightforward answers in
Rushdie's fiction: indeed, it piles paradox on paradox.

CHAPTER ONE

The Rushdie Canon

ANKHI MUKHERJEE

'I admit it: above all things, I fear absurdity', sighs Saleem Sinai, Rushdie's best-loved literary creation and author stand-in (Rushdie 1981: 9). Rushdie may have recalled the sentiment at finding himself embroiled in two rather absurd (unrelated) episodes in the brief span of autumn 2011 and winter 2012. Rushdie had joined Twitter in September 2011, only to find the twitter handle @SalmanRushdie taken. 'Who are you? Why are you pretending to be me?' thundered Rushdie in the somewhat less convincing persona of @SalmanRushdie1. 'Followers' took advantage of the confusion by needling the author with questions which only the real Rushdie would have insider knowledge of. 'Where did the great Pakistani poet Faiz Ahmed Faiz seek sanctuary when he was hounded by a mob?' ventured journalist Omar Waraich from Islamabad. 'Under my aunt Begum Majeed Malik's carpet, in her cellar in Karachi', Rushdie replied. 'Now stop it everyone. It's becoming dull.' Despite the obvious vexation, Rushdie excitably took to tweeting the opening lines of a new short story, 'A Globe in Heaven', promising a single tweet each day, posting ten tweets all at once instead. Unpropitious start notwithstanding, Rushdie today seems to be at home @SalmanRushdie, where his definitive line is 'I yam what I yam'. Media reports and blogs suggest that he might even be enjoying this jape, organizing 'literary smackdowns' (between, say, *Bridget Jones's Diary*, *White Teeth* and *Gawain and the Green Knight*, all of which begin on New Year's Day) or indulging in a spot of wordplay on burning issues of the day ('The marriage of poor Kim # Kardashian was krushed like a kar in a krashian').

The second absurdity assumed chaotic contours in January 2012, when, on the eve of Rushdie's visit to the Jaipur Literary Festival (JLF), the author was apparently lied to by intelligence agencies in India about assassination squads posting dire threats to his life (the agencies denied that they had released any such information). As journalist, writer and JLF founder William Dalrymple, echoing other political commentators, explains in a *Guardian* article (28 January 2012), Rushdie's trip to India had fatefully clashed with an election in the crucial north Indian state of Uttar Pradesh, for which the vote of the Muslim community would be a key determining factor. Soon after the official announcement of Rushdie's participation in the literary festival, Maulana Abdul Quasim Nomani of the Deoband madrasa had issued a ban on Rushdie's presence in India, an indictment that revived graphic memories of the burning acts surrounding the reception of Rushdie's *The Satanic Verses* by a section of the Muslim populace in India, which had most certainly not read the book. It was unsurprising that the move would be unchallenged by the Rajasthan government, which was busy making amends with its Muslim voters following an incident of police violence (toward Muslims), but it was indeed shocking that not one political party, not even the Congress Party with its vaunted secular ideals, offered immunity and a warm welcome to one of India's most celebrated writers. The author sensibly cancelled his visit so as not to endanger lives at the festival, and the organizers settled for a virtual chat via video link instead. This too had to be scrapped at the last minute when large groups of Muslim activists descended on the property promising violent riots and 'rivers of blood' were the link telecast live.

Symptomatic as they are of the perils of modern existence, be it the imposture of identity dogging social networking sites, or the discrepant speeds and developments of global and local narratives (if literary festivals like the JLF represents the idea of literature without national borders, the Deoband madrasa stands for a local site of resistance immune to the seductions of Indian modernity's englobing aspirations), I cite these episodes primarily for the way in which they tragic-comically question the ontology of 'the real Salman Rushdie'. Maverick trickster or long-suffering artist? High priest of the freedom of expression or incorrigible attention seeker? Visionary revisionist or troublemongerer? According to Faisal Devji, 'this celebrated author has been reduced to a kind of billboard upon which almost any cause can be advertised': if, for supporters, Rushdie represents the free expression of ideas, he also becomes, for his detractors, a potent emblem of blasphemy and heresy. Rushdie, says Devji, 'is no longer a writer at all but more like one of his own fictional characters, Gibreel Farishta to some and Mahound for others.' The *Independent* tellingly ran its report on Rushdie's Twitter misadventures under the title 'Would the real Salman Rushdie please tweet up?' (19 September 2011). But this obfuscation of 'textual' and 'authorial' intention, to use Amir Mufti's terms of differentiation (1991: 99), or the historical Rushdie with a diegetic author function, was the defining characteristic of the *Satanic Verses* controversy which erupted in February 1989. As Gayatri Spivak pointed out in the aftermath of the Rushdie affair, here is a writer who has unwittingly halted poststructuralist play by literalizing the 'death of the author,' one whose aesthetic production has been the site of such an interception of 'the global *lebenswelt*' or 'the praxis and politics of life' that a 'mere reading' of the novel has become impossible (Spivak 1993: 244). This essay looks at some of the ways in which Rushdie has not merely entered the Western canon, but has come to stand for the counter-canon of postcolonial Anglophone literature himself.

'How very enchanting, I have often thought, Rushdie's imagination must be for that whole range of readers who have been brought up on the peculiar "universalism" of "The Waste Land" . . . and the "world culture" of Pound's *Cantos*', muses Aijaz Ahmad (1991: 1462). The carefully careless appropriations and polyglot ascriptions of the Modernist writers valorize what Ahmad calls 'the idea of the availability of *all* cultures of the world for consumption by an individual consciousness': the *Cantos*, for instance, can be read as an exemplary instance of metropolitan cultural consumption, with 'the sages of ancient China jostling with the princely notables of renaissance Italy, with Homer and Cavalcanti in between, all in the service of a political vision framed by Mussolini's fascism' (1462). Despite the dazzling technical innovations to capture the alienation, fragmentation and anomie of a cultural elite, Ahmad points out that in none of the major modernists 'was the idea of the fragmented self, or the accompanying sense of un-belonging, ever a source of any great comfort' (1463). Salman Rushdie is in the vanguard of the post-1960s intellectual culture that uses the ideology and aesthetic strategies of Anglo-American modernists to sidestep the vexed modalities of belonging in their cultural predecessors and advocate instead an 'excess of belonging': 'the writer not only has all cultures available to him as resource, for consumption, but he actually belongs in all of them, because he belongs in none' (Ahmad 1991: 1463). Or, as Rushdie puts it, in the words of the *ayah* Mary Pereira's lullaby in *Midnight's Children*:

> Anything you want to be, you kin be,
> You kin be just what-all you want. (383)

This overoptimistic formulation defines Saleem Sinai's imbrications in multitudes of histories, not just those of the family and its radiating circles, but also his imaginative relationships, which serve to defamiliarize the unitary webs of cultural identity. It is also, of course, as Saleem avers, the greatest of all lies 'spoken in the night,' as borne out by his precipitate disintegration from the strain of being 'so-many too-many persons' (463).

Rushdie's 'Outside the Whale,' which overtly sets itself up in a reactive mode against Orwell's 1940 essay, 'Inside the Whale', charts the curious turn of argument whereby Orwell, who had, in the beginning of the piece, described apolitical writers as 'plain idiots', gravitates nevertheless to a fatalist stance of quiet endurance: 'Seemingly there is nothing left but quietism – robbing reality of its terrors by simply submitting to it. Get inside the whale – or rather, admit you are inside the whale (for you *are*, of course) . . . simply accept it, endure it, record it'

(Rushdie 1991: 95). It is, however, a 'whaleless world', Rushdie remarks, and there can be no 'easy escapes from history' (101). Elaborating on the genre of Raj fiction, Rushdie demonstrates how even mediocre and seemingly anodyne instances of empire nostalgia surreptitiously carry on the ideological work of a colonial past. Paul Scott's *Raj Quartet*, for instance, perpetuates through form and structure the very ethic that it purports to condemn. Despite its gallery of unsympathetic British characters, the form insists that it is the lives of the British officer class that matter. 'It tries to taste Indian, but ends up being ultra-parochially British,' Rushdie comments (90). Unsurprisingly, then, formal innovation is key to Rushdie's politics of the novel and symptomatic of his rejoinder to Orwell's quietism: 'rowdyism', or 'in place of the whale, the protesting wail' (99).

'It is an *intellectual* fiction whose aesthetic pleasures lie at the level of the phrase and the idea', remarks Timothy Brennan of Rushdie's corpus (1989: 115). As Brennan and others have observed, Rushdie's novels work best as satires whose state of animation and verbosity often mask the lack of development of character or plot; they serve also to present alternative or aesthetic histories elided by official narratives of nationalism, globalization and modernization. In *Midnight's Children* he memorably describes this process as pickling or 'chutnification', whereby 'memories, dreams, ideas' are preserved and strategically unleashed on an 'amnesiac nation' (443). In his novels of the postcolonial nation state and the postcolonial globe, Rushdie substitutes distorted temporality for the linear, calendrical time of nations, divided and disintegrating heroes in place of the unified subject of enunciation, a vortex of image and memory fragments for the perceived coherence of realist representation, 'two or three or fifteen' instead of monocultural claims of identity (*Satanic Verses*, *SV* 102). Rushdie uses parody and pastiche, not just in the 'random juxtaposition of different discourses' but also as 'imitation and citation' (Mufti 1991: 110). To quote Mufti again, parody and pastiche could be said to work with the same formal intention, 'marking the texts' hesitation with regard to notions of originality and purity, on the one hand, and their self-critical sense of affiliation, on the other' (110). The ironic assemblages of disparate materials – high and low cultural forms, Eastern and Western narrative traditions, the idea of colony and the idea of metropolis, various genres and modes of discourse – show the pluralist heritage and affiliations of global citizens, but are also testimony to the belated writer's anxiety of influence: how is meaning made from the formlessness of conflicting selves 'joggling within these bags of skin?' or 'how does newness enter the world?' (*SV* 519, 8).

In what follows, I shall examine three key aspects of Rushdie's invention of the English novel with special attention to the visual culture of the novels, the transformation motif in his mobility narratives and his rewriting of the canon.

The Talisman of the Perforated Sheet

First, the 'that holey, mutilated square of linen', which comically sets the paradigm of alternative reading strategies in *Midnight's Children*:

> Aadam Aziz's visits to the bedroom with the shaft of sunlight and the three lady wrestlers became weekly events; and on each occasion he was vouchsafed a glimpse, through the mutilated sheet, of a different seven-inch circle of the young woman's body. (25)

Nothing is as it seems in *Midnight's Children*. The landowner Ghani, in whose house (and with whose daughter) Aadam Aziz carries on the tableau of synecdochal medical inspections, is a blind man claiming to be a connoisseur of European paintings. Aziz himself is a man of 'altered vision': his five years away in Germany has led to such a widening of his perspective that the valley of Kashmir appears narrow and 'utterly enclosed' (11). He falls in love with the fragments of the girl he sees through the hole in the sheet – 'I swear her bottom blushes' (29) – setting the tone for a novel that equates its hoarding of broken wholes of stories in little pickle jars with 'acts of love' (461). The novel shores inspired and expedient uses of fragmented vision: Amina Sinai's act of assiduously loving and accepting, bit by bit, her partner in a marriage of convenience; Lifafa Das's 'Dunya dekho' (see the world) peepshow, with discrete images that the powers of suggestion would mobilize into a totality; Saleem's own virtual tour of India, Taj Mahal to the Meenakshi Temple, from the clock tower; and finally, the authorial act of improvising endings from the scraps, shreds and fragments of memory, for 'the story you finish is never the one you begin' (426).

In *Shame*, fragmented vision is less associated with the high spirits of modernist experimentation than with the literal act of partition 'that chopped up the old country and handed Al-lah a few insect-nibbled slices of it, some dusty western acres and jungly eastern swamps that the ungodly were happy to do without' (61). The narrator, who says he has come to know Pakistan 'in slices', is forced to 'reflect that world in fragments of broken mirrors' and reconciled to the 'inevitability of the missing bits' in his fictionalized biography of the country (69). (Reflecting on the process of writing his definitive 'India' book in North London, Rushdie's describes his own cultural position thus: 'It may be that when the Indian writer who writes from outside India tries to reflect that world, he is obliged to deal in broken mirrors, some of whose fragments have been irretrievably lost'; Rushdie 1991: 11). He hears voices that mock his peripheral knowledge – *'Outsider! Trespasser! You have no right to this subject!'* – and, unlike Saleem, succumbs to momentary self-doubt: 'is history to be considered the property of participants solely?' (28). Again, can the politics of access of the cosmopolitan writer, neither insider nor rank outsider, at home everywhere and nowhere, be claimed as a privileged double perspective, 'a stereoscopic vision . . . in place of 'whole sight'? (Rushdie 1991: 19). In *Shame*, the undermining of the unitary subject of history results in a full-blown crisis of representation: the historiography of the novel is cobbled together from scraps of gossip and family scandals whirling around Iskander Harappa and Raza Hayder, fictionalizations of President Zulfikar Ali Bhutto and his ouster, General Zia. Moreover, Rushdie allows the 'excessively masculine tale' of 'sexual rivalry, ambition, patronage, betrayal, death, revenge' to be overtaken by the marginalized stories of peripheral women (173). *The Moor's Last Sigh* gives us Aurora Zogoiby, the 'smartyboots metropolis' rejoinder to the debunked celluloid myth of 'Mother India', who, like Saleem Sinai, denounces realistic representation for a pluralistic 'epic-fabulist manner' (139, 174). She calls her erroneous and iconoclastic re-imaginings of history 'not Authorized Version but Aurorised Version' (225). Aurora's most fecund period of artistic creativity, her Moor paintings, are described as an 'interweaving' of history, myth, hallucinatory visions, so accelerated that it is like dancing to music 'without caring for the message in the song' (227). The valorization of talismanic fragmentation continues in the *The Satanic Verses*, where the 'untranslated man' Gibreel inevitably auto-destructs, succumbing under the pressure of remaining steadfastly joined to his past, while Saladin Chamcha, who starts out as a toady, an ingratiating 'creature of *selected* discontinuities' (427), is allowed to re-invent himself.

The legacy of the perforated sheet works in the service of representing what Sir Darius Xerxes Cama in *The Ground Beneath Her Feet* calls 'outsideness': 'outcastes, lepers, pariahs, exiles, enemies, spooks, paradoxes' (42–3). Such 'outsideness' pertains equally to those who don't belong in what Edward Soja calls the 'spatialized ontology' of globalized nation-states (1989: 118), and those who chose to remain outside the frame: 'The only people who see the whole picture are the ones who choose to step out of the frame' (43). For generations of Anglophone and diasporic writers after him, the half-truths and partial truths of Rushdie's historical novels, their irrepressible excess of literary language and form, the partiality for the lurid, vivid, fragment over judicious reconstructions, have been highly influential, even when such influence is acknowledged in the mode of disavowal. In a novel like Arundhati Roy's *The God of Small Things* (1997), Rushdie's style manifests itself in the way the structure of the book tells a counter-narrative to the story that seems to sequentially unfold. Alternating between the narration of the past in even chapters and the present in odd ones, the novel worries the question of beginnings, voice and silence in a way reminiscent of *Midnight's Children* and *Shame*. Roy sneaks in a sly reference to Rushdie when Mammachi writes to the manager of 'Padma Pickles', seeking advice on pickling methods (167). In contrast to Saleem's small gain of 'chutnification' and pickling history in manageable lots, however, Mammachi's business is a disaster. As Alex Tickell points out, her pickles do not gel – 'too thin for jelly and too thick for jam' (2007: 30) – and the jars leak (47). If Rushdie made his unreliable narrator suspend selfhood for the catalytic transmission of story, Roy makes the story itself too idiosyncratic and broken to pose as *grand récit*. If Saleem is handcuffed to history, Estha and Rahel, born from separate but simultaneously fertilized eggs, inhabit a 'dizygotic' private vision of plenitude resistant till the end to 'Edges, Borders, Boundaries, Brinks and Limits' (3).

Zadie Smith's *White Teeth* (2000) strongly evokes the hallucinatory reality of the London portrayed in *Satanic Verses*, a city where 'you have no choice but to cross borders and speak in tongues' (Bhabha 1994: 13). The Babel of Glenard Oak School (Brent School Report 1990: 67 different faiths, 123 different languages), which frustrates the homogenizing energies of state-sponsored multiculturalism, recalls the 'deafening manytongued terrifying' noise Saleem Sinai internalizes in the auditorium of his head (162), while the novel's critique of the rebranding of Britishness in millennial London has uncanny echoes of Rushdie's mistrust of socially produced nation-space, in the subcontinent as well as postcolonial, multiracial England. The multiple, often opposing, histories and backstories that Smith catalogues in *White Teeth* are also, of course, incentives for aesthetic inaugurals. As with Smith's Alsana, 'the life you lead is a midnight thing, always a hair's breadth from the witching hour' (14).

The Rebirth Bug

Rebirth and reinvention are inseparable from Rushdie's reformulation of the *Bildungsroman*. As Rushdie says himself, the form of *Midnight's Children*, especially its metonymically proliferating narrative, represents 'the Indian talent for non-stop self-regeneration' (Rushdie 1991: 16). Characters are subjected to violent changes of heart, diabolical transformations, reincarnations and transmogrifications. Rebirth takes many forms in the novels: Saleem's loss of memory in *Midnight's Children* ('I, he, had begun again' 350), which marks the narrative's benumbed switch from India to Pakistan; Ormus and Vina's posthumous ubiquity in the cable multiverse in *The Ground Beneath Her Feet* ('I thought they were supposed to be *dead*, but in real life they're just going to go on singing' 575); Rashid Khalifa's recovery of his voice at the end of *Haroun and the Sea of Stories*. 'We have been made again', says a minute old woman of the African, Caribbean, Indian, Pakistani, Bangladeshi, Cypriot and Chinese diasporas in London (Rushdie 1987: 414).

The renewal of self often takes place in an uncanny register, associated with narcissistic feelings of omnipotence and animistic thinking. As Freud states, the uncanny arises 'when the distinction between imagination and reality is effaced' ('The Uncanny' 244). *Midnight's Children* is a classic example of the obfuscation of fantasy and reality to create new maps of belonging. What does it mean to love one's country, the novel seems to ask. Rushdie says elsewhere that it means that 'its shape is also yours, the shape of the way you think and feel and dream' (Rushdie 2002: 195). Saleem Sinai's life has been 'transmuted to grotesquerie by the irruption into it of history' (Rushdie 1981: 57). Born at the moment of India's independence from British rule, and 'fathered, you understand, by history' (139), Saleem is bestowed with a magical prescience and telepathy that causes him to anthropomorphize the destinies of India. He becomes a media technology, a disembodied intelligence that channels and broadcasts collective social imaginings. He inherits, as does the newly minted nation, the unshaped but 'multitudinous histories of the land' (172), and shares with it a longing for form and meaning. Saleem defines and dreams his world and suffers the dystopic aftermaths of such utopian dreams. At times, the misadventures of Saleem's boyhood and puberty are reactive responses to those of the young adult state: at others, they are immediately responsible for catastrophic local or national events. Saleem is a fantasist who uncannily becomes a creator of alternative realities: he is India itself, the unwitting repository of an epic memory, as well as being an Indian agent of self-determination and postcolonial nation-building.

Saleem's genealogy is confused and conjectural. Raised in an upper-class Muslim household, he is actually a changeling, the biological son of poor Hindu parents, or, if the author is to be believed, a Hindu mother and her extramarital interest, the Englishman Methwold. Like his 'grandfather', Aadam Aziz, Saleem is a 'half-and-halfer' (18), an Anglo-Indian uneasily negotiating modernity and tradition, India's lost past and the immanent time in which nationalist and colonialist definitions of the country are contested. The absurd salience of his birth moment leads to an 'uncorking', whereby Saleem progressively loses any claim to singularity and becomes a milieu, an abstract and corporate subject. His head buzzes with the 'inner monologues of the so-called teeming millions' (166). He uses his gift of telepathy to infiltrate the private lives of private and public figures at first, but that infantile scene of peeping soon gives way to a new urgency of what Spivak calls 'the worlding of the world' (Spivak 1990: 1). Saleem renews himself by becoming a federation of equals and opposites, a democratic community of sentiments and aspirations that would give form and shape to a seemingly amorphous new nation:

> Because the feeling had come upon me that I was somehow creating a world; that the thoughts I jumped inside were *mine* . . . as current affairs, arts, sports, the whole rich variety of a first-class radio station poured into me, I was somehow *making them happen*. (174)

Saleem selects 581 surviving children from the 1,001 born in the first hour of India's independence, children both freakishly gifted like him and 'different'. The midnight babies, privileged by Saleem as fabricators of the national narrative, are, however, themselves emplotted and victimized in the course of the novel. The Midnight's Children's Conference is truly finished when Saleem is given a 'sperectomy', which lets out all hope from his body. The last section of the novel sees Saleem marginalized, penalized and castrated; his silver spittoon, an enduring symbol of memory and conjuration, is bulldozed away. The joyous communal chorus that was MCC dies down as Indira Gandhi ushers in the continuous midnight of a two-year long Emergency and Rushdie's *bildung* ends with a violent fantasy of discombobulation. Saleem is pulverized to 'specks of voiceless dust' (462), but perhaps another renewal has begun in that these could also be the specks of commemorative ink on paper.

Gibreel Farishta, whose stage name testifies to the first of many acts of self-invention, is yet another creature of reincarnation. First, his reversal of fortune from working class oblivion to the nurturing mentorship of his boss, Babasaheb Matre, who facilitates his break in films ('Boy like you is too damn goodlooking to carry tiffins on his head all his life' (Rushdie 1987: 23), followed by his phenomenal success in theological movies. Then there is his unexpected recovery from a freak on-set accident that left him haemorrhaging inside his skin: this, in turn, leads to a monumental loss of faith and a ham-eating metamorphosis. Finally, he commits career suicide after a transformative encounter with Alleluia Cone, who enjoins change, and suffers yet another miraculous rebirth in 'Proper London' after escaping the hijacking of an Air India jumbo. However, for all his 'new beginnings and metamorphoses', Gibreel subscribes, we are told, to the fallacious idea of the self as being "homogenous, non-hybrid, "pure"'" (427). Unsurprisingly then, he is precipitately disarticulated and made absurdly discontinuous after he is 'born again' on an English beach (31). India's reigning king of celluloid theologicals becomes an unwitting instrument in an act of theological revisionism in the twentieth century that Amir Mufti has described as 'a sweeping rearrangement and rethinking of the terms of Muslim public culture' (Mufti 1991: 97).

'To get his mind off the subject of love, and desire, he studied, becoming an omnivorous autodidact, devouring the metamorphic myths of Greece and Rome, the avatars of Jupiter, the boy who became a flower, the spider woman, Circe, everything' (Rushdie 1987: 23–4). In the animistic universe of *Satanic Verses*, the Ovidian characters so loved by Gibreel Farishta in his formative years come to lurid poetic and political existence: 'change-for-fusion, change-by-conjoining', as Rushdie says in Ovidian cadences of the love song that is *The Satanic Verses* (Rushdie 1991: 394). The subversive fusing of animal, human, ideas and cultures, national borders and identities is not merely an act of defying 'the absolutism of the Pure' (394). Rushdie's Ovidian extrapolations are also his homage to the proleptic power of discourse, which has liberating as well as oppressive implications. This is evident in the episode where Saladin

Chamcha turns into a demi-goat and is whisked away to a Detention Centre for troublesome migrants. There he finds a fashion model turned man-tiger or manticore, businessmen from Nigeria who had grown tails, holidaymakers from Senegal who had turned into snakes during transit.

> 'But how do they do it?' Chamcha wanted to know.
> 'They describe us', the other whispered solemnly. (168)

Against this model of coercive regimes of modern power and knowledge is Rushdie's tale of the poet Baal, whom Ionnis Ziogas likens to Ovid's Orpheus, the magic of whose lyre stayed his eventual execution in the hands of the Thracian matrons. When his twelve wives are incarcerated and about to be executed under the 'new immorality laws', Baal's song moves their gaolers to tears. 'I am Baal', he says, 'I recognize no jurisdiction except that of my Muse' (391), a small triumph for the artist before he is captured and beheaded. Saladin Chamcha, that anglicized creature of willed discontinuities and multiple voices, is allowed a final role reversal, where he embraces the consolation of an imagined community, which in turn makes possible a bittersweet homecoming. Transformed by his stay in the ethnic ghetto of Brickhall, the city 'visible but unseen' by the denizens of Proper London, Saladin Chamcha, reconciled to his humanity and redeemed through his own self-acceptance and the forgiveness of others, is ready for a transmutation breathtaking in its simplicity. The 'bizarreries' of his old English life firmly behind him, Saladin Chamcha, 'toadji', or the old apologist of empire, goes home to Bombay, daring finally to speak of his 'newly discovered racination' (Suleri 1992: 196) as 'renewal' and 'regeneration' (*SV* 534).

'Europe Repeats Itself, in India, as Farce'

In his *Financial Times* review of *The Enchantress of Florence*, a novel that brings medieval Florence to the court of Akbar, and shows how the spirit of Renaissance was not simply confined to Europe, but had Mughal, Ottoman and Persian flowerings, John Sutherland astutely observes the following: 'What point is it making? That there is as much unclash as clash.' Salman Rushdie's rewriting of the canon could be similarly read cultural conversation and a form of translation, whereby he arrogates to the author-function of his works the prerogative of knowing how 'other realities are conjugated' (Rushdie 1981: 246). Saleem Sinai is a 'swallower of lives' (*Midnight's Children, MC* 9): 'to understand me, you'll have to swallow a world' (283). Rushdie's mimesis of the Western canon of literature takes place in the mode of what Spivak terms as postcolonial 'citation, reinscription, rerouting the historical' (1993: 244). In a *Paris Review Interview*, he reveals his strong identification in the post-Fatwa years with authors whose writerly lives were fringed with personal tragedies:

> Ovid in exile, Dostoevsky in front of the firing squad, Genet in jail – and look what they did: the *Metamorphoses, Crime and Punishment,* everything that Genet wrote is prison literature. I thought, well, if they can do it, I can have a go at doing it. (January 1, 2008)

The grounds of Rushdie's long-standing fascination with Ovid are revealed in his review of Christoph Ransmayr's *The Last World,* an inter-weaving of the textuality of *Metamorphoses* with the life of the historical Ovid: the bitter exile in Tomis on the shores of the Black Sea; the eternal story of dissidence and tyrannical despots; the turning of banal and barbaric lives into the mythopoeic; his big nose, which earned for Ovid the nickname Naso (*Imaginary Homelands, IH* 291–3). Rani Harappa's ekphrastic shawls in *Shame* are borrowed from Arachne's graphic weav-ings of the depredations of a corrupt, patriarchal state. Alleluia Cone's death from the high tower in *Satanic Verses* mirrors that of Psyche, while stuttering Sisodia is a veritable Echo. Ovidian text erupts in the guise of cloudforms, 'ceaselessly metamorphosing, gods into bulls, women into spiders, men into wolves' (Rushdie 1987: 6), and in the story of the latter-day Eurydice and Orpheus, Vina Apsara and Ormus Cama, set against the invention of the metamorphosing form of Rock 'N' Roll in *The Ground Beneath Her Feet.* Moving on from Ovid, the roll call of Anglo-American classics that constitute the hauntology of a Rushdie novel is long: *The Satanic Verses* alone alludes to Blake's *The Marriage of Heaven and Hell,* Bulgakov's *The Master and Margarita,* Joyce's *Ulysses* and *A Portrait of the Artist as a Young Man,* Hemingway's *Moby Dick* and Calvino's *Invisible Cities.*

Similarly, the influence of the grand, authorizing narratives of the East – *The Arabian Nights, Panchatantra, Katha Sarit Sagar,* Ramayana and *Mahabharata,* Farid-Ud-Din Attar's *The Conference of Birds,* not to mention the *Qur'ān* – dominate Rushdie's work. Commenting on his appropria-tion of the Indian epic and folktale, Kumkum Sangari states:

> The informality of the epic structure – the scope for interpolation, digres-sion, accretion, in addition to its self-ascribed status as history or *itihaas* – has allowed it in the past to represent ideological collectivities as well as to permit the expression of contesting world views. (Sangari 2002: 20)

The terms of Rushdie's engagement with the classical canon, both Eastern and Western, are relatable to the kinds of creative discord that Emperor Akbar in *The Enchantress of Florence* associates with the realization of true harmony: 'difference, disobedience, disagreement, irreverence, iconoclasm, impudence, even insolence' (310). To read is to reread, refind, and rewrite. In *Haroun and the Sea of Stories,* the process of

'Pagination and Collection' of the Guppee army is a powerful allegory of the textual revisionism that is characteristic of Rushdie's canonical extrapolations. The Guppee soldiers are literally pages, thin persons in rectangular uniforms that 'rustle exactly like paper' (116). As Aron Aji points out, the reorganization of the pages could be read as the inventive acts of critical appraisal the *suras* of the *Qu'rān* encourage: in each new reading, 'the existing ones are neither destroyed nor undermined but brought together in new, harmonious and compatible wholes' (124). Rushdie's fond evocation of the elephant God, Ganesha, the narrator of the epic Mahabharata, too flirts with blasphemy. If he gleefully associates the Hindu god with the long-nosed, sexually maladroit scribe of *Midnight's Children*, he makes Aurora in *The Moor's Last Sigh* directly take on the deity by dancing a pagan elephant dance on the cliffs on the day of the Ganpati festival. Gibreel Farishta achieves superstardom after the theological *Ganpati Baba*, all trunk and ears. 'The seductions of his fame had grown so great that . . . young ladies asked him if he would keep the Ganesh-mask on while they made love, but he refused out of respect for the dignity of the god' (25).

While references from South Asian popular culture pepper Rushdie's prose, especially in the 'India' novels, it is harder to locate the influence of canonical literature in vernacular languages from the subcontinent in the same. This is partly due to Rushdie's disenchantment with the more communal, nationalistic aspects of vernacular India. In a telling episode in *The Moor's Last Sigh*, a novel that unremittingly pits plural, often incompatible, realities against ideas of 'pure India' championed by the religious rightwing, Camoens Gama attends a gathering in Malgudi, a small town on the banks of the river Sarayu, to hear Mahatma Gandhi speak. Rushdie here is channelling *Waiting for the Mahatma* (1955), of whose author, R. K. Narayan, Naipaul said that 'Narayan writes in English of Indian Life' (*Literary Occasions* 25). While the simplicity of rural Indian life moves Camoens, he is put off by the 'God stuff': In the city we are for secular India but the village is for Ram' (55). If Rushdie's overwrought prose strikes a startling contrast with Narayan's plain style, it also marks a cynical attitude toward transparency, whether in Narayan's untroubled use of a global and national language (English) to describe regional lives and rural politics, or in the simple message of syncretism in the Gandhian *dhun* or melody that Camoens sees galvanizing the gathering: 'they say *Ishwar and Allah is your name* but they don't mean it, they mean only Ram himself, king of Raghu clan, purifier of sinners along with Sita', Camoens notes (*The Moor's Last Sigh* 56). The conspicuous lack of reference to the vernacular canon of literature from the subcontinent is no doubt related to Rushdie's notorious pronouncement in the *Vintage Book of Indian Writing* that prose writing in English in the 50 years of the country's independence (1947–97) was proving to be 'a more interesting body of work' than cultural productions in India's 16 official languages. He goes on to add that the 'still burgeoning,

"Indo-English" literature represents perhaps the most valuable contribution that India has yet made to the world of books' (x). As Debjani Ganguli comments, 'In one rhetorical sweep, India's best-known literary celebrity in this era of global English had rubbished centuries of India's fabled linguistic and literary plenitude, and tainted its contemporary indigenous literary productions as inward looking' (650). It would seem that for Rushdie the vernacular is interchangeable with the parochial, while English becomes the only fitting medium of secular urban cosmopolitanism: what Rushdie once lauded as the 'the Indian talent for non-stop self-generation' (Rushdie 1991: 17), clearly, happens only at the level of the *English* language, albeit a hybridized, contextual and unmistakably 'vernacular' English.

'One universe, one dimension, one country, one dream, bumpo'ing into another, or being under, or being on top of': this is how Aurora describes her utopian project of painting Moorish Spain, 'a romantic myth of a plural, hybrid, nation', over the reality of divided, sectarian India (Rushdie 1995: 226, 227). J. M. Coetzee sees in Aurora's Mooristan a working model of Rushdie's own palimpsest-like aesthetic recall: 'not overpainting India in the sense of blotting it out with a fantasy alternative, but laying an alternative, promised-land text or texturation over it like gauze' (*Stranger Shores* 202). The ubiquitous traces of canonical works in the cycles of Rushdie's own 'palimpsestine' belie a childish logic of plenitude that disavows lack. 'Like the taxonomy of migrancy, Rushdie provides what may be called an oneiric multiplicity, the dream as legitimating matrix' (Spivak 1993: 253). Disavowing the Oedipal logic of supplanting the law of the father through acts of creative misprision, Rushdie argues for a model of self-generation and perpetuation – the child as the father of man – wherein parents are not always accidental but elected, sometimes half consciously, and the belated novelist's literary output perpetuates, instead of cancelling, the 'polyglot family tree' of his predecessors such as Gogol, Cervantes, Kafka, Melville, Machado de Assis: 'it is perhaps one of the more pleasant freedoms of the literary migrant to be able to choose his parents' (Rushdie 1991: 20–1).

Salman Rushdie and the Rise of Postcolonial Studies: *Grimus*, *Midnight's Children* and *Shame*

ELEANOR BYRNE

Great writers generate the current that powers the lights by which their work is read. A measure of Rushdie's significance as a writer is the way his work has stimulated a new critical vocabulary, a new 'tool box' of analytical concepts. His work has been integral to the growth of ideas and issues known as 'post-colonial studies'. This chapter, looking at his first three novels, focuses on two aspects of this, two areas central to this field and to Rushdie: the idea of migrancy and the formation of the nation after Empire. There are many forms of migrancy (economic, exilic, émigré or refugee) and 'it is the immigrant writer who is best equipped by [a] kind of double vision to come up with the corresponding new literary forms' (Cook 1994: 23). Rushdie has also narrated the complex histories of anti-colonial national struggle and described the interwoven and often violent birth of nations out of Empire. This chapter then explores these issues in *Grimus*, *Midnight's Children* and *Shame* and in the critics who address them.

Grimus: False Starts and False Voices

Immediately, there is a problem. Salman Rushdie's first novel *Grimus* (1975) does not at first sight fit the 'narrative' I have suggested. It was not widely reviewed, and where reviewed, not well received, as Rushdie himself comments: '*Grimus* . . . to put it mildly, bombed' (Rushdie 1991: 1). Moreover, there is a critical consensus that *Midnight's Children*, *Shame* and *The Satanic Verses* might most usefully be understood as a trilogy (Proctor 2012) which leaves *Grimus* rather unaffiliated. It is a first novel but, in some ways, it is 'out of sequence'. Damian Grant's account indicates its perceived failings, '*Grimus* is a young man's novel; it is over-ambitious, over-literary, philosophically overheated; a novel of ideas, in the doubtful sense that it is the ideas that run the show – it may be considered premature' (Grant 1999: 27).

Some writers appear to 'find' their voice immediately: their first novel seems to speak both to their personal co-ordinates and to their readership, and to the political and national culture of an era. *Midnight's Children* did this, but *Grimus* just doesn't *sound* like his next two. Its lack of recognizable and defined voice at the heart of the narrative is ultimately what Rushdie laments:

> I feel very distant from *Grimus*, mainly because I don't like the language it is written in. It's a question of hearing your own voice, and I don't hear it because I hadn't found it then. (Rushdie 1985: 123)

In this light, *Grimus* appears as a false start, springing forward before the starter's gun has gone off, that forces the racer to return to the blocks to try again. The falseness of voice appears as a kind of faithlessness to its owner.

However, its perceived failures are as interesting as the later successes, and latterly literary critics have returned to the text looking for embryonic forms of the key critical themes and formal innovations associated with his subsequent work. As James Proctor notes,

> [U]nlike his subsequent writing, all of which reveals a firmly geographical imagination (despite and perhaps because of its preoccupations with dislocation), there is a certain boundlessness about Rushdie's first novel, which critics like Timothy Brennan have argued explain its neglect. What is suggestive in terms of the later fiction is Rushdie's fascination with the central ideas of admixture and migration. (2009)

Some of these readings or re-readings are convincing, as they suggest the novel carries seeds of later more fully realized preoccupations of Rushdie and postcolonial studies, which with the benefit of hindsight we can now uncover.

The most important of these is the relationship between migrancy and form. Mujeebuddin Syed, for example, comments that by 'combining mythology and science fiction, mixing oriental thought with Western modes, *Grimus* is in many ways an early manifesto of Rushdie's heterodoxial themes and innovative techniques' (Syed 1994: 135). Catherine Cundy is slightly less forgiving, but writes that the protagonist is 'a nascent and tentative study of migrant identity' (Cundy 1992: 128). *Grimus* was written by Rushdie as an entry for the publisher Victor Gollancz's Science Fiction Prize. Whilst it did not win, it was published but not on a science fiction category list. This might have been a publicity and marketing decision but it also reflects the wide variety of genres being invoked and explored in the novel. Set in a future landscape, the narrative falls somewhere between a quest and a saga, and demonstrates a fascination with multiple internal dimensions and external realities that does give some credence to the view that Rushdie's later interest in cultural translation, migration, borders and inbetweenness acted out in form can be seen here.

The novel follows the adventures of Flapping Eagle, a young Amerindian cast out from a fictitious tribe, the Axona, as he traverses a version of the 'real' world, mostly by sea, on a quest in search for Grimus, a god like creator, who has given him an elixir of eternal life: Flapping Eagle has tired of this gift after over 700 years of travelling. He seeks Calf Island, a mythical timeless place where all the inhabitants, Grimus's victims, also exhausted by their immortality live together in the city of K. He eventually finds it, falling through a hole in the sea, and he realizes that the purpose of his quest is to kill Grimus: Grimus himself wishes for and has planned this conclusion. The novel ends with Grimus's death and the disintegration of the 'reality' of Calf Island.

Grimus's locations are largely drawn by Rushdie from several other fictions. Depending on one's perspective it is overly derivative, or innovative in its attempts to weave a hybrid narrative out of two distinct literary and religious traditions. Notably it blends allusions to the Sufi poem, *The Conference of Birds*, by Farid ud 'Din Attar, and Dante's *Commedia:* it is preoccupied with the exploration of interior and exterior landscapes involved in the search for meaning and God. Grimus's name is a reversal of the name of a mythical bird, the Simurg, the goal of the birds' quest in *The Conference of Birds*. The 30 birds in the poem all have character flaws that represent different aspects of human frailty: none are suited to be a leader. They begin the quest to find the Simurg to be their leader and finally arrive at a lake where they see their own reflections in the water. Flapping Eagle repeats this journey. Indeed, Flapping Eagle is Grimus's physical double, although he is the last to know this (he doesn't set eyes on Grimus until late in the novel): his companions, however, have known this for some time and this has in turn affected their treatment of him, their reading of his 'fate' and their response to his own requests to be guided to Grimus. Flapping Eagle's guide in his quest up Calf Mountain is Virgil Jones, clearly modelled on Dante's Virgil in the *Commedia*.

Whilst poorly received by readers and critics alike at the time, this model of cultural and literary hybridity in *Grimus*, even only partially formulated, is precisely what many critics praise in his later work. Similarly his exploration of the ways in which the postcolonial migrant experiences themselves as a provisional subject, both at home and a stranger in both their counties of origin and destination, a blender of traditions and a translated subject, is evident in the portrayal of Flapping Eagle. In his depiction of the pains of immortality in chapter six, in a long italicized passage, there is a clear sense of a kind of rehearsal of the pains of migrant subjectivity.

He was the leopard who changed his spots, he was the worm that turned. He was the shifting sands and the ebbing tide. He was moody as the sky, circular as the seasons, nameless as glass. He was Chameleon, changeling, all things to all men and nothing to any man. He had become his enemies and eaten his friends. He was all of them and none of them [. . .] Stripped of his past, forsaking the language of his ancestors for the languages of the archipelagos of the world, forsaking the ways of his ancestors for those of the places he drifted to.

Immorality is a metaphor here for the experience of migration: the troubles of humans made immortal stem from the need to adapt endlessly to the multiple worlds and times, to the experience of loss and remaking. These are parallel, Rushdie suggests, to the experience of a postcolonial migrant subject, remaking themselves in a new location. *Grimus* is perhaps most interesting then in the ways that it has not quite grasped the subject under its own nose, exploring the migrant condition through a series of ciphers and fantasy landscapes, only rarely able to name the losses and gains of the migrant subject.

Midnight's Children and the Rise of Postcolonial Studies

Midnight's Children has been widely judged as one of the best novels of the second half of the twentieth century and Rushdie's finest: its narrative drive and energy is not surpassed by any of his successive novels. It has what Søren Frank terms a 'hypercanonical' status in the West (Frank 2010: 187), a status reinforced by having been voted the 'Booker of Bookers', the 'best' book to have won the Booker Prize since its inception in 1969.

However, the Booker itself is open to postcolonial irony: as Graham Huggan notes, the original Booker company ran distribution networks on sugar estates in Guyana (Huggan 2001: 106–7). Huggan is suspicious of the prize, seeing in it a contradictory influence on contemporary literary production. While *Midnight's Children* has been globally celebrated for its eloquent and evocative explorations of questions of identity, history, colonial legacies and national imaginings, critically scrutinizing the British legacy in India, it has also been criticized for reproducing India as an exotic site of imaginary magic events (the film poster for the 2012 production of Midnight's Children, directed by Deepa Mehta, which shows, sepia-tinted, a young Indian woman dancing in traditional dress, might be accused of this, perhaps). Huggan argues that while ostensibly

Midnight's Children is a radically revisionist novel, a work of historiographic metafiction that shows the inescapably ideological character of historical facts . . . this has not prevented the novel being read – and judged accordingly – as a surrogate guidebook, or as a medley of incomplete historical narratives that engage with India's (post-)imperial historical past. While deconstructive of historical accuracy, *Midnight's Children* has still been accused of being inaccurate; while critical of the commodification of an Orientalised India, it has profited precisely by circulating such commercially viable Orientalist myths ... Its author has been rewarded, not so much for writing against the Empire, but for having done it so amenably, with such obviously marketable panache. (2001: 115)

Huggan's comments demonstrate a level of critical anxiety about the saturation of the postcolonial field by Rushdie, and his popularity with Western audiences is sometimes read as potentially a sign of complicity with a Western readership's Orientalist desire to 'see' India as more colourful, teeming, sensual and dreamlike, than the industrialized West, a projection that fails to account for the material legacies and ongoing effects of Imperialist power and globalization. It is exactly this sort of anxiety that often features in the teaching of postcolonial studies. However, I want to focus on two other concepts, tied to migrancy and the nation, that are central and that stem from Rushdie's work: hybridity and the relationship between nation and form.

Hybridity

The study of postcolonial literatures in universities is a relatively new phenomenon replacing what was previously termed 'Commonwealth Literature'; something that Rushdie notoriously claimed 'did not exist' (Rushdie 1991: 61–70). For Rushdie the term 'commonwealth literature' risked 'creating a ghetto mentality amongst some its occupants' (63). Crucially for Rushdie, writers placed in this category were praised for having written work that could be seen to be 'wholly' from the culture from which they were seen to belong and books 'which mix traditions or which seek to consciously break with tradition are often treated as highly suspect' (66). The fetishization of 'authenticity' that this entailed was anathema to Rushdie's own literary project at the time.

One aspect of this fetishization of 'authenticity' lies in the very choice of language in which to write. The rise of English to the status of global language is clearly yoked to the influence of the British Empire and its imposition of English as the language of administration and education across its colonies. The subsequent unravelling of Empire in the post-war era produced a range of questions and debates about the choice of English (as opposed to an indigenous language) as the language for administration, education and – crucially – self-expression in newly independent nations such as India, Pakistan, Kenya or Nigeria. There was a very famous debate between Ngũgĩ wa Thiong'o, a Kenyan, who argued that writers from the former colonies should use their own languages to build their own communities, and the Nigerian Chinua Achebe, who argued that using, and subtly altering English, would give their writing a much greater audience and so spread its message further. In relation to these debates, Rushdie argued that Indian culture was necessarily eclectic, 'we possess a mixed tradition, a mélange of elements as disparate as ancient Mughal and contemporary Coca-Cola American . . . Eclecticism, the ability to take from the world what seems fitting and to leave the rest, has always been a hallmark of the Indian tradition' (Rushdie 1991: 67). This provided one form of answer to these questions as well as the central idea in *Midnight's Children*: the idea of mixing called 'chutnificaition' or, in the term celebrated by the critic Homi Bhabha, *hybridity*.

This 'chutnificaition' occurs at the level of form. If one of the failed projects of *Grimus* was to produce a hybrid narrative that could accommodate Eastern and Western literary traditions, *Midnight's Children* is widely praised for succeeding in doing so. Many genres constitute its hybridity: 'saga, *Bildungsroman*, autobiography, national history, myth, legend, the picaresque, epic, slum-naturalism, magical realism, essay, prophecy, satire, comedy, tragedy, surrealism' (Frank 2010: 187). Its literary forebears are also too many to ever fully account for, but it reflects the double literary and cultural inheritance that Rushdie experienced as a boy growing up in Bombay watching both Bollywood and American movies. Rushdie cites his own influences in general as 'Gogol, Cervantes, Kafka, Melville, Machado de Assis', all of whom might be found in this novel, but also clearly makes use of the structures of the *Mahabharata*, and *One Thousand and One Nights*. The narrative is written and told in front of an audience, an implied reader and Padma, who sits at Saleem's feet as Ganesha sat at Vyasa's to take down his story. Interestingly this is a reversal though, as Rushdie himself notes, Saleem gets his references to Hindu mythology badly mixed up and ignores his own clear similarities to Ganesha – 'elephantine nose and dubious parentage' (Rushdie 1991: 25). Saleem also pictures himself as Scheherazade telling stories to delay his execution. As Saleem maps himself onto history and recasts the history of India as an extended family saga, it becomes clear that his memory sometimes fails him, he offers frequent digressions from the main narrative trajectory in the style of Laurence Sterne's *Tristram Shandy* (1767), whose narrator finds he has not even reached the account of his own birth until volume III.

Form and the Nation in 'Double Time'

The central conceit of *Midnight's Children* is that the fate of its protagonist narrator Saleem Sinai is to be born at the stroke of midnight, the moment of Indian independence. The events in his own life will always be tied to the fate of India as a nation. Midnight's Children are the 1,001 children born in the first hour of India's independence, all with marvelous gifts, who Saleem gradually 'tunes into' like a radio after an accident, whilst spying on his mother from the laundry basket in his parents' bathroom, causes him to acquire telepathic powers. The narrative is told through interplay of analepsis and prolepsis (flashback and flash-forwards), with key events in the narrative sometimes hinted at, like a movie trailer which offers selected highlights of the next part of the narrative, revealing the conclusion rather than adhering to convention of suspense. The narrative moves between different times and narrative voices as Saleem stages the writing of his childhood experience while he works in a pickle factory, writing his autobiography during the evenings and retelling it to Padma. He claims that there is an explicit parallel between writing literature, its ability to preserve history, and memory, and the preservation of fresh vegetables in the pickling process: thus, as I've suggested, the 'chutneyfication of history'.

For Franco Moretti, *Midnight's Children* disrupts the very tradition of the novel as a Eurocentric form, reorienting the 'centre of gravity' from a narrow European circuit to a 'truly worldwide literary system' (Moretti 1996: 249). Moretti suggests that *Midnight's Children*, with other novels, ushers in a new dynamic and a new aesthetics for the novel. Moretti includes it in a much longer discussion of Gabriel Garcia Marquez's celebrated *One Hundred Years of Solitude* (1968) in which he discusses the impact of the Latin American literary boom of the late 1960s and the 1970s:

> [N]o postwar work has been greeted by the Old World with more enthusiasm than *One Hundred Years of Solitude*. Does this mean that Garcia Marquez's novel really belongs like it or not, to the Western tradition? Not exactly. Or rather, it half belongs to it (just like *Midnight's Children*, which I shall often mention too): sufficiently at home to make itself understood – but also sufficiently alien to say different things. And to succeed, moreover, in solving symbolic problems that European literature was no longer able to work through. (1996: 233)

Moretti notes that the writing often critically identified under the heading of 'Magical Realism', in which he includes both Rushdie and Marquez, 'takes the *avant garde*, and sets its feet on the ground'. Moretti is referring here to European modernist writing which he characterizes as having experimented extensively with form, polyphony and technical complexity, but at the expense of the anthropocentric, of the human and of voice. In *Midnight's Children* the opposite happens, and polyphony is re-motivated: there are many languages in the novel, because India is divided into many cultures, and Saleem, with his extraordinary hearing, manages to hear them all. The technical complexity remains, but it is *naturalized* (Moretti 1996: 234).

Saleem's telepathic power to which Moretti is referring here does not sit comfortably in the fictional world of his childhood, the 'magic' is not accepted as part of an everyday marvellous reality, but shocks and horrifies his parents when he confesses, 'I heard voices yesterday. Voices are speaking to me inside my heard. I think – Ammi, Abboo, I really think – that Archangels have started to talk to me' (164). Saleem cites both Moses on Mount Sinai and Muhammad on Mount Hira, before offering his own comic diminutive, 'I heard voices on a hill' (163). The Midnight's Children's Conference, or MCC, radio and telepathy signal a new relationship between public and private spheres. The parliament inside Saleem's head numbers 581 surviving children, referencing the members of the Indian Parliament, while the MCC also represent the initials of the most famous cricket club in the world (Marylebone Cricket Club) at Lords in London. Rushdie points up the irony of this icon of post-independence India re-installing at its centre a figure for the metropolis. As metaphors are made literal they appear darkly comic. For Stephen Slemon turning the debate specifically to the postcolonial context, 'the magic realist narrative recapitulates a dialogical struggle within culture's language, a dialectic between codes of recognition inherent with the inherited language' (that of the colonizer) and 'those imagined codes – perhaps utopian or future oriented – that characterize a culture's original relations with the world'. Magical realism as a postcolonial form, he argues, enables a 'foreshadowing of history so that the time scheme of the novel metaphorically contains the long process of colonisation and its aftermath and a thematic foregrounding of gaps absences and silences produced by the colonial encounter' (Slemon: 19).

Frederic Jameson's controversial essay 'Third World Literature in the Era of Multinational Capitalism' had already identified what he saw as a constant in literary texts from what he termed the 'Third World':

> What all Third World cultural productions seem to have in common and what distinguishes them from analogous cultural forms in the first world – they are to be read as what I will call national allegories, even when, or perhaps I should say, particularly when their forms develop out of predominantly western machineries of representation, such as the novel. (Jameson, 1986: 69)

Whilst he acknowledges that this is a sweeping hypothesis he stands by it as a structural form applicable to non-First (Western capitalist) or Second (Socialist) World countries. Jameson's point was that the Western novel had historically observed a split between private and public spheres, with the novel seeing its material as the private sphere, separate from the world of economics and politics. This, he argued, did not apply to Third World texts, which even when seemingly about the private, 'necessarily project a political dimension in the form of a national allegory. 'The story of the private individual destiny is always an allegory of the embattled situation of the public-third-world culture and society' (72). He goes on to argue that allegorical structures do actually exist in Western writing but are deeply embedded in First World literary production, unconscious rather than conscious. An example of a critical excavation of such a text might be Edward Said's reading of Jane Austen's *Mansfield Park* that unearths the economics of slavery and plantation culture in the Caribbean upon which the foundations of Mansfield Park are built, and extrapolates from this the moral bankruptcy of the family hierarchy within.

Postcolonial critics have had mixed responses to this model. Questioning the sweeping nature of the claim, Aijaz Ahmad rejects a definition of the 'Third World' as defined by its experience of 'externally inserted phenomena', that is, the experience of national oppression under colonialism (Ahmad 1987: 20). But Neil Lazarus has defended Jameson's view arguing that 'only on the terrain of the nation can an articulation between cosmopolitan intellectualism and popular consciousness be forged' (Lazarus 1994: 216). What both critics share with Slemon is the idea of postcolonial nations as 'split', narrating themselves *both* as newly dynamic modern anti-colonial states that draw on, or operate in dialogue with, European models of governance *and* as sites of tradition, where a spiritual world, family structures and everyday practices and belief are claimed as the essence of national culture. It is this split that all three see as giving rise to the Magical Realist form, the disjuncture between the two modes. For postcolonial critic Homi Bhabha, this means that narratives of nation have to be understood as 'double'; 'the nation's people must be thought in double time', as they signify their present national ambitions through a mobilization of particular customs or beliefs with origins that may precede the birth of the nation itself (Bhabha 1994: 297).

Midnight's Children also seems to rehearse this dynamic of a kind of dialogue between intellectualism and popular consciousness through the conceit of Saleem and Padma's relationship. Saleem, very much as an intellectual, attempts to narrate the history of his life, and metaphorically that of the nation to Padma, one of its citizens, and finds himself in constant dialogue with her. She is a critic not a silent receiver of history's narratives. The narrative of postcolonial nation then is constructed between them, as Saleem tries to 'please' Padma, to make his account credible to popular consciousness that she embodies. Yet at the same time this might be reversed and he might be viewed as attempting to write a love story to her, to seduce her, with ever more incredible narratives of nation that speak of the intellectual's desire for 'the ordinary people' as originators of an authentic tradition on which to build the nation. 'Padma is certainly leaking into me. As history pours out of my fissured body, my lotus is quietly dripping in, with her down-to-earthery, and her paradoxical superstition, her contradictory love of the fabulous' (38). This exchange allegorizes the process by which the double narrative of the nation gets created.

For Bhabha, 'the society of the nation in the modern world is 'that curiously hybrid realm where private interests assume public significance and the two realms flow unceasingly and uncertainly into each other like waves in the never-ending stream of the life process'. Rushdie literalizes this through the mapping of Saleem's body onto the nation, the body politic. Bhabha notes 'the body has always stood for the people and the revolutionary nation in postcolonial theory', notably this goes as far back as in Fanon's writing where he refers to the colonized as occupying a 'zone of occult instability', this is a medical term for a set of underlying conditions that produce different symptoms in the shoulder and arm. The medical term for physical ailments turns into a metaphor for the psychic condition.

In *Midnight's Children*, Saleem is highly conscious of the allegorical claims of his narrative, even speaking of himself being burdened with metaphor. In his current form he is a shadow of his earlier self, a broken man, cracked, falling apart, has been forcibly sterilized and long since abandoned the dreams he associated with the 1,001 children of Midnight, of using his and their special powers to create a new India. His body has borne the same fate as that of the nation. His face looks like a map of India, as Saleem's sadistic geography teacher Zagallo delights in pointing out, 'In the face of thees ugly ape you don't see the whole map of India?'(231) As Neil Ten Kortenaar observes, the metaphor of the nation as a body is made literal and therefore comical; if India were a person it would be grotesque like Saleem (Kortenaar 2005: 35).

Shame and the Palimpsest Nation

The darkly comic richness of this self-conscious use of polyvalent metaphors and extended allegories as a kind of voicing of and playing out of this narrative 'problem' for the postcolonial nation is one that Rushdie continues to use in this next novel *Shame* (1983). In *Shame* Rushdie continues to pursue his interest in exploring the conditions of possibility for postcolonial nations, here focusing on the other nation he can claim, if only partially, to 'belong' to, Pakistan. 'Although I have known Pakistan for a long time I have never lived there for longer than six months at a stretch' (69). The effect of this is to foreground the narrator's complex claims to be able to write about a country he has 'learned in slices' (69). The narrator foregrounds his own migrant status, 'I, too, know something of this immigrant business. I am an emigrant from one country (India) and a newcomer in two (England, where I live, and Pakistan to which my family moved against my will) (85). Whilst the events are located in Pakistan, the narrator is elsewhere, rehearsing his own legitimacy as narrator which is compromised by his ambiguous relation to the nation. Like *Midnight's Children* it attempts to map a political history, that of Pakistan, onto the fortunes of one extended family, it also becomes a means to explore more generally the experiences of being a migrant postcolonial subject and 'finds' a perfect metaphor for this condition in the figure of translation, one that will be subsequently extensively used by postcolonial critics. Brendon Nicholls comments on this: as 'Rushdie's fiction is keenly aware, translation always addresses at least two places, whether it involves a movement between a source language and a target language, or the migrant's movement across borders and cultures' (Nicholls 2007).

The narrator notes that the origins of the country's name might be read as symptomatic of this broader condition of migrancy, 'It is well known that the term Pakistan, an acronym, was originally thought up in England by a group of Muslim intellectuals [. . .] – So it was a word born in exile which then went east, was borne-across or trans-lated, and imposed itself on history; a returning migrant, settling down on partitioned land, forming a palimpsest on the past' (87). Pakistan itself contains a sizeable immigrant population caused by the movement of peoples during the years surrounding Partition. From its inception then Pakistan had its own *Mohajirs* – outsiders and immigrants – a term used against Bilquis Kemal, whose bodily transformation mirrors the violence of Partition, her past in India disappears in flames, her naked body re-clothed by her husband to be, Raza Hyder.

Pakistan's peculiar position as a postcolonial nation that was 'invented' at the point of partition with India in 1947 makes it a rich site for speculations about the country as a kind of collective imagining. Rushdie considers this as a kind of writing over, of history and memory, so that the figure of the palimpsest, a kind of writing over the top of a text that already exists, suggests itself as a useful metaphor for the process of bringing Pakistan into being as a nation. 'A palimpsest obscures what lies beneath. To build Pakistan it was necessary to cover up Indian history, to deny that Indian centuries lay just beneath the surface of Pakistani standard time. The past was rewritten there was nothing else to be done' (87). This affects the protagonist of the novel, Omar Khayyam Shakil, who is 'a peripheral hero', never quite the centre of his own story, afflicted with vertigo, with a sense of being at the edge of things, inverted. As in *Midnight's Children*, Omar Khayyam's body stands in for the body politic, his name borrowed from the Persian poet, who the narrator notes, 'was never very popular in his native Persia' (29) but was read in translation in the West. 'Dizzy, peripheral, inverted, infatuated, insomniac, stargazing, fat: what manner of hero is this?' our narrator asks (25). In fact his story is almost entirely over-shadowed by that of the central conflict between Iskander Harappa and Raza Hyder, who represent Zulfikar Ali Bhutto and Muhammad Zia-ul-haq respectively. For Sara Suleri, this does not just indicate how marginal the nation is to the power struggle between these two men, it also suggests something about Rushdie himself as a narrator from outside Pakistan: 'Omar Khayyam serves very little function in the plot of *Shame*, other than to represent the narrator's more self-punishing impulses, his sense of being an inept body in a discourse of history' (Suleri 1992: 188).

Of Omar Khayyam's many flaws the one most extensively explored is that which the book also bears as its title, Shame. Omar is instructed by his three mothers not to feel shame, and as a result lacks any moral centre. Rushdie's narrator struggles to explain the meaning of shame as he tries to 'translate' without losing the complexity of meanings with regard to cultural and language differences: '*Sharam*, that's the word. For which this paltry "shame" is a wholly inadequate translation [. . .] A short word, but one containing encyclopaedias of nuance' (33). As the narrative progresses, an inability to feel shame appears to afflict all the key characters, and acts as a figure for the epistemic and structural violence that those in power wield in Pakistan. As it is inadmissible to the Isky/Harappa dynamic, its repression from the public sphere means that it becomes embodied in the private one, in the most private and privileged site of identification within the nation, the female body. The figure of Sufiya Zinobia is a complex one in the book, a hybrid of many ghosts. Primarily she bears the story of another girl, a victim of an 'honour killing' (in itself a problematic term for violence perpetrated against women) in the East End of London. It is translated to Pakistan and merged with Omar's bride to be, who is born blushing and appears to soak up the unfelt shame for the nation. This shame eventually transforms her in to a violent monster. *Shame* closes with Sufiya's self-destruction and the decapitation of Omar Khayyam, all that remains is a 'silent cloud, in the shape of a giant grey and headless man, a figure of dreams' (286).

Conclusion

The hybridity that stems from migrancy and the complex development of the nation, as allegory (or not) are central themes in Rushdie's work: they are, as I have shown, central in postcolonial studies too. In this chapter, I have argued that these two, the fiction and the criticism, have been wound together, and it is through coming to both that we uncover a richer sense of meaning in Rushdie's fiction.

CHAPTER THREE

Rushdie as an International Writer: *The Ground Beneath Her Feet, Fury, Shalimar the Clown* and *The Enchantress of Florence*

MARIANNE CORRIGAN

Introduction

> Mapping the world is a new challenge, which is essentially what Rushdie has taken up in his works, both thematically and through his philosophy of representing, which has been compared to the metaphor of the rhizome used by Gilles Deleuze.
>
> Thomsen 2008: 94

In the introduction to *A Thousand Plateaus*, the French philosophers Gilles Deleuze and Félix Guattari set out their cultural concept of the rhizome. Based on the organizational framework of botanical roots, spreading like grass without a central 'core', the rhizome is an idea concerned with the principal of inter-connectivity: as Deleuze and Guattari argue, any 'point of a rhizome can be connected to anything other, and must be' (Deleuze and Guattari 1987: 7). A rhizome is non-hierarchal; it functions through a series of connections as opposed to feeding into a centre or a chain of command. Therefore, for Deleuze and Guattari, the rhizome is not a homogenous or totalizing system, it functions through pluralisms as opposed to conforming to one ideal. More specifically, the rhizome represents a network which is constantly undergoing a process of change; the only 'constant' aspect of the rhizome is that of its inter-connectivity. A modern-day, non-biological example of the rhizome would be the internet.

Mads Rosendahl Thomsen, as my epigraph suggests, finds a link between the rhizome and Rushdie's fiction. What is particularly interesting about Rushdie's writing, especially his twenty-first century novels, is the way in which they register the inter-connective networks of contemporary culture. History, religion, popular music, folklore and global culture coexist and connect with each other within Rushdie's novels, in what we can identify as rhizomatic narratives of globalization. The ideological focus of the novels *Midnight's Children*, *Shame* and *The Satanic Verses* on the deconstruction of colonial, hegemonic constructs, both culturally and politically, lead critics such as Revathi Krishnaswamy to locate his work as 'cross-pollinated by postmodernism and postcolonialism' (Krishnaswamy 2005: 91) and Sabrina Hassumani to argue that Rushdie is 'a postmodern writer whose subject is the postcolonial moment' (Hassumani 2002: 18).

In contrast, however, Timothy Brennan has argued that Rushdie is more appropriately identifiable as an 'international' (Brennan 1989: 17) writer, while Stephen Morton describes the 'worldliness' of his fiction, before going on to note 'the important contribution Rushdie's writing makes to understanding the relationship between imperialism, political violence and religion in the twenty-first century' (Morton 2008: 16). Drawing on these two important critical positions – Rushdie's internationalism and his worldliness – this chapter will look at Rushdie's later novels, *The Ground Beneath Her Feet*, *Fury*, *Shalimar the Clown* and *The Enchantress of Florence*, and examine how Rushdie's interest in globalization and cultural connectivity have helped to define him as an international writer in the twenty-first century.

Globalization

In *Globalization and Culture*, John Tomlinson argues that globalization 'refers to the rapidly developing and ever-densening [sic] network of interconnections and inter-dependences that characterize modern social life' (Tomlinson 1999: 2). While Tomlinson identifies the elements of inter-connectivity and interdependence which lie at the heart of the contemporary phenomenon which is globalization, it is not only modern social life which sees its effects: globalization is principally an economic process. The successful international distribution of consumerist goods and services by transnational companies, as well as the arrangement of current global economic markets, relies heavily upon institutions and organizations operating in unison as a 'whole' global power, as opposed to in isolation as individual nation states. In terms of consumer culture, globalization has seen the internationalization of products and services which were previously specific to certain geographic localities. While this process can be traced back to the Industrial Revolution and the importation of sugar, spices and precious metals by the British during the period of Empire, the process has intensified to such an extent that it is now accepted as standard to be able to walk into Tesco in England in the middle of the night on a Tuesday and purchase a dragon fruit which has been sourced from Israel. The availability of such a product in this context seemingly erases epistemological notions of time and space by closing the geographical distance which one would ordinarily have to travel in order to find this item, as well as considerably reducing the length of time it would take to arrive at such a location. In order to begin to comprehend the huge role of globalization in contemporary social and cultural patterns of consumption one only has to apply this thinking to the majority of other imported foodstuffs, electrical products or clothing which are presently available for purchase in the English supermarket.

The collocation of seemingly random images, foodstuffs, material goods or culture in one space, such as a supermarket, is itself a social and cultural symptom of the economic networks of globalization. David Harvey registers a comparison between this assembling of foodstuffs and the assembling of media images derived from differing geographic contexts in a homogenized viewing format which has been designed for ease of consumption by the viewer. Harvey describes how it is possible for viewers to 'experience a rush of images from different spaces almost simultaneously' (Harvey 2011: 13). Essentially, what Harvey describes is the repackaging or reassembling of products or digital images in a format which is designed to maximize their consumption.

How is this form of 'cultural collating' relevant Rushdie? It is clear that his novels reflect the process of assembling cultural 'products' or narratives through the ways in which he lifts stories or characters from different geographic locations, religious texts, historical accounts or cultural contexts, and jumbles them up together within the space of his novels for the reader's consumption. Consequently, we can see how the economic dimension to globalization is mirrored through the cultural form of the novel. If globalization involves, and is characterized by, the de-territorialization and the re-territorialization of frontiers, then Rushdie's later novels both engage with a bordered world but seek ways to look beyond it, through the reconfiguration of cultural material to form new rhizomatic connections within the space of the novel.

The Ground Beneath Her Feet

The Ground Beneath Her Feet is an intertextual exploration of the myth of Orpheus and Eurydice, set against a distorted, historical narrative documenting the development of rock music from the 1950s up to the 1990s through Rushdie's fictional super group VTO. VTO are Bombay-born Vina Apsara and Ormus Cama, both talented yet troubled singers who go on to become huge global pop music stars. When Vina vanishes during a devastating earthquake, Ormus continues to search for her in what manifests as a contemporary exploration of Orpheus' quest for Eurydice following her disappearance into the underworld. Moving away from concerns with examining the postcolonial nation state, the novel marks the beginning of Rushdie's narrative explorations of globalization, through an examination of the ways in which music is produced, circulated and consumed at the end of the twentieth century.

Popular music was, and remains, one of America's greatest exports. In the 1950s, the music was ideologically associated with notions of freedom and individuality; a post-war generation who rejected the austerity of their parents. Yet it is equally important to register the fact that the post-war economic and cultural dominance of America over European countries and developing nations in the 1950s resulted in a form of hegemony which was neither overtly political nor military, yet was certainly identifiable through the exportation of cultural products such as rock and roll music. Often the music may have been that of marginalized groups within society, such as black recording artists, yet the corporations who produced, marketed and circulated the products were the ones who profited, rather than the artist. Furthermore, this transference of a cultural product, such as music, and its accompanying ideologies, from an economically dominant nation to an emerging economy is an example of cultural imperialism. Bernd Hamm and Russell Charles Smandych define cultural imperialism as 'a by-product – sometimes intended, sometimes unintended, but always inevitable – of political and economic imperialism' (Hamm and Smandych 2005: 24).

Yet in *The Ground Beneath Her feet*, Rushdie attempts to register a resistance to the cultural domination of American music on a global scale by constructing a narrative whereby Ormus is the true inventor of rock and roll music, thus diversifying, or polluting, the seemingly homogenizing effect of American popular music:

> So according to Ormus and Vina's variant version of history, their alternative reality, we Bombayites can claim that it was in truth our music, born in Bombay like Ormus and me, not 'goods from foreign' but made in India, and maybe it was the foreigners who stole it from us. (96)

However, this strategy is problematic as both Rai and Vina do indeed accept the promises of capitalism and relocate to America, where Vina's iconicity and status as a global star sees her image commodified in various cultural forms for international consumption. Ormus and Vina are musical superstars in the same vein as artists such as Michael Jackson, Tina Turner or Elvis Presley. Rushdie also examines the important aspect of commodification to the transference of forms of cultural art (such as music), across geographical or cultural boundaries. As an international star, Vina essentially becomes a brand name, which can be used to endorse and subsequently market numerous products for international consumption: 'Her diet book and her health and fitness regime will become world-wide best-sellers. Later she will successfully pioneer the celebrity exercise video and license a range of organic vegetarian meals, which, under the name Vina's VegeTable, will also succeed' (394).

Through a portrait of Vina as an international, cultural icon, Rushdie begins to examine the tension between artistic value and economic value. *The Ground Beneath Her Feet* highlights the difficulties for an author or musical artist in maintaining any form of agency over their music once it has been released into the sphere of the global markets for purchase. Control over the very consumption of a cultural product can become an impossibility due to the de-territorializing effects of globalization, which seemingly erases geographic boundaries to create a consumer market which is universal, rather than concentrated in a specific region. Whilst music is portrayed as a deeply artistic form in the novel, problematically, it is also through music that Vina herself is commodified. Her songs and image become international merchandise which is marketed and consumed through the inter-connective economic and cultural channels brought about by globalization.

Fury

Set in America at the turn of the twenty-first century, Rushdie's ninth work of fiction, *Fury*, examines how consumerism, globalization and technological cultures such as gaming have connected to radically reconfigure concepts of self and identity in contemporary Western culture and society. Celia M. Wallhead argues that the novel marks Rushdie out as a 'global, international writer' (Wallhead 2002: 170), whilst Chhote Lal Khatri discusses the novel's attempt to register a 'universal dimension to the cause of fury' (Khatri 2006: 163). Rushdie's protagonist Professor Malik Solanka is a middle-class, economic migrant, who, driven by a fierce personal fury, abandons his wife and child in favour of a new life in America. Solanka is a dollmaker by profession; his prize creation is the Doll 'Little Brain', who sparks a cultural and media frenzy which ultimately begins to represent everything he despises about contemporary American materialism; in effect, Solanka unwittingly aids the expansion of an acquisitive culture which, in reality, disgusts him. The growth of Little Brain's cultural empire mirrors the rise of Barbie through her status as a global icon: both are dolls; both have doll-family members which are available for consumers to purchase; and both dolls have been awarded an identity and lifestyle into which consumerist society is able to buy:

> Little Brain: first a doll, later a puppet, then an animated cartoon . . . Little Brain moved to Brain Street in Brainville, with a whole family and neighbourhood posse of Brains: she had an older brother called Little Big Brain . . . and even a laconic cowboy movie star neighbour (John Brayne). (96)

In contemporary Western society, the body, and in turn selfhood, necessitates the consumption of mass-manufactured commodities for its expression. From the fashion industry to the automobile trade, the consumer is continually invited to invest in products which promise to enhance and improve the body and self: the message is clear, identity is intrinsically linked to artifices and material goods. *Fury* is thematically interested in how the virtual world represents a global space where consumers are able to enhance and alter their image through avatars, digital photography and the acquisition of new virtual identities in the online gaming sphere.

As the novel progresses, consumer demand for his products sees Solanka becoming increasingly immersed in the development of a virtual empire based around his doll-inspired creations. Solanka's complex virtual world revolves around the story of the Puppet Kings: a sci-fi adventure involving battles between various imaginary tribes.

> On the website, as it came into being, visitors would be able to wander at will between the project's different storylines and themes . . . Each of these in turn would lead to further pages, plunging ever deeper into the multidimensioned world of the Puppet Kings, offering games to play, video segments to watch, chat rooms to enter, and, naturally, things to buy. (187)

Through Solanka's creation of the virtual narrative 'The Puppet Kings', Rushdie illustrates the participation of contemporary society in active – as opposed to passive – consumerism. The market which Solanka targets does not simply consume his products in an 'inactive' manner, that is, by simply purchasing the figurine of a doll. Instead, the consumerist process becomes one of participation, whereby the consumer is invited to partake in active involvement with the product in question by interacting with the computer game, entering the chat rooms and ultimately immersing him or herself further in the virtual world.

The construction of identity through a set of virtual codes which are recognizable to other participants in the game in question, connected to one another by a globalized, rhizomatic electronic network, marks the beginning of Rushdie's exploration of how culture connects within audiovisual environments, such as the internet or the online gaming world. Towards the end of *Fury*, Solanka experiences a disturbing merging of the real and virtual worlds when a group of revolutionaries burgle a toy shop in Mildendo, Lilliput-Blefuscu, and steal a supply of Kronosian Cyborg masks and costumes. A political countercoup ensues in the form of living activists who have taken on the identities and aesthetics of the cyborg Puppet Kings. Here, the novel explores cultural anxieties regarding the online world taking over the organic world, as culturally we interact more and more with digital technology.

In addition to its exploration of global, gaming culture and consumerist society, *Fury* also explores the ways in which the virtual world offers a new lease of life to the traditional, linear format of the story. As opposed to a definite beginning and end, which exist within the traditional binding and involve the progressive turning of pages, the virtual game has the capacity to continue and evolve and contains multiple levels, possibilities and outcomes, all of which interconnect through a rhizomatic narrative. Here, we see how Rushdie has moved from examining the indigenous forms of oratory explored in *Midnight's Children*, to an interrogation of how the global, rhizomatic space of the internet has emerged as a space where new forms of narrative emerge in the twenty-first century.

Shalimar the Clown

Shalimar the Clown represents a shift in Rushdie's thematic focus from the cultural aspects of globalization explored in *The Ground Beneath Her Feet* and *Fury* to the political dimension, with specific attention to the military conflict in the disputed territory of Kashmir and the threat of international terrorism in the wake of the 9/11 attacks. In January 2000, Rushdie argued that 'the defining struggle of the new age would be between terrorism and security' (Rushdie 2002: 326) and *Shalimar the Clown* sees Rushdie exploring these themes through a complex, inter-connective narrative. The novel engages with a more historical consideration of globalization, through its allegorical and thematic examination of recent US neo-liberalist foreign policy and its relationship to the militarization of Kashmir. Shalimar begins life in Rushdie's fictional Kashmiri village of Pachigam as a talented performer who falls in love with a young girl called Boonyi. However, his tale is one of loss and tragedy, with both his relationship and country disintegrating, principally as a result of the complex cultural and political connections between Kashmir and America. When Max Ophuls, the American ambassador to India arrives in Pachigam to watch a production, he encounters, and is mesmerized, by Boonyi. Boonyi deserts Shalimar to become Max's lover, and as a result of his wife's affair with Max, Rushdie's anti-hero eventually becomes consumed with feelings of hatred and death: feelings which, fuelled by the preaching of the 'Iron Mullah', the leader of a terrorist group, subsequently translate into a desire to instigate murderous acts and witness bloodshed. Shalimar resolves to kill the American ambassador, and begins to formulate a plan to travel to America.

Shalimar's signature trick during his time spent as a performer with the village entertainers is to walk the tightrope: he

> remembered his father teaching him to walk the tightrope, and realized that travelling the secret routes of the invisible world was exactly the same. The routes were gathered air. Once you had learned to use them you felt as if you were flying, as if the illusory world in which most people lived was vanishing and you were flying across the skies without even needing to get on board a plane. (275)

Rushdie's description of travelling through the 'secret routes' of the 'invisible world' registers the complex and often clandestine networks which enable the transfer of information between terrorist organizations. Here, Rushdie is highlighting how the networks of inter-connectivity and interdependence which characterize globalization can be viewed in a negative light, as a result of the ways in which terrorist groups such as the IRA or al-Qaeda are able to communicate more effectively due to global communication networks. Stephen Morton argues that *Shalimar the Clown* sees Rushdie attempting 'to find a literary form appropriate to describe the transnational social and political relations that underpin globalisation' (Morton 2008: 131). As discussed at the beginning of this chapter, in terms of form, Rushdie's novels represent networks through the ways in which they draw together cultural, religious and historical information to explore the ways in which culture circulates and connects. *Shalimar the Clown* registers a relationship between novelistic form and theme by exploring the connection between the interpersonal events which unfold in a small Kashmiri village, and the political drama which plays out on the global, geopolitical stage.

Interestingly, the novel seeks to expand upon one of the principal themes of *Midnight's Children*, with his exploration of the magic realist concept of 'Historical Anchoring' or 'felt history' (Faris 2004: 23): terms used to describe the allegorical identification of a character, on a drastically physical level, with the events which are unfolding in his or her country. In effect, felt history is a magic realist technique to explore the connection between nation and individual. In *Shalimar the Clown*, Rushdie maps the militarization of Kashmir through the body of Boonyi, and her sexual relationship with Max. Having left Shalimar to be Max's lover, the American dream quickly begins to sour for Boonyi, as she turns to food and prescription drugs in an attempt to physically fill the spiritual void which results from having abandoned her husband: her

> appetite had grown to subcontinental size. It crossed all frontiers of language and custom [. . .] Inevitably her beauty dimmed. Her hair lost its lustre, her skin coarsened, her teeth rotted, her body odour soured, and her bulk – ah! Her bulk – increased steadily, week by week, day by day, almost hour by hour. Her head rattled with pills, her lungs were full of poppies. (203)

Boonyi's consumerism gradually morphs into a grotesque, self-destructive force. The aspects of her traditional 'Kashmiri self', her love of dance, culture and the spiritual, have been destroyed by the effects of gross consumerism; Boonyi finds herself ruined by gorging on the American dream, an example of the ills of excessive capitalism. As Neil Murphy summarizes: 'she grows fat, bloated and poisoned by the excessive use of Western consumer goods' (Murphy 2008: 354). Boonyi's body becomes a site of conflict between the spiritual and the physical; East and West, Kashmir and America; Shalimar the Clown and Ophuls. Through a complex inter-connective narrative which interrogates post-9/11 political polemic of religious fundamentalism and its symbiotic relationship with attitudes of anti-Americanism, Rushdie constructs a narrative exploration of global geopolitics in the twenty-first century.

The Enchantress of Florence

An intertextual exploration of historical accounts of Renaissance Florence and both the Ottoman and Mughal Empires, *The Enchantress of Florence* is a departure in thematic terms from Rushdie's previous works of fiction. The plot travels across continents, from the Mughal court of Akbar to Renaissance Florence, while simultaneously engaging with the cultural and philosophical ideas of the historical periods in question. The novel represents a more historical consideration of globalization, examining tropes of cultural and political connectivity by joining the historical periods of the Ottoman and Mughal empires with that of Renaissance Florence. While *The Ground Beneath Her Feet, Fury* and *Shalimar the Clown* are novels which mark Rushdie out as an international writer concerned with the exploration of global consumer culture and international politics in the twenty-first century, *The Enchantress* represents a desire to examine globalization and cultural connectivity within a more ancient historical context. Through the role of his picaresque storyteller, Mogor dell'Amore, also known as Ucello di Firenze and Niccolo Vespucci, Rushdie draws together specific moments in both Indian and European history, as well as a particular focus on the cross-cultural connections among myth, magic and folklore.

In terms of cultural connectivity, *The Enchantress of Florence* is representative both materially and metaphorically of the concept of the novel as a network, as a result of the complex intertextual rhizomes which constitute its narrative. The plot is populated by a mixture of historical, fictional and magical characters, all of whom interact with each other within the textual framework; the result is an uncanny amalgamation of fact and fiction. The Italian writer and philosopher Niccolò Machiavelli is a prominent character in the novel, and interestingly, Rushdie treats him with particular sympathy:

[A]fter fourteen years of loyal service the people had shown that they did not care about loyalty. The people were fools for power. They had allowed il Machia to be taken down into the underground bowels of the city where the torturers waited. Such a people did not deserve to be cared for. They did not deserve a republic. [. . .] The people had wanted his death, or at least had not cared if he lived or died. In the city that gave the world the idea of the value and freedom of the individual human soul they had not valued him and cared not a fig for his soul's freedom, nor his body's integrity neither. (300)

Rushdie's intertextual use of Machiavelli in the novel exemplifies how historiographically defined notions of self and identity may be reimagined within the space of fictional narrative. In Rushdie's case, the Machiavelli who appears in *The Enchantress of Florence* does little to embody the characteristics of political deceit and deception which have been synonymous with the name of the historical figure of Machiavelli since the sixteenth century. Here, Rushdie seeks to explode received historical truths regarding established notions of character and identity, and attempts to explore how concepts of citizenship may be reconfigured through textual migrancy.

Indeed, migrancy is a key theme in *The Enchantress of Florence*. In many ways, the text revisits some of *The Satanic Verses'* principal thematic concerns through an exploration of migrant identity and marginality. Mogor dell'Amore is a protagonist who maintains close links with the picaresque hero. He typically occupies the status of 'other' or 'outsider', and is repeatedly identifiable as a 'non-citizen' through his status of migrant. Dell'Amore occupies the role of outsider to the social contexts within which he finds himself, yet must find a means through which to function appropriately in such situations in order to ensure his survival. The ability of the picaresque hero to occupy a variety of roles, to perform, is an integral aspect of his self. Indeed, it is through this role-play that such a character is able to challenge dominant hierarchies and interrupt established social and political structures. The subversion of dominant political or cultural ideologies has always been of interest to Rushdie. *The Enchantress of Florence* raises the question of how hegemonic constructs uphold their power within social contexts by registering narrative forms of storytelling, such as myth, folklore and the novel, which allow the sustenance of ideologies through generations.

Conclusion

Clearly, through a close critical reading of *The Ground Beneath Her Feet, Fury, Shalimar the Clown* and *The Enchantress of Florence*, we can see how the discourses of globalization and culturally connectivity have emerged as the principal thematic concerns of Rushdie's later fiction. The postcolonial ideologies relating to acts of resistance and the deconstruction of imperial hegemony which are explored in *Midnight's Children* have given way to a more global consideration of culture and politics at the turn of the twenty-first century. From *The Ground Beneath Her Feet* onwards, Rushdie's fiction is more identifiable as international in its geographic, cultural and political scope, centring on discourses of globalization, consumer culture, terrorism and migration. Both *The Ground Beneath Her Feet* and *Fury* thematize global commodity culture through their explorations of the manner in which both music and identity have become lucrative sites for the process of material consumption.

In turn, they problematize the figure of the artist, musician or creator of literary texts, as a result of his or her problematic participation in this process. *Fury* is especially concerned with examining the route of commodification which a text undergoes in order to market and circulate it for consumption, whereas *The Ground Beneath Her Feet* employs the narrative of a small-town musician turned international superstar to ask questions regarding artistic integrity and ownership, within a climate of transnational consumerist culture. It is interesting that Rushdie himself, as early as 1982, began to identify himself as an international writer, arguing that 'we are inescapably international writers at a time when the novel has never been a more international form' (Rushdie 1992: 20). Taken within the wider context of his argument, Rushdie is referring here to the ways in which the 'culture and political history of the phenomenon of migration' (20) gives writers who have geographically relocated access to culture, literature and histories which supplement their own. The result is a complex, hybrid mix of history and culture which stems from the wider processes of migrancy and movement which occur through globalization. While subject identity, citizenship, migrancy and belonging are central concerns of postcolonial discourse, such concerns are also global concerns which are not limited to the geopolitical sphere of nations who have converted from colonial status to independence. As we can see from a close reading of these recent novels, through an examination of globalization and cultural connectivity, Rushdie explores the long and often complex history of migrancy and the cultural encounters which have helped to shape contemporary notions of self and citizenship in the twenty-first century.

Postcolonial Secularism and Literary Form in Salman Rushdie's *The Satanic Verses*

STEPHEN MORTON

In an article first published in the *Guardian*, Anshuman A. Mondal emphasizes how Rushdie's concern in *The Satanic Verses* 'seems to have been with the loss of faith, not the nature of faith – and he takes it for granted that such a loss is a good thing' (Mondal 2009). Mondal's critique of Rushdie raises some important questions about the way in which Rushdie's 'secularist faith' is mediated in and through the literary conventions of postmodern satire, and about the transnational structures of public address in which the novel participates (Singh 2000). How is the Nehru-inspired 'secularist faith' of *Midnight's Children* translated in the fictional world of *The Satanic Verses*? And to what extent does *The Satanic Verses* disavow its complicity in Orientalist representations of Islam through its use of postmodern literary techniques? In so far as *The Satanic Verses* combines fantastical accounts of flying film stars and a migrant character who turns into a half-man, half-goat figure with a social commentary on police brutality and race politics in 1980s Britain, the novel can be seen to conform to the conventions of the European novel as a secular cultural form. More specifically, as Andrew Teverson has argued, *The Satanic Verses* uses the conventions of Menippean satire – a form of satire that 'sets the scandalous and "profane" against the normative and holy' – in order to raise questions about the meaning of revelation, and to situate the Qur'an in the historical context of its production (Teverson 2007: 149). By borrowing from Arabic and Urdu literary forms and the narrative conventions of Bombay cinema, *The Satanic Verses* certainly engages with literature and culture from the Muslim world. Yet, as this chapter suggests, by framing these references in the satirical narrative of the novel's two migrant-protagonists, *The Satanic Verses* runs the risk of subordinating its engagement with Islam and history to the secular values of the European novel. Rushdie's fictional engagement with Islam and its history in *The Satanic Verses* may attempt to take the epistemological claims of Islam seriously in order to make sense of the political uses of Islam in Iran, Egypt and Pakistan. And in this respect, *The Satanic Verses* can be seen to participate in broader debates about women and Islam, and about the role of Islam in the struggle against Western imperialism, as we will see. Yet as this chapter suggests, both the rhetorical stance and the literary form of *The Satanic Verses* have also worked to undermine the novel's attempt to engage readers in a dialogue about Islam and modernity.

Rushdie's Defence of *The Satanic Verses*

In an interview with David Frost, Rushdie argued that he wanted to present Muhammad as a more human figure:

> To show [Muhammad] as a human figure wrestling with the political and social realities of his prophesy and of his revelation flirting with compromise, rejecting it and renewing the strength of his message, in my mind that doesn't make him a lesser figure. It makes him a more human and understandable and comprehensible figure. (Rushdie 2001: 147)

Such a defence of Rushdie's representation of the Prophet Muhammad in *The Satanic Verses* might seem like a rational defence of the novel. Yet, as the anthropologist Talal Asad argues in *Genealogies of Religion*, Rushdie's representation of the Prophet Muhammad as a human not only devalues his status as a sacred figure in the Qur'an, it also assumes a culturally specific meaning of the human that can be universally applied to all cultures:

> Several commentators have suggested that the sexual episodes in the novel's account of the Prophet serve to humanize him. This may indeed be so. But the assumptions constituting that humanity are themselves the product of a particular history. Thus, in the Christian tradition, to sexualize a figure was to cut him off from divine truth, to pronounce him *merely* (sinfully) human; in the post-Christian tradition of modernity, to 'humanize' a figure is to insist on his sexual desire, to disclose in it, by a discursive stripping of its successive disguises, his essential human truth. (Asad 1993: 292)

In Asad's argument, what is particularly problematic about *The Satanic Verses* is not the novel's criticism of Islam per se, but that the 'force of [Rushdie's] criticism depends on the fact that he is situated in a Western liberal tradition and is perceived to be addressing an audience that shares it' (295). In this respect, Asad suggests that *The Satanic Verses* is a form of what Mahmood Mamdani calls bigotry, or hate speech, because it uses the cultural codes and secular values of European literature to suggest that religious faith is an inherent sign of folly or madness (Mamdani 2007).

Talal Asad's criticism of *The Satanic Verses* on the grounds that it mocks the religious beliefs of British Muslims from a position within the post-Christian cultural and literary traditions of the British liberal intelligentsia are insightful, but in focusing on Rushdie's rhetorical stance as a writer who is addressing an educated, secular, liberal and middle-class British readership, he overlooks the way in which *The Satanic Verses* also became the site of a global political debate about the relationship between Islam and Western modernity. Such a reading has been developed by the literary critic Aamir Mufti, who situates *The Satanic Verses* in terms of a broader debate about the meaning and role of Islam as a political ideology as well as a religious ethos in the years since the Iranian revolution of 1979 (Mufti 1999: 51). In Mufti's argument, *The Satanic Verses* raises questions about the role of women in modern Islamic communities; the place of secular political concepts, such as nationhood, citizenship, democracy and social justice in Islam; and the role of Islam in the struggle against the economic, political and cultural imperialism of the West (51). In doing so, Rushdie seems to challenge the revolutionary Islam of conservative intellectuals such as Maulana Mawdudi, Sayyid Qutb and Ayatollah Khomeini to define revolutionary Islam as a 'revolt against history' (Rushdie 1992: 384). For Rushdie, Islamic revivalism is not 'a religious event', but rather 'a political event that is almost always nationalist in character' (380). What is more, by demonstrating that the birth of Islam was an event that took place in history, *The Satanic Verses* clearly challenged the conceptual premises upon which Khomeini's Islamic revivalism was based. Indeed, as one commentator put it, the 'death sentence' pronounced by Iran's Ayatollah Khomeini 'has as much to do with Khomeini's sense of his role in the larger Islamic community' and his aspiration to 'the leadership of the Islamic world' as it does with 'the content of Rushdie's book' (Bakhash 1988: 236).

The reception and translation of *The Satanic Verses* among some Muslim readers may in some cases differ significantly from the reception of the novel among Muslim and non-Muslim readers familiar with the conventions and values of modern European literature. Indeed, the novel's circulation in what Mufti calls 'the Islamic public sphere' involved the public relations officer of the Islamic foundation in Leicester photocopying and mailing the offending passages in the novel to the embassies of 45 Islamic countries, including Iran (70). What is more, the fact that the 'militant opposition to the novel' was based on 'a realist and fragmented reading' (66) suggests that the reception of the novel within the Islamic public sphere framed *The Satanic Verses* in terms of the hermeneutic codes of Qur'anic exegesis rather than the cultural codes of modern literature, in which the fictional allusions to the life of the prophet Muhammad are one part of a more complex narrative.

To read *The Satanic Verses* as a work of literary fiction would thus seem to be to read the novel in terms of a secular cultural tradition which is imbricated in the history of European colonial modernity. For the secular category of imaginative literature in English has its provenance in the civilizing mission of nineteenth-century British imperialism (Asad 1993: 290). Yet the assumption that the secular category of literature and the non-secular category of Qur'anic interpretation are mutually exclusive is to reinforce the opposition between the secular and the religious that *The Satanic Verses* calls into question. In this respect, the British government's defence of Salman Rushdie's *The Satanic Verses* as a work of imaginative literature or culture is no more objective than the angry response of some readers to the novel's depiction of the Prophet Muhammad.

The so-called Rushdie affair – in which the Ayatollah Khomeini called upon Muslims around the world to kill Rushdie on February 14, 1989, and the British government defended Rushdie's right to free speech by offering him state protection against this death threat – could be seen to exemplify what the conservative Harvard political scientist Samuel Huntingdon called the 'clash of civilisations' between the West and the Islamic world. For the conventions and meanings of Western civilization and its literary culture, which *The Satanic Verses* assumes, are not shared by *some* of the novel's readers. Yet *The Satanic Verses* also seeks to interrogate this reductive dichotomy between the civilizations of the West and the so-called Islamic world by exploring the experience of the postcolonial migrant in the Western metropolis. The novel does this by juxtaposing the fictional experiences of South Asian migrants in 1980s London with episodes from the life of the prophet Muhammad, references to Bombay cinema, popular culture and world literature. This juxtaposition of South Asian migration to Britain with the Prophet's exile in seventh-century Medina suggests that the novel decentres – or, to use Gibreel Farishta's term, 'tropicalises' – London's status as an imperial metropolitan centre. By satirizing characters such as Mahound and the Imam, however, *The Satanic Verses* also seems to criticize traditional scholastic and literal interpretations of the Qur'an. Rushdie's critical engagement with Islam may make sense if it is situated within the tradition of Urdu and Persian poetry; but, as suggested below, the literary form of *The Satanic Verses* as an Anglophone novel also locates it within a European literary tradition. The hybrid literary form of *The Satanic Verses* may imply that it is a work of global fiction which aspires to synthesize different cultural traditions. But the danger of this hybrid literary form is that it transforms the scriptural foundations of Islam into an aesthetic object, and thereby subordinates Rushdie's fictionalized version of Islam to the secular values of the West.

Provincializing Europe and Reading the Non-Secular in *The Satanic Verses*

If we take Rushdie's suggestion in 'In Good Faith' seriously, and read *The Satanic Verses* as an examination of revelation as an event that takes place inside history, however, it is possible to read Rushdie's treatment of miraculous events in the novel as an attempt to make sense of historical events through a non-secular epistemological framework. Such an approach to Rushdie's magical realism corresponds with what the South Asian historian Dipesh Chakrabarty calls provincializing Europe, or the process by which the social, economic and political legacies of European colonialism are negotiated and translated in different postcolonial societies (Chakrabarty 2000). Crucial to Chakrabarty's definition of provincializing Europe is the process by which secular concepts such as democracy, capitalism, citizenship and history are translated and understood in radically different non-secular epistemological paradigms. By applying this term to *The Satanic Verses*, I want to consider how the novel negotiates and translates the histories of South Asian migration and race politics in 1980s Britain through the non-secular framework of Islamic history, literature and culture. In doing so, I want to suggest that Rushdie's magical realism in *The Satanic Verses* emphasizes the importance of religion as an epistemological framework for making sense of postcolonial modernity from the diasporic standpoint of a secular British Indian Muslim. This is not to say that Rushdie's representation of religion as a system of knowledge in *The Satanic Verses* is always progressive; on the contrary, in the case of Gibreel Farishta's dreams and delusions, religious understanding is presented as a form of paranoia/schizophrenia. Yet, as the chapter proceeds to consider, Rushdie's representation of the Ayesha pilgrimage in *The Satanic Verses* offers a counterpoint to the dogmatic interpretations of the Qur'anic scriptures advocated by Mahound/Gibreel and the anti-historical Imam in the novel. By doing so, *The Satanic Verses* encourages a more open, subjective approach to Islam that recognizes the coexistence of the secular and the religious in the modern postcolonial worlds of Rushdie's fiction. In this respect, as I suggest in the conclusion, the rhetorical structure of *The Satanic Verses* brushes against the grain of Rushdie's faith in secularism.

Migration and Postcolonial Modernity in *The Satanic Verses*

One of the central ways in which postcolonial modernity is thematized in *The Satanic Verses* is through the idea of migration. Just as Rushdie's novel *Shame* uses the experience of the *hirjat*, or an exalted form of migration that has its roots in the flight of the Prophet Muhammad from Mecca to Medina (Raza 2003: 55), to register the experience of migrant characters who were forced to move from India to Pakistan after partition, so *The Satanic Verses* rewrites passages from the life of the Prophet Muhammad to register the experience of migration from India to Britain in the late twentieth century. In doing so, Rushdie parallels the Prophet's search for his identity during his exile in Medina with the identity crisis experienced by the novel's two protagonists, Gibreel Farishta and Saladin Chamcha, during and after their fantastical migration to London (Jussawalla 1999: 88). In some respects, the identity crisis of the two protagonists in *The Satanic Verses* mirrors the novel's preoccupation with migration as an ontological condition of postcolonial modernity. If migration is understood as a particular kind of ontological condition – a way of inhabiting a place one does not feel entirely at home in while also nostalgically imagining a homeland somewhere else – *The Satanic Verses* stages this condition through the figure of the double: a figure which the psychoanalyst Sigmund Freud described as *unheimlich*, or unhomely in his essay on 'The Uncanny'. This doubleness is exemplified in part seven of the novel, where the narrator asserts that Chamcha and Gibreel are 'conjoined opposites [. . .] each man [is] the other's shadow' (426). Whereas Gibreel wishes to remain 'continuous' (427) with the imaginary homeland he left behind, Chamcha embraces his impure, hybrid identity as a British South Asian.

Gibreel and Chamcha's opposing responses to the unhomely condition of their migration are played out through a struggle for recognition in the post-imperial metropolis of 1980s London. The opening chapter of the novel represents Saladin Chamcha and Gibreel Farishta falling from Air India flight 420 – a symbol of postcolonial modernity – after it has been blown up by a Sikh terrorist group above the English Channel. The destruction of the plane and the miraculous survival of Saladin Chamcha and Gibreel Farishta develop this philosophical dimension of the novel further by raising questions about the possibility of reincarnation or life after death. For, as Saladin and Gibreel fall from the plane, Gibreel's body is taken over by an invisible force that commands him to fly and sing a song in 'a language he did not know to a tune he had never heard' (9); as he does so, both Gibreel and Saladin 'began to slow down' (9). The responses of Gibreel and Saladin to this apparently miraculous event are significant because they represent two different ways of thinking about religion in the novel. Whereas 'Gibreel never doubted the miracle', and 'never stopped saying that the gazal had been celestial', Saladin Chamcha 'tried to reason it out of existence' (9). Chamcha's secular and sceptical approach to their survival seems to be supported by the narrator's subsequent description of Gibreel as an Indian movie star, whose 'big break arrived with the coming of the theological movies' (24). This reference to theological movies is significant because it draws attention to the novel's artifice, and suggests that the story of Saladin and Chamcha's survival is itself a fictional construct, which could be part of a movie script. Such a reading of this episode may appear to be consistent with Talal Asad's argument that *The Satanic Verses* is a work of postmodern literary fiction, and as such it is a product of Western culture and its secular values. Yet Gibreel's belief in the miracle also implies a way of understanding his survival of the aeroplane crash and his migration through a non-secular epistemological paradigm.

The Satanic Verses and Its Arabic and Urdu Literary Precursors

Gibreel's reference to 'the gazal' in the passage cited above also suggests an alternative reading of the novel, which situates *The Satanic Verses* in a Persian and Urdu literary tradition. The 'gazal' or ghazal is a form of lyric poetry written in couplets with a regular metre and rhyme scheme. Each of these couplets encapsulates a complete theme, such as romantic love or the love of a mystic for his God (Russell 2003: 297); as a consequence, the ghazal seems to lack a unified theme (287). Bedouin poets originally developed the ghazal in Arabic during the late sixth century; it was later adopted in Persian, and was disseminated to North India by Sufi mystics in the twelfth century; subsequently, the ghazal was developed in Urdu during the period of the Mughal Empire (Schimmel 1975). During the twentieth century, the Urdu ghazal came to symbolize Muslim decadence within India and 'an imperial culture in decline' (Mufti 2004: 245). By alluding to this poetic form and its cultural history within India, Rushdie thus locates his engagement with the Islamic world in terms of India's Muslim cultural inheritance.

If the song that Gibreel Farishta is prompted to sing as he falls from Air India flight 420 is a celestial 'gazal', it is the Persian and Urdu literary genre of the *dastan* that provides a rich intertextual resource for the narrative structure and geographical location of *The Satanic Verses*. As the literary critic Feroza Jussawalla explains, the *dastan* is characterized by 'a long-winded stream of consciousness tale that incorporates many related and sometimes loosely strung-together frame tales and assorted humorous anecdotes' (Jussawalla 1999: 95). Furthermore, the plot of the *dastan* covers 'a broad geographical area including most of the world known to the medieval geographers [and] takes place in an indefinite time, generally said to be long in the past' (96).

As well as being a long-winded narrative, *The Satanic Verses* certainly takes place across a 'broad geographical area' and in 'an indefinite time'. While the novel begins with a plane crash above the English Channel in the late twentieth century, chapters 2 and 6 of *The Satanic Verses* are situated in seventh-century Jahilia; and chapters 4 and 8 (the Ayesha chapters) are located in late-twentieth-century India. Rushdie's framing of the Jahilia chapters and the Ayesha chapters within the dream sequences of Gibreel Farishta is also consistent with the framing devices and stream of consciousness style that Jussawalla associates with the *dastan*.

Moreover, if Gibreel's dream sequences are read as an extended interior monologue, it is possible to situate Rushdie's use of Islamic history in terms of the migrant experience in late-twentieth-century British society. In Jussawalla's account, Rushdie's satirical representation of historical events from the life of the prophet Muhammad is part of a 'long tradition of Indian Islamic writers who both criticized Islam and yet were deeply part of the post-Mughal literary/religious tradition' (94) in India. The imperative behind Rushdie's satirical representation of Islam is, however, different from that of other writers in this tradition such as the nineteenth-century Indian writers 'Ghalib and his student Altaf Husain Hali, Bahadar Shah Zafar and Dagh' (94) in that Rushdie uses the form of the Anglophone novel to reinterpret the Qur'an rather than the poetic forms conventional to the Persian and Urdu literary traditions that Jussawalla invokes. In so doing, Rushdie violates what Homi Bhabha calls 'the poetic license granted to critics of the Islamic establishment' (Bhabha 1994: 226).

Gibreel's dream work in *The Satanic Verses* is certainly an attempt to make sense of his identity both as a migrant and a Muslim in postcolonial British society. Yet, the crucial question remains: By re-inscribing the Qur'an within the context of postcolonial British society, does Gibreel's dream work 'place the authority of the Koran within a perspective of historical and cultural relativism'? (226), as the postcolonial theorist Homi Bhabha suggests; or does this dream narrative interpret the post-Christian liberal values of twentieth-century British society within a non-secular frame of reference by defining modern British society as a contemporary form of Jahilia?

The section of the novel entitled 'Mahound', which is set in seventh-century Jahilia, is reported from Gibreel's point of view as a migrant in twentieth-century Britain. Gibreel's dream narrative of the story of Mahound is represented as a theological film: 'Gibreel: the dreamer, whose point of view is sometimes that of the camera and at other moments, spectator' (108). While the story of Mahound is represented as a Bombay film adaptation, in which Gibreel is both the audience and the central character, he is nonetheless afraid of the 'self his dream creates' (109). Gibreel's fear is initially articulated as a form of stage fright – 'the kind of fear you feel when you're on a film set for the first time' (109) – but it is subsequently described as a fear of not having the authority to communicate the words of God: '*Mahound comes to me for revelation, asking me to choose between monotheist and henotheist alternatives, and I'm just some idiot actor having a bhaenchud nightmare, what the fuck do I know, yaar, what to tell you, help. Help*' (109). Gibreel's pleas for help in this passage point towards a recognition of a tradition of Qur'anic interpretation, about which he feels unqualified to comment.

Later in the novel, the role that Gibreel plays takes over his psyche, and he begins to speak 'verses in Arabic, a language he did not know' (340). That these verses are a repetition of the *gharaniq* or 'birds' verses cited in Al-Tabari's *Annals* is significant because it suggests that the voice that possesses Gibreel is that of the Devil rather than God. This is not to suggest, however, that Gibreel's dreams and visions simply confirm or deny the existence of God or the Devil. Indeed, as Roger Y. Clark has persuasively argued, the voice that possesses Gibreel is that of Rushdie's satanic narrator, whose manipulative behaviour recalls that of the character Iago in Shakespeare's *Othello* as well as the figure of Satan in al-Tabari's *Annals*: 'Rushdie inserts key elements of the satanic verses incident into this Shakespearean drama when the possessed Chamcha whispers doggerel satanic verses over the telephone, thus driving Gibreel into a monstrous green-eyed jealousy' (Clark 2001: 130). For Clark, the 'satanic narrator's mode of operation' in *The Satanic Verses* is a diabolical form of indeterminacy, which 'moves in and out of the text in order to insinuate that there is no such thing as a single, transcendental Meaning and Unity' (131). Such a reading of the satanic narrator in *The Satanic Verses* is premised on the view that 'critics have focused on the worldly politics of the Rushdie Affair rather than the otherworldly politics in the text itself' (129). What Clark implies but does not explicitly say is that the narrator's movement 'in and out of the text' also juxtaposes the worldly and otherworldly dimensions of the novel. In this respect, the narrative structure of *The Satanic Verses* represents what the deconstructive literary theorist Paul de Man calls an allegory of reading, in which the rhetorical organization of a literary text draws attention to the necessity of the text's misunderstanding (de Man 1983: 136). For in combining the worldly and otherworldly dimensions of the novel, Rushdie prevents readers from deciding with any certainty whether a satanic narrator has possessed Gibreel Farishta, or whether Gibreel is a Prophet, or whether he is suffering from mental illness. Yet, as Rushdie has frequently suggested, this textual indeterminacy has a political purpose: to expose the invention and interpretation of Islam in and through history, while also creating a fictional space for exploring the structure of belief.

The narrative juxtaposition of the worldly and otherworldly dimensions of the novel, which contributes to the textual indeterminacy of *The Satanic Verses*, is perhaps most clearly exemplified in Gibreel Farishta's attempt to bring moral and religious redemption to 1980s London. Like Jahilia in the seventh century, London is presented as an ungodly metropolis of 'masks and parodies' (320); a city that Gibreel attempts to 'redeem [. . .] all the way from A to Z' (322). This geographical mapping of Gibreel's religious mission in London is later rendered futile as Gibreel realizes that 'the city in its corruption refused to submit to the dominion of the cartographers, changing shape at will and without warning' (327). In order to control the moral 'corruption' that he perceives in London's shifting urban space, Gibreel sets on a path of destruction with a flame-throwing trumpet, which he calls 'Azraeel, the Last Trump, the Exterminator of Men!' (448). Gibreel uses this trumpet as an instrument of divine judgement to execute a group of sex workers and their pimps outside Kings Cross station, whom he confuses with the twelve sex workers behind the curtain at Jahilia. In this juxtaposition of the worldly space of 1980s London and the otherworldly space of Jahilia, Rushdie highlights the way in which Islam is produced in and through history. Whether Gibreel's violent rampage is a figment of his deluded imagination or a brutal act of murder committed in the name of religious judgement, his actions reinforce the narrator's characterization of Gibreel as an 'untranslated man' (427), or a migrant who refuses to assimilate to the liberal and secular values of late-twentieth-century British society.

Gibreel Farishta and the Identity Formation of British Muslims

Rushdie's characterization of Gibreel Farishta as an untranslated man, who 'has wished to remain, to a large degree, *continuous* – that is, joined to and arising from his past' (427) also raises an important question about his identity as both a South Asian migrant and a former actor who believes he is one of the fictional characters in a theological feature film. Such a question corresponds with debates about British Muslim identity in contemporary Islamic studies. In the introduction to *Islams and Modernities* (1993), Aziz Al-Azmeh argues that the angry responses of British Muslims to the representation of the Prophet in *The Satanic Verses* are based on a coherent cultural identity that had to be invented. In Al-Azmeh's argument, this fictional identity was based on a 'sentimentalist view of a spurious, unsullied reality prior to the corruption of the present', which 'is neither "real" nor old, but is a recherché cluster of modes of visible behaviour which are said by certain Islamist authorities to represent the "true prior reality" – one that British Pakistani Muslims had never known until recently, for it is not only traditions that are invented, but also collective memories' (Al-Azmeh 1993: 8).

Al-Azmeh's critique of the idea that Islam is a coherent and unified culture and religion outside of history also seems to echo Rushdie's fictional reinvention of the life of the Prophet Muhammad in *The Satanic Verses*, and his characterization of the Imam as a figure who is against history and the measurement of time (211–15). While some of Rushdie's critics take issue with *The Satanic Verses* on the grounds that the novel fails to present an accurate historical account of the life of the Prophet Muhammad, *The Satanic Verses* stages the impossibility of recovering such a coherent history by exposing the lacunae, contradictions and multiple meanings embedded in early historical sources such as al-Tabari's *Annals*. One example of this staging is seen in chapter 5 of the novel, in which the Prophet's scribe, Salman, alters the words of God as the angel Gibreel dictates them to the Prophet:

> Here's the point: Mahound did not notice the alterations. So there I was, actually writing the Book, or re-writing, anyway, polluting the word of God with my own profane language. But, good heavens, if my poor words could not be distinguished from the Revelation by God's own Messenger, then what did that mean? What did that say about the quality of the divine poetry? (367)

In this passage, Salman al-Farsi draws attention to the material and textual basis of the Prophet's revelation, which is also at the same time a 'recitation' (364). By incorrectly transcribing this recitation, Salman not only questions the reliability and authenticity of primary historical sources, but also starts to question his faith in God. This fictional account of Salman al-Farsi's incorrect transcription of the Prophet's words may correspond with a similar passage in al-Tabari's *Annals*, in which Abdullah ibn Sa'ad, one of the Prophet's scribes, temporarily lost his faith after an incorrect transcription of the Prophet's words went unnoticed. But this assumes that *The Satanic Verses* is a realistic representation of Islamic history rather than a fictional representation of the way in which Islamic law has been invented and interpreted *in history*. Such a fictional representation may encourage further reflection on the ambivalence and multiple meanings of Islamic history, but this representation not only presupposes a readership familiar with the codes of contemporary European literature it also takes for granted that readers will be willing to accept the claim that the history of the Prophet Muhammad is an invented narrative.

In this respect, Gibreel's revelations in *The Satanic Verses* may seem antithetical to and discontinuous with the novel's representation of postcolonial migrants in the fictional district of Brickhall in 1980s London. The literary critic Ian Baucom contends that Gibreel's attempts to 'tropicalise' or reclaim the streets of London mirror the riots in Brickhall (Baucom 1999). Yet this is to collapse Gibreel's desire to punish the moral corruption that he perceives in 1980s British society as an avenging angel and the genuine political grievances of black Britons against racist discrimination and social exclusion.

Rushdie's representation of Saladin Chamcha's experience of police brutality and racism as an illegal South Asian migrant who washes up on the shores of Hastings, his depiction of Dr Uhuru Simba's death in police custody and the subsequent riot that erupts in Brickhall in response to Dr Simba's death certainly suggest that *The Satanic Verses* is sympathetic to the political cause of anti-racism and the riots in Brixton of 1981. This sympathy is, however, complicated by a distinction that the narrator of *The Satanic Verses* makes between the secular, hybridized idea of the self exemplified by Saladin Chamcha and the coherent, essentialist idea of the self embodied by Gibreel Farishta: as 'homogenous, non-hybrid, [and] "pure"' (427). Rushdie's narrator asserts that the idea of the self that Saladin Chamcha symbolizes is false and therefore evil, while Gibreel, 'to follow the logic of our established terminology, is to be considered "good" by virtue of *wishing to remain*, for all his vicissitudes, at bottom an untranslated man' (427). The narrator also inverts this distinction by claiming that the idea of cultural purity is itself insufficient. In so doing, Rushdie's narrator seems to valorize the hybridized, secular migrant over the non-secular migrant who refuses to assimilate to the cultural values of the host nation.

The Coexistence of the Secular and the Religious in the Ayesha Chapters

In the chapter titled 'Return to Jahilia' the satirical poet, Baal, nails his poetry to the prison door after his capture by Mahound, an act that recalls Martin Luther nailing his 95 theses on the Castle Church door at Wittenburg in 1517. This parallel with the reformation is significant because it suggests that the figure of the writer/author in *The Satanic Verses* also wishes to bring about a reformation in Islam – a reformation that Rushdie explicitly called for in 2005. But this would be to overlook the significance of Mahound's statement, which he makes as Mahound's soldiers lead Baal to his execution: 'Writers and whores. I see no difference here' (392). For Mahound, 'Writers and whores' are identical in so far as they both transgress social rules and conventions. As a consequence, both groups are regarded as a threat to the social and political order. Indeed, the 12 sex workers at the curtain threaten Mahound's authority by pretending to be his wives. As Rushdie has suggested in an interview, this strategy of inversion serves to exemplify the way in which 'women have been bought and sold' as both wives and sex workers (Rushdie 2001: 222). It also implies that the figure of the postcolonial writer has been bought and sold in the global literary marketplace. Moreover, as suggested below, it is through the female character Ayesha that a rethinking of Islam is most clearly articulated in *The Satanic Verses*.

Rather than merely criticizing the commodification of female sexuality, *The Satanic Verses* suggests that it is women who offer an alternative vision of Islam to that offered by Gibreel Farishta and the Imam. Indeed, it is Ayesha and Mirza's pilgrimage from the Indian village of Titlipur to Mecca that offers a more progressive model of Islam. In 'the two sections [of the novel] that mirror and transform the Mahound sections', Ambreen Hai argues that Ayesha 'becomes the female migrant leader of archetypal postcolonial migrants and of believers in a prominent future' (Hai 1999: 37). What is more, Ayesha is the sworn enemy of the Imam, who during his exile in London broadcasts radio messages calling for a revolution against Ayesha and against history. If the anti-historical Imam in *The Satanic Verses* is a fictional caricature of the Ayatollah Khomeini, and his period of exile in Paris prior to the Iranian Revolution in 1979 (Brennan 1989: 156), Ayesha seems to offer a more progressive approach to Islam. Ayesha's diagnosis of Mishal Akhtar's cancer and her encounter with the Angel Gibreel, who encourages her to lead the villagers of Titlipur on a pilgrimage to Mecca, suggests that she is herself a prophet. What is more, Ayesha's ability to persuade the villagers to follow her on the pilgrimage contrasts strikingly with the coercive and destructive methods of Mahound and the Imam.

The tragic ending of this pilgrimage, in which many of the pilgrims die in the attempt to cross the Arabian Sea, might seem to discredit both Ayesha's promise of a miraculous parting of the Arabian Sea, and the religious faith that such a promise represents. Yet this tragic ending is less significant than the rational debate that the pilgrimage provokes. Like Gibreel Farishta and Saladin Chamcha's fall from the Air India aeroplane, aptly named the *Bostan* (the Arabic word for garden or heaven), Ayesha's pilgrimage across the Arabian Sea is a test of the pilgrims' faith. Moreover, it is Mirza Saeed's persistent scepticism and arguments against the pilgrimage – to save his dying wife, Mishal – that offers a counterpoint to Ayesha's religious belief. While Mirza accuses Ayesha of being a 'God-bothered type from ancient history' (238), Mishal criticises Mirza's 'imported European atheism' (238). And, in response to Ayesha's assertion that the waters of the Arabian Sea will part in order to allow the pilgrims to travel to Mecca from Titlipur, Mirza asserts that the 'mystical experience is a subjective, not an objective truth'. As a consequence of this scepticism, he predicts that the 'waters will not open' (239). Mirza's secular view that the mystical experience is subjective would seem to be confirmed by the way in which the pilgrimage is perceived as it proceeds to the Arabian Sea. For the police and some extremist religious elements the pilgrimage is regarded as a 'sectarian demonstration' (474); it is subsequently branded the Ayesha Haj and denounced as an attempt to 'incite communal sentiment' (488). Furthermore, some of these extremist groupings distribute leaflets arguing that 'Padyatra, or foot-pilgrimage, is an ancient, pre-Islamic tradition of national culture, not imported property of Mughal immigrants' (488). Such a communalist reading of the pilgrimage is, however, undermined by the Brahmin toy merchant Sri Srinivas' perception of Ayesha as having the 'identical, same-to-same face' as the Hindu goddess Lakshmi (476). Srinivas' misrecognition of Ayesha as Lakshmi thus implies that the religious identity of the pilgrims is less significant than their belief in the prophet Ayesha.

While the narrator appears to reinforce Mirza Saeed's assertion that 'mystical experience is a subjective not an objective truth' (239), Mirza's experience of being-towards-death following the drowning of Mishal and the other pilgrims in the Arabian Sea implies that Mirza has himself lost the argument with Ayesha and Mishal about the parting of the

Arabian Sea. For as Mirza drifts towards unconsciousness, he has a vision of the sea pouring over him, and Ayesha stepping miraculously out of his wife's body (506). As the pilgrims start to struggle underwater, Ayesha repeatedly commands Mirza to 'Open', an order that he stubbornly refuses to obey until he realizes that Ayesha is drowning:

> She was drowning, too. He saw the water fill her mouth, heard it begin to gurgle inside her lungs. Then something within her refused that, made a different choice, and at the instant that his heart broke, he opened.

> His body split apart from his adam's-apple to his groin, so that she could reach deep within him, and now she was open, they all were, and at the moment of their opening the waters parted, and they walked to Mecca across the bed of the Arabian Sea. (507)

Ayesha's appeal to the secular landlord Mirza to 'open' is on one level a demand for Mirza to recognize the coexistence of the theological and the secular in an era of postcolonial modernity. But, as Sara Suleri has argued, Ayesha's injunction to 'open' from the standpoint of a woman and a Muslim is also a sign of Rushdie's feminization of Islam (Suleri 1992: 202–6). Against the dogmatic monotheism of Mahound and the anti-historicism of the Imam, Suleri suggests that Ayesha embodies a more open and inclusive approach to Islam, which encourages dialogue and debate rather than foreclosing it. In this respect, *The Satanic Verses* might appear to parallel the attempts by Muslim women writers such as Assia Djebar, Leila Abouleila and Fatima Mernissi to articulate the position of women in Islam. The problem with this reading, however, is that it ignores Rushdie's rhetorical stance as a secular Muslim writing from a former centre of Western imperial power in a cultural form that is associated with the post-Christian liberal values of that former imperial centre to a Muslim reading public that may or may not share those values. As a consequence, there is a danger that Ayesha may be read as a convenient counterpoint to an Orientalist stereotype of Islamic fundamentalism rather than encouraging readers to reflect on the position of women in Islam.

As we have seen, *The Satanic Verses* is structured around a series of unstable binary oppositions such as the sacred and the secular, the hybrid and the pure and the worldly and the otherworldly. For Rushdie, this textual indeterminacy may be an attempt to historicize Islam, and to create a fictional space for exploring the structure of belief. Yet this textual instability does not simply work to secure the secularist faith of which Rushdie speaks in essays such as 'In Good Faith'; it also paradoxically serves to enact a return of the religious, or a mode of thinking about the otherworldly that subverts the literary conventions of the novel which attempt to contain it.

CHAPTER FIVE

Revisiting *The Satanic Verses*: The *Fatwa* and Its Legacies

ANSHUMAN A. MONDAL

The controversy that engulfed Salman Rushdie's fourth novel *The Satanic Verses* and the *fatwa* issued in response by then–Supreme Leader of the Islamic Republic of Iran Ayatolloh Khomeini remains to this day an iconic register of the radical intractability of cultural difference. While the episode apparently confirms the idea that 'Western' and 'Islamic' cultures are discrete entities whose values cannot be reconciled, in this essay I will argue that it in fact demonstrates the way in which cultural difference is *produced* by the dynamics of power that determine cultural encounters. Indeed, if the dominant reading of the *fatwa* has been to suggest that Islamic and Western norms and values are untranslatable, I will show how the episode can be read otherwise to reveal that cultural difference emerges because 'culture' is both translatable *and* untranslatable. Moreover, this is the necessary condition for the emergence of cultural hybridity, that form of 'cultural difference' which, for Bhabha, occupies the 'Third Space' *between* cultures, where 'newness enters the world' (Bhabha 1994: 39). This is particularly germane to any discussion of the *fatwa* because the novel that provoked it rests on a claim to uphold the value of hybridity over and against those monolithic and essentialist notions of culture articulated by Khomeini's *fatwa*.

Liberal commentaries on the *fatwa*, both then and during the coverage marking its twentieth anniversary, slipped easily from outrage at Khomeini's 'barbarism' to disgust at the putative 'barbarism' of Islam in general. This speaks to the desire to translate (and thereby domesticate) alternative vocabularies of moral and cultural value articulated from within and in the name of Islam into the terms of secular-liberalism. But that desire is simultaneously thwarted by the *fatwa*'s outlandish intransigence towards Western secular-liberalism's normative enterprise, so these slippages *also* articulate a distance induced by the fear of an incomprehensible Other located *beyond* the limits of Western (read: universal) knowledge and culture. While the universal reach of Western cultural values is required in order to pass judgement on the barbarism of Islam, its limits are exposed by the inability to bring it within the frame of the 'knowledg*able*'. In that sense, the *fatwa* is a 'limit-text' that demonstrates what Bhabha calls 'the ambivalence of cultural authority', which emerges during the attempt 'to *dominate* in the name of a cultural supremacy which is itself produced only in the moment of differentiation' (Bhabha 1994: 34; see also Mondal 2008).

Within this overdetermining frame, the *fatwa* itself and its continuing legacies have been more specifically determined, first, by the imbalance in power relations that structured this particular cultural encounter: while liberal rhetoric during the controversy positioned itself as a defender of fragile freedoms by speaking truth to power, the blithe dismissal of all Muslim objections (not just the *fatwa*) was, in fact, a *performance* of its actual cultural hegemony. This perhaps accounts for why the twentieth anniversary of the *fatwa* was marked by a re-inscription, a repetition with a difference. While many of the prominent Muslim protagonists of the 'Rushdie affair' within the British context – foremost among them, Ianayat Bunglawala, former spokesperson for the Muslim Council of Britain, and Ghayasuddin Siddiqui, who was then a leading member of the Tehran-backed Muslim Institute (see Bunglawala 2007 and 2008) – have, in the intervening years, adapted or retracted their positions *vis á vis* the novel and the issues it raised concerning the respective limits of freedom of expression and religious liberty (as has the Islamic Republic of Iran itself, specifically with respect to Khomeini's *fatwa*), liberal positions in the controversy have not altered in any significant respect. Indeed, the events of 11 September 2001 and the subsequent 'war on terror' have further entrenched them. Thus, writing in *The Observer* just before the twentieth anniversary, Andrew Anthony concluded that 'there is nothing more sacred than the freedom to question what is sacred' (Anthony 2009). Likewise, on the day itself, Lisa Appignanesi invoked John Mortimer (the writer and barrister who defended Penguin during the *Lady Chatterley's Lover* case) in suggesting that 'it was almost the duty of writers to offend' (Appignanesi 2009). Both these statements reprise, almost to the letter, the positions taken up by Rushdie and his defenders during the controversy over *The Satanic Verses*, both before and after the *fatwa*. Appignanesi echoes Rushdie's famous catechism, 'what is freedom of expression? Without the freedom to offend, it ceases to exist' (Rushdie 1991: 36) and Anthony reprises Rushdie's sacralization of literature in 'Is Nothing Sacred?' (despite his assertions to the contrary) on the basis that '[l]iterature is the one place in any society . . . where we can hear *voices talking about everything in every possible way*' – where nothing *can* be sacred because to make something sacred is 'to set [it] apart', and thus remove it from that scrutiny (Rushdie 1991: 416).

Rushdie himself has significantly hardened his position on Islam and Muslims, and both the emergence of what has been called the 'New Atheism' and the backlash against 'multiculturalism' have bolstered the liberal conviction that surfaced during the Rushdie affair concerning the cultural obduracy and 'backwardness' of Islam (Rushdie 2003:

Anthony 2008; Malik 2009; Bradley and Tate 2010). These trends have accompanied the rhetoric of the 'war on terror' and the 'clash of civilizations' articulated by a resurgent neo-liberalism and has resulted in a re-alignment of right- and left-wing liberalisms promoting a united front in the face of a common cultural foe: Islam.

The result of this re-alignment has been the fetishization of freedom of expression as a totem of Western culture, and of liberalism as the register of its cultural supremacy (notwithstanding the numerous contradictions within the West that this glosses over). While right-wing neo-liberals and left-leaning social liberals make uneasy bedfellows, they have converged in the wake of the *fatwa* into a strategic alliance that identifies a conflict between the West and the so-called Islamic world. Neo-liberals identify 'Islam' as a geopolitical enemy that must be overcome to maintain the economic and military superiority of the West, whilst social liberals characterize it the *locus classicus* of illiberalism. This has been accompanied by a shift towards a more 'muscular' liberalism that has been articulated by both right and left liberals, most recently by the current British prime minister, David Cameron (*Guardian* 5 February 2011; see also Mondal 2011).

Once again, this rhetoric is usually defined by its addressee: Islam. On the right the usual inflection is to exclude Muslims and Islam from 'our' cultural 'norms and values', which 'they' must 'learn' in order to demonstrate their integration into society; many left liberals have also subscribed to this culturalist turn in arguments about integration, but among them there is also an emphasis on an absolutist conceptualization of freedom of expression in which *any* limit on not just the right but the exercise of free speech is deemed to be an erosion of '[o]ur established and long-fought for liberties to read or not read what we like' (Appignanesi 2009). As we have seen, this was an argument put forward by Rushdie himself in the wake of the *fatwa* and has since become common currency in liberal circles: the right to freedom of expression *ceases to exist* without the 'right' to offend. This invokes an 'all-or-nothing' argument that invariably conjures up a liberal nightmare in which 'any sentence might turn out to be a death sentence' (Anthony 2009).

That this absolutist position on freedom of speech can (in its current version) be traced back to the repercussions of the *fatwa*, and has been invoked each time a subsequent Muslim-related freedom of expression controversy has ignited (e.g., over the publications of cartoons representing the Prophet in the Danish newspaper *Jyllands-Posten*) but *not* during other freedom of expression controversies (such as the furore over the 'offensive' remarks directed at the granddaughter of the actor Andrew Sachs by Russell Brand and Jonathan Ross on the BBC) underscores the point that this rhetoric – like the corollary rhetoric within economic neo-liberalism which extends the negative definition of liberty as freedom from restraint into the economic sphere, from 'the free play of ideas' to the free market – is still performing a gesture of cultural supremacy. Its purpose is to position 'Islam' outside the frame of 'freedom' and, therefore, of civilization (there is a corresponding gesture of *inclusion* in which liberalism's 'tolerant' credentials are burnished by admitting those Muslims who, in effect, subscribe to the norms and values of liberalism). Indeed, these same liberals unhesitatingly defend the principle of *limiting* offensive speech (under the rubric of 'hate speech') when it is deemed racist or anti-semitic, which suggests that the argument is not *just* about the limits of legitimate expression, but rather what Bhabha calls 'the ambivalence of cultural authority.' (One can read 'ambivalence' literally in the sense of 'dual value' or, more colloquially, as 'double-standard').

If one of the most notable legacies of the *fatwa* has been the ideological realignment of liberalism another has been the exposure of a faultline that secular-liberal intellectuals had long since imagined to have been rendered obsolete: between secular and non-secular ways of thought and being. Certain prominent Muslim opponents of Rushdie during the controversy may have shifted their position *vis á vis* the permissibility of the novel within the context of freedom of expression, but they have not retracted their original claims that the novel was 'offensive' to Muslims – indeed, whilst the jurisdiction of Western notions of freedom of expression may well have been extended in the intervening period by the increasing attenuation of Muslim opposition to it within Western countries, the divergent and discrepant *readings* of the novel from secular and non-secular (predominantly Muslim) perspectives remain unresolved.

Part of the difficulty in translating the controversy over *The Satanic Verses* into a mutually productive dialogue lies in the fact that the readings of the novel put forward by Rushdie and his secular champions are not acceptable – or even recognizable – as such to their Muslim interlocutors because the respective axioms of moral judgment concerning 'the relative value of the sacred and the profane', are divergent and irreconcilable. Beyond this initial and fundamental schism are other untranslatable codes, conventions and axioms which register the radical heterogeneity of cultural difference and speak to irreducibly discrepant ways of reading not just this (or any) text but also the social text of human experience. The controversy, and the *fatwa* in particular, rendered visible a limit to secular discourse (be it liberal or otherwise) that had hitherto not been apparent to those who had become accustomed to its putative universalism. This is perhaps another reason why the terms of the controversy over *The Satanic Verses* have been repetitively rehearsed in each successive confrontation over freedom of expression, because the *fatwa* could be read not just as a challenge or an affront to secular-liberal notions of juridical rights, but also a trauma in which an irreducible 'Other' irrupts within the projected parameters of Western selfhood and interrupts its universal reach.

There are, of course, risks here in reproducing or reinforcing the 'clash of civilizations' thesis that has determined and dominated so much of the discourse mediating the encounter between 'the West' and 'Islam' since the *fatwa*, and indeed the *Satanic Verses* controversy is ostensibly the point of departure for the idea itself as formulated by Samuel Huntington. (The original article which Huntington published in *Foreign Affairs* quotes Bernard Lewis' essay 'The Roots of Muslim Rage', and adopts its defining optic on Islam as its own. Lewis' article was itself a response to the Rushdie controversy.) What I would like to suggest, however, is not that the *fatwa* somehow represents all Muslims and articulates the essential 'core' of a civilizationally coherent and homogenous Islam. Instead, the *fatwa* can be seen as a counter-offensive *gesture* that reveals alternative ways of reading human experience, history and moral value that *exceed* the paradigms of Western secular thought. The fatwa is only one among a multiplicity of such subaltern possibilities, but its presence as a *fissure* in dominant regimes of secular representation renders visible that which normally remains invisible because while such regimes of representation constitute Western discourse as universal through their exclusion and/or domestication of 'otherness', the *fatwa's* moral and legal outrageousness as well as its unequivocal endorsement of violence *performed* a resistance to secular universalism that could be neither ignored nor assimilated. Indeed, this may be why Khomeini transgressed the due process and juridical proprieties of Islamic as well as Western secular law.

The problem of recovering and representing alterity without exercising an epistemic violence that recuperates it as merely an Other to the dominant (and dominating) logic of the Self – that is, without (mis-)translating it – is one of the central problematics within postcolonial studies. That is to say, roughly, a central problem with European thought is the difficulty in seeing and understanding non-Western people and ideas without, as it were, instantaneously measuring them by European standards and concepts. It is also one of the central concerns within Salman Rushdie's fictional work, and this is one of the reasons why his work is such an integral part of the postcolonial counter-canon. Moreover, it is something that Rushdie himself has spoken of as being one of the main preoccupations of *The Satanic Verses*. He states that the novel is 'a serious attempt to write about religion and revelation from the point of view of a secular person' (Appignanesi and Maitland 1989: 41) and that 'it is by no means always hostile to faith' (Rushdie 1991: 396). Indeed, he goes on to say, 'the most secular of authors ought to be capable of presenting a sympathetic portrait of a devout believer' (417). But many of the criticisms advanced by Muslim opponents during the controversy rested upon the charge that, in this respect, *The Satanic Verses* failed to represent Islam and Muslims as anything but Other in a manner reminiscent of, if not directly reproducing, the discourse of Orientalism as outlined by Edward Said (Akhtar 1989; Sardar and Wyn-Davies 1990; Ahsan and

Kidwai 1993). The critical question, then, is whether or not Rushdie succeeds in representing the alterity of religious faith from a secular point of view.

However, this question in turn rests on whether or not the novel successfully mediates between secular and non-secular ways of thinking and being. Does it enable a secular sensibility to inhabit and thereby empathize with, and understand, religious experience, albeit imaginatively and temporarily, or does it, in fact, subordinate the singularity of the one (religious experience) to the dominating perspective of the other (secularism)? Or, to put it slightly differently, does the text inhabit a space *in-between* the secular and the non-secular, that hybrid (Third) space where alterity can emerge as neither an extension of the Same nor as an alien Other but as something else besides, that space where 'newness enters the world'? The trope of hybridity in *The Satanic Verses* is, therefore, crucial to addressing these questions, not least because, in Rushdie's own words, the novel is 'love song to our mongrel selves' (Rushdie 1994: 294).

The Satanic Verses is a novel that responds to two questions that frame the narrative and determine its thematic concerns: 'How does newness come into the world?' (8) and 'What kind of idea are you?' (335). Both of these converge upon the figure of the hybrid, which appears in many forms throughout the novel, beginning with its epigraph, which, by invoking Daniel Defoe's *History of the Devil*, also evokes one of his other works, 'The True Born Englishman', a poem which satirically observes that such a creature is, in fact, a 'het'rogenous thing' that has emerged from the numerous migrations and conquests, the many cultural infusions and racial incursions that have punctuated British history since ancient times. This is one of the main themes of a novel that addresses the racist exclusivism of British nationalist identity during the period of Thatcherite ascendancy. From the outset, therefore, Rushdie juxtaposes migration – Defoe's Satan is a vagrant with no fixed abode – with hybridity and then, in the arresting opening scene, fuses this with another of the novel's main tropes, metamorphosis. The episode concludes with the question,

> 'How does newness enter the world? How is it born? Of what fusions, translations, conjoinings is it made? How does it survive, extreme and dangerous though it is? What compromises, what deals, what betrayals of its secret nature must it make . . .? (8)

As the novel progresses, the narrator periodically asks the other question, 'WHAT KIND OF IDEA ARE YOU? Are you the kind that compromises, does deals, accommodates itself to society, aims to find a niche, to survive?' (335) The echo of discourses surrounding immigration and integration in late-twentieth-century Britain aligns both these questions to the phenomenon of migration. As Rushdie would later write after the *fatwa*: 'If *The Satanic Verses* is anything, it is a migrant's eye view of the world. It is written from the very experience of uprooting, disjuncture and metamorphosis . . . that is the migrant condition . . . from which, I believe, can be derived a metaphor for all humanity' (Rushdie 1991: 394).

The narrative therefore rests on a set of axiomatic principles concerning the value of migration, its ability to foster change, transformation and renewal, and the necessity of compromise in order to ensure survival. Since metamorphosis, migration and compromise all produce 'hybrid' formations in one form or another, the novel valorizes hybridity and its attendant 'ethic of impurity' as a fundamental principle of historical development that invokes Darwin's theory of natural selection: adaptability is the key to survival. (Both Shabbir Akhtar and Bhikhu Parekh have attributed the phrase 'ethic of impurity' to a statement made by Rushdie in one of the publicity interviews he gave prior to the novel's publication; they did not, however, cite the source; Akhtar 1989: 18; Parekh 1999: 74). Rushdie speaks of the 'argument between purity and impurity' in his essay 'In Good Faith' (Rushdie 1991: 394).)

This ethic of impurity is the basis for the novel's exuberant dismantling of established structures of thought and patterns of belief, and its insistent interrogation of 'orthodoxies of all types', in particular those aligned to the 'ethic of purity'. Foremost among these are the cultural codes of chauvinistic nationalism (such as Thatcherite Conservatism) and the moral codes of established religion (such as Islam).

The ethic of impurity, as expressed by *The Satanic Verses*, therefore has a dual provenance, one avowedly secular and historical, the other theological and metaphysical. While the former tackles the binaries of 'insider/outsider' constructed along racial, cultural and, indeed, religious lines, the latter explores the nature of good and evil and, using what Roger Clark has identified as a 'satanic narrator', upsets and confounds traditional, religiously sanctioned moral imperatives as a means of interrogating the religious beliefs that both produce and are produced by them (Clark 2001).

Thus, on the one hand, the novel clearly endorses Zeeny Vakil's 'ethic of historically validated eclecticism' against 'the confining myth of authenticity' that Saladin Chamcha espouses until he accepts and embraces his hybrid identity. On the other hand, as with other dichotomies, the novel consistently throws the distinction between good and evil into doubt, sometimes inverting them, sometimes blurring the distinction between them, and at other times insisting on their interrelatedness, even interpenetration. The narrator goes to some length to explain that 'the separation of functions, light versus dark, evil versus good . . . [is] a pretty recent fabrication. Amos, eighth century BC, asks: 'Shall there be evil in a city and the Lord hath not done it?' (323)

Throughout the novel, this pattern is repeated in relation to both the secular and religious narratives: the 'ethic of impurity' establishes dichotomies only to collapse them again. At the same time, however, there is a contrary current running through the novel in which there is a *divergence* between the secular and religious registers with respect to the key trope of compromise, which is itself a deconstructive trope insofar as it involves the overcoming of oppositions. On the one hand, the theme of compromise and pragmatism is linked to hybridity and figured as a secular virtue with respect to history, but on the other it appears to be a symptom of religious failure – a pragmatic acknowledgement of the need to dilute the 'purity' of faith in the face of (secular) reality.

The avowedly secular Saladin's fortunes, for example, only begin to improve after he begins to compromise his devotion to a particular myth of British national 'authenticity' in favour of a hybrid identity that accommodates both his British and Indian selves. At his lowest point he witnesses a 'chimeran graft . . . two trees that had been bred into one . . . If such a tree were possible, then so was he' (406). The closing passages of the novel, in which Saladin not only accepts his hybrid identity but recuperates it by returning to India to make peace with his father (a representative figure of Indian nationalism), not only deconstructs the insider/outsider oppositions set up by nationalism itself, but also ironically renders him 'whole' in a way denied to his rival and antagonist, Gibreel, whose quest for wholeness is predicated on a rejection of 'moral fuzziness' in favour of the 'stark, imperative oppositions' (354) that he believes constitute the true faith of a religious believer.

At no point does the novel contradict this idea that true religious faith is unambiguously aligned with the 'ethic of purity'. Acts of compromise by religious characters are shown to be signs of weakness and a betrayal of fundamental principles, and are seen as such by the characters themselves. This, in turn, throws into doubt the authenticity of the various revelations that appear in the narrative, and the divinity from which they supposedly emanate. The novel's representation of the episode of the 'satanic verses', for instance, rests on the question 'Is Allah so unbending that he will not embrace three more [goddesses] to save the human race?' (111). The answer to this profoundly moral and theological question is, however, predicated on the exigencies of power. *'Any new idea, Mahound'*, says the narrator, *'is asked two questions. The first is asked when it's weak: WHAT KIND OF IDEA ARE YOU?'* The Prophet's doubts, such as they are, are a consequence of his political marginalization and his eventual rejection of compromise, even when weak, testifies to the view that true faith involves 'the path of purity and not of base compromise' (272). Likewise, in the 'Ayesha' narrative the 'satanic verses' episode is reprised when the modern and secular Mirza Saeed offers Ayesha a compromise at precisely the moment when her power is fragile and vulnerable. Like Mahound, she is initially tempted but eventually rejects the compromise even though she is in a position of weakness: 'His offer had contained an old question: *What kind of idea are you?* And she, in turn, had offered him an old answer: *I was tempted but now I am renewed; am uncompromising; absolute; pure'* (500).

The idea that Islam, in particular, is totally antithetical to compromise and the hybridity to which it is aligned is made explicit by the narrator:

> [Islam is] *the cussed, bloody-minded, ramrod-backed type of damnfool notion that would rather break than sway with the breeze . . . The kind that will almost certainly, ninety-nine times out of a hundred, be smashed to bits; but, the hundredth time, will change the world.* (335, original emphasis)

Islam is here figured as an exception to the text's principle of historical development through hybridity. It is the one-in-a-hundred phenomenon where the ethic of purity establishes itself, survives and even thrives. However, this essentializes Islam as a system of belief that is 'outside' history; it has, in effect, remained unchanged for over fourteen hundred years. Ironically, this is complicit with the Islamist understanding of Islam as a 'pure' religion that transcends history, which Rushdie avowedly contests. (Rushdie is not averse to essentializing gestures when it suits him, despite his ethic of impurity. He writes, '[i]n our beginnings we find our essences. To understand a religion, look at its earliest moments' (Rushdie 1991: 424; see also Mondal 2013). Moreover, the text is here displaying what the anthropologist Johannes Fabian has termed 'allochronism'; that is, in portraying Islam as a religion that remains essentially unchanged, it is marked as a superseded way of life that may coexist with modernity but is not 'co-eval' with it. Islam (and religion in general) is a remnant of 'another time', not an integral and valid way of living 'in our time' (Fabian 1983: 143). It is part of humanity's infancy, not its maturity. *The Satanic Verses* thus rehearses a classic secularist gesture, which enables secularism itself to monopolize the ground upon which 'modern' ways of thinking and being can be realized.

From this perspective, the modernization or reform of Islam that Rushdie calls for, and elsewhere acknowledges as part of its history, is rendered impossible. For if newness does enter the world through 'conjoinings' and 'hotch-potch', a 'bit-of-this and a bit-of-that', then Islam's 'purity' speaks to an inability to accommodate the plurality and multiplicity on which such a process depends. As such, its renewal and reform is precluded. The opening words of *The Satanic Verses* are: 'To be born again, first you have to die' (1). The refrain is repeated with a difference on the last page, 'if the old refused to die the new cannot be born' (547). The implication is clear: the death of Islam, or at least its Allah, is the prerequisite for a new sort of Muslim. And what could a 'born-again' Muslim look like after such a death? Only a secularized Muslim for whom faith is a matter of private belief, a reproduction of the Subject produced by Western secularism.

In the context of a novel that celebrates multiplicity and hybridity, this characterization of cultural difference as a zero-sum game – for a new culture to emerge another must die – is absurdly contradictory unless we put it into the context of a secularism which requires the 'death' of religion in order to constitute itself – symbolized by Gibreel Farishta's suicide at the end of the novel. Given that the secularism to which Rushdie subscribes already takes for granted the death of the Christian God, the novel's focus on Islam becomes more significant because its late-twentieth-century resurgence was perceived as a threat to secular hegemony (one that was ironically, albeit indirectly, reinforced by the novel's publication and the subsequent controversy).

Thus, a text that seeks to challenge 'orthodoxies of all kinds' reinforces a secularist orthodoxy which believes that religion no longer has anything to contribute to human development (and, indeed, is positively obstructive). As a consequence, *The Satanic Verses* is unable to extend its dismantling of the binary oppositions that uphold established patterns of thought to those governing secularism. In a famous and oft-cited passage, the narrator asks, 'What is the opposite of faith? Not disbelief. Too final, certain, closed. Itself a kind of belief. Doubt' (92). This opposition between faith and doubt is the basis for what Malise Ruthven has called the novel's 'theology of doubt', and it is the governing structuring principle through which the text explores religious faith from a secular point of view (Ruthven 1990: 17). Like all theologies, however, the 'theology of doubt' revered by *The Satanic Verses* is a structure that rests on a foundation that must, in order to uphold the structure, lie outside the structure itself; as a result, all the oppositions *within* the structure can be dismantled, but the foundational principle or *logos* cannot; it is beyond 'play' (Derrida 2001). Therefore, in the novel's 'theology of doubt' the opposition between faith and doubt is itself beyond doubt. The opposition is never dismantled within the novel *because it cannot be done*; without it the novel would not be what it is.

But what happens when the novel's 'theology of doubt' is itself put into doubt from an alternative critical position which does not take as axiomatic the antinomy between faith and doubt? If *The Satanic Verses* is a 'love song to our mongrel selves', what kind of reading might emerge if we 'mongrelize' the very thing it cannot, namely if we put our faith in doubting the 'theology of doubt'?

One might begin by acknowledging that the divergence between the secular and theological interests of the novel revealed by the trope of compromise speaks to a wider, more significant, discontinuity. Samir Amin defines as 'metaphysical' those forms of thought that seek 'totalization' by absorbing and superannuating the singular into the 'system', the particular into the general and the concrete instance into the abstract concept (Amin 1988: 28). From that perspective, the opposition between the religious and the secular is blurred because both secular and religious thought can be metaphysical. Secularism articulates its own metaphysical ambitions, for example, in such totalizing ideologies as nationalism, or in the fetishizing of a capitalized Reason, or in its invocation of historical Progress. In this respect, *The Satanic Verses* oscillates between the metaphysical and its opposite, the 'hermeneutic'; between the grand narrative, the global perspective, the totalizing gesture, and the suspicion, interrogation and dissolution of all these things, which is principally focused on the figure of the 'hybrid'.

Insofar as the novel approaches religion, however, the balance of emphasis tilts towards the metaphysical, for there is at its core a grand ambition, as we have seen, to dethrone God by mounting, in the name of a 'satanic' narrator, an adversarial attack on the foundational principle of divinity itself. It thus produces an anti-theology that seeks to displace religion *in its totality*. This totalizing gesture is profoundly metaphysical, as is its treatment of religious faith purely in terms of its claims to Truth. Turning Rushdie's question around, one might ask: 'What is the opposite of doubt?' It is by no means obvious that the answer should be 'faith' because that answer depends on a definition of faith that is synonymous with the more obvious and precise answer, namely 'certainty'. 'Faith' is here read purely as dogma and placed within an epistemological frame as opposed to an *experiential* one; in other words, 'faith' is defined by its *explicability* within a particular form of Reason rather than the multiplicity of (inexplicable) truths that might be derived from the singular, irreducible experience (or 'event') of faith. Thus, when Rushdie asks, 'if we accept that the mystic, the prophet is sincerely undergoing some sort of transcendental experience, but we cannot believe in a supernatural world, then what is going on?' we might, in turn, ask: 'What is *he* in fact *really* asking?' (Rushdie 1991: 408). In staging his exploration of religious faith in such terms there is clearly a tension between exploring and empathetically understanding the sincerity of the experience in ontological terms (an empathy that is not actually upheld by the novel), and *explaining* the experience as an epiphenomenon of some other, deeper, more 'truthful' phenomenon that involves translating the singularity of the experience into a 'system' of knowledge. We can notice, too, that the tension itself involves precisely the separation of knowledge and experience, faith and reason that characterizes post-Enlightenment thought (Caputo 2001: 42–9). Rushdie's exploration of faith, then, subscribes to the binary forms of thinking that establish and police the boundaries that, in other respects, he vigorously contests in the name of the 'hybrid', the 'postmodern' and the 'postcolonial'.

Ironically Rushdie's grand metaphysical ambition is bound to the very metaphysics it contests. Roger Clark observes that Rushdie's method is to employ a 'satanic' narrator provocatively to induce 'sympathy for the devil' (the song, by The Rolling Stones, is referenced several times in the narrative) in order to confound and upset established notions of good and evil and thereby call into question the Divine *logos* on which they rest (Clark 2001: 131). But engaging in a cosmic war against God suggests that this narrator is, in fact, a believer; he *must* believe in God for why would he oppose something he does not believe exists? I read this as symbolic of a wider filiative relation between the novel's secularism and the 'religion' it contests.

This is illuminated by an ethical problem that only arises because of the narrator's 'satanic' orientation. Put simply, it is this: the 'satanic' character Saladin (who physically embodies the 'satanic' – and secular – ethic of the text) commits a diabolic act (the enunciation of his own 'satanic verses') that leads, eventually, to the deaths of Allie Cone, Whisky Sissodia and Gibreel. The text does not sidestep or abjure his responsibility, 'how to explain his overwhelming feeling of guilt, of *responsibility*: how to tell her that these killings were the dark flowers he had planted long ago?' (542–3); however, not only is Saladin not punished, he is also the one major character who survives and, indeed, is *redeemed*, 'in spite of all his wrong-doing, weakness, guilt . . . he was getting another chance' (547). This poses a moral problem for a text that ultimately seeks to establish a framework of human existence, and a moral code, that is not founded on belief in a supernatural deity and the putatively rigid systems of thought and morality – the 'rules, rules, rules' (363) – that are derived from it (as symbolized in Baal's transition from polytheism to godlessness). For, despite the 'satanic' method, the ineluctable problem is that the text cannot espouse a 'satanic' ethics that exonerates Saladin's responsibility for the deaths of other human beings. This is a responsibility established by the same 'religious' moralities that are thrown into question by the text: 'Thou shall not kill.' The result is an *aporia* that is resolved by the paradoxical invocation of a religious gesture. Gibreel's suicide is an act of sacrifice that absolves Saladin of his 'sin'/guilt (and of having to 'explain' himself). It is only this return of the religious repressed that makes possible, and complete, Saladin's redemption and moral rehabilitation, although this is quickly repressed once more by a secular formulation: 'there was no accounting for one's good fortune' (547).

Thus, *The Satanic Verses* cannot divest itself of conventional (religious) morality, not least because 'religion' is an ineluctable part of human ethical development. Once this is admitted, it can only be dismissed by focussing purely on religion as an epistemological 'error', thereby excising its ethical dimension. In the Ayesha narrative, the effects of this displacement can be seen both in the way that religious faith is fetishized as an uncompromising dogmatism, and in the way that such certainty leads, inevitably, to inhumane and unethical behaviour; hence the grotesque episode in which a crowd emerging from a mosque stones a two-week old baby to death. This suggests that 'religion' is in a state of 'arrested development' ethically as well as historically; religious belief is shown to be inimical to even minimal standards of moral behaviour.

Notwithstanding this rather uncompromising disavowal, the return of the religious repressed signals an inability to uphold secularism's governing oppositions between the religious and secular, between faith and reason – and, indeed, it exposes the fictitiousness of these oppositions. Not only does a religious sensibility return in the form of a redemptive sacrifice at the end of the novel, so too does it emerge in the form of several liberal humanist pieties that are revealed once the postmodern stylistic pyrotechnics of the novel are stripped away. Rushdie displaces faith in God only to replace it with his own articles of faith, not just in hybridity as a kind of ontology of history – it is its very nature – but also a belief in the redemptive power of a transcendental Love ('It all boiled down to love'; 397) and forgiveness. Such ideas about Love and forgiveness represent *continuities* with prevailing religious discourses and these tropes demonstrate how secularism, despite giving every appearance of being committed to a materialism that sees the world 'as it really is' and speaks, in Barthes' words, 'with the "Voice of Nature"' is, in fact, a system of belief with its own shibboleths.

The Satanic Verses is, therefore, a classic statement of secular liberal humanism, and it rehearses the same universalizing gestures deployed by its liberal defenders during the controversy it ignited. The radical excess of cultural difference, as represented by Islam, is encircled and domesticated by a secular scepticism, the dominance of which is insistently reasserted over its efforts to empathetically represent the experience of religious belief. A novel that professes to be a 'love song to our mongrel selves' and a challenge to 'orthodoxies of all kinds' cannot imagine a hybrid position between the religious and the secular and ultimately reinscribes and reinforces the categorical distinctions of secularist orthodoxy. Insofar as the figure of the hybrid in the novel represents an attempt to disrupt the master logic of Western universalism, we must conclude by noting the ethical failure of a text that purports to speak up for difference but ultimately betrays that ambition.

Salman Rushdie's Post-Nationalist Fairy Tales: *Haroun and the Sea of Stories* and *Luka and the Fire of Life*

ANDREW TEVERSON

It is almost always impossible to tell when a story was first told and when it was first written down, or how it was transmitted, and impossible to say when the last telling and final version of a story will be. Good stories pay little attention to cultural or linguistic frontiers. The student of story collections finds himself adrift on an ocean of stories, an ocean which is boundless, deep and ceaselessly in motion.

Irwin 1994: 64–5

In our deepest natures we are frontier-crossing beings. We know this by the stories we tell ourselves.

Rushdie 2002: 408

Towards the end of the eighteenth century, a powerful alliance was forged between the popular traditional tale and the idea of the nation. The principal advocates of this alliance were a group of poets and intellectuals in Germany under the influence of the philosopher Johann Gottfried Herder (1755–1804), who had argued, in the teeth of a long, rationalist tradition stretching from Plato to Locke, that traditional narrative and poetic remains, far from being frivolous distractions, should be understood as agents of national renewal. Folk tales and folk songs, Herder believed, were the fragmentary embodiments of the spirit of a homogenous national people (the 'volk'), and they reflected the essence of the nation in its purest, most antique form. To preserve these remains was, therefore, to perform a signal service to the national idea: it helped root the nation in a sense of its long and dignified past and it gave the nation's people a basis for cultural regeneration in the present. These potent arguments gave impetus to the collection and preservation of national folk narrative archives throughout Europe. In Germany, they inspired the Brothers Grimm to start collecting the tales that would result in their voluminous *Kinder- und Hausmärchen* (Children's and Household Tales, 1812–57); in Finland they motivated Elias Lönnrot's assemblage of epic songs, the *Kalevala* (1835–49); in Norway they gave impetus to Jorgen Moe and Peter Asbjornsen's *Norske Folkeeventyr* (*Norse Folktales*, 1841–4); and in Serbia they encouraged Vuk Stefanović Karadžić in his composition of *Srpske Narodne Pripovijetke i Zagonetke* (*Serbian Folktales and Riddles*, 1854). In each case, these collections presented the fictions they anthologized as chronicles of the history of a nation, and as guarantors of the durability of the national soul.

As experienced folklorists such as Jacob and Wilhelm Grimm well knew, however, traditional tales are Janus-faced in so far as their reflection of cultural identity is concerned. On the one hand, folk tales are narratives which settle comfortably in one place, take on the colouration of local practice and come to express the world views of the people who disseminate them. But on the other, folk narratives are unruly, border-crossing fictions that, far from endorsing national particularism, have circulated between cultures, across borders, in writing, in performance, in speech, for centuries. At the early stages of the Grimms' collection, it was convenient for them to emphasize the Germanic character of their tales, confronted as they were by an aggressive, expansionist Napoleonic imperialism, and a Germany that was more than half a century away from unification. The Grimms, however, were also fully aware that every one of their *hausmärchen* had international paradigms, and that their collection was, therefore, as expressive of international cross-connections and cross-fertilizations as it was of the particularity of the German spirit and the uniqueness of the German folk vision. In the second edition of the *Kinder- und Hausmärchen*, accordingly, published between 1819 and 1822 when the Napoleonic threat was no longer current, this international dimension of the fairy tale comes to the fore in a long essay on Italian precursors for the German fairy tales, and in a host of notes that trace the complex genealogies of the Grimm tales. 'In their search for linguistic and historical roots of German folk-tales', Christa Kamenetsky notes, 'the Grimms were preoccupied with Germanic traditions yet never to the point of overlooking possible influences from other cultures or cross-cultural variants. In fact, searching out variants in other cultures was one of the main objectives of their notes' (1992: 26). In this respect too, the Grimms followed their mentor Herder, for whom, according to F. M. Barnard, 'nationalism and internationalism were not currents that ran in opposite directions but rather successive stages of historical development' (Barnard 1965: 86).

The relationship between folk narrative and nationalism also preoccupied the poets, novelists and playwrights of anti-colonial movements in the twentieth century. In the main, this preoccupation took the form of an endorsement of Herder's argument that traditional narratives operate as vehicles of cultural self-definition in periods of oppression and cultural erosion. In Kenya, for instance, as Ngugi wa Thiong'o has shown, one of the first imperatives of the counter-colonial struggle against British cultural imperialism was to recover and revivify

banned native traditions and use them in the present to 'make statements of resistance' to British power (Ngugi 1993: 88). Comparably, in
the Caribbean, Kamau Brathwaite has emphasized the necessity for
writers of African heritage to recuperate the traditions of their mother-
lands in response to the over-emphasis upon European heritage in the
colonial education system (Brathwaite 1984: 8–13). Such uses of tradition
differ in important respects from the uses of popular tradition made a
century or more previously in Europe: they reject the Eurocentrism of
nineteenth-century folk nationalism, they also resist the tendency, in
evidence in some forms of Romantic Nationalism, to retreat from the
politics of the present by seeking shelter in the mythologies of the past
(as Fanon insists in 'On National Culture' (1961), the pursuit of folk narrative tradition by post-colonial nationalists is inert if it is shaped only
by 'despairing, broken-down nostalgia', but becomes a dynamic part of
contemporary political struggle if its function is 'to bring conflicts up
to date and to modernise the kinds of struggle which the stories evoke';
Fanon 1994: 49, 47). Nevertheless, it remains the case that the novelists,
poets and playwrights of the early anti-colonial movement may be said,
distantly, to conform to the most dominant conception of folk traditions
established by Herder and Grimm at the dawn of the nineteenth century: they saw these traditions as essentially national resources with
nationalist functions. It is for this reason that Anthony K. Appiah argues
that the 'early novels' of anti-colonial writing, '[i]n one respect . . . seem
to belong to the world of eighteenth- and nineteenth century literary
nationalism'; they are fictions which 'are theorized as the imaginative
recreation of a common cultural past that is crafted into a shared tradition by the writer' (1991: 349).

The post-colonial engagement with folk traditions has not remained
static, however. Since the 1960s, as Appiah and others have demonstrated
(see Lazarus 1990 and Jani 2010), disillusionment with the practice of
nationalism in post-colonial states has resulted in a growing suspicion of
nationalist politics and the models of culture associated with it. Writers
such as Yambo Ouologuem in Mali (Appiah 1991), Chinua Achebe (in
his later novels) in Nigeria (Appiah 1991), Ayi Kwei Armah in Ghana
(Lazarus 1990), and Salman Rushdie, Amitav Ghosh, Rohinton Mistry,
Shashi Tharoor and Vikram Chandra in India (Jani 2010) have, in different ways and in different contexts, begun to 'look away from the nation
as a potential site for fulfilling the promises of decolonisation' and to
use their fiction to promote cosmopolitan models of identity that tran-
scend the nation (Jani 2010: 7, 50). As might be expected, this reaction
against nationalist politics has produced a corresponding and logically
consistent reassessment of the 'nativist' discourses that have been used
to support ideas of the nation. More than ever, post-colonial writers are
making use of traditional fictions, but in recent decades these fictions
are used increasingly, not to establish the 'coherence and the *telos* of the
nation' (Jani 2010: 8), but to disrupt it by demonstrating that cultures

are never formed in isolation, but through a centuries-long process of cross-fertilization and exchange. In this respect at least, writers of the later post-colonial period, having rejected the Romantic Nationalist alliance between folk narrative and nation, revisit another aspect of the argument made by Grimm and Herder: they seek to use traditional fictions to foreground the 'international transmission of culture', and to use this conception of culture to undermine absolutist ideas of cultural difference and the hierarchies of power they have been used to reinforce (Herder [1772] 1969: 173–4).

At the forefront of the post-nationalist literary movement in Indian writing is Salman Rushdie, whose *Midnight's Children* represents the first high-profile critique of Indian nationalist politics after the disillusioning period of 'Emergency' rule initiated by Indira Gandhi in the late 1970s (Jani 2010: 50). Perhaps more than any other single writer in the period, Rushdie has come to be associated with the satirical critique of nationalist politics, and with the use of aesthetic practices (hybridization, eclecticism, intertextuality) that disrupt homogenizing discourses such as nationalism. The present essay seeks to explore this reaction against nationalism from the point of view of Rushdie's approach to folk tradition, and it does so by considering the political and cultural objectives of his uses of folk tradition in his children's novel *Haroun and the Sea of Stories* (1990) and its 'companion' (Rushdie 2010b), written 20 years later, *Luka and the Fire of Life* (2010). These fictions, it is argued, are especially useful in illustrating the cosmopolitan attitude to folk and fairy tales in Rushdie's work for two reasons. In the first place, they demonstrate, with particular clarity, the ways in which Rushdie foregrounds the cosmopolitan and transnational nature of tradition in order to support cosmopolitan and transnational conceptions of culture and nation. In the second place, as children's fictions and overt fantasies, they allow Rushdie to depict, more optimistically than elsewhere, a utopian model of culture, in which the plurality of community is underwritten by the plurality of the stories it tells. In both respects, these fictions illustrate an idea that is central to this essay: that fairy tales are regarded as politically efficacious in recent post-colonial writing, not because they describe the nation but because they describe how culture transcends the nation.

Haroun and *Luka*

Haroun and the Sea of Stories was written by Rushdie for his first, and then only, son Zafar (middle name: Haroun) and dedicated to him in a touching acrostic poem which emphasizes the capacity of storytelling to connect father and son. It is the story of an inventive young boy named Haroun, who travels to the earth's invisible second moon Kahani ('story' in Hindi), where he becomes embroiled in a war between two communities: the Guppees, who talk a great deal ('gup' means gossip) and the

Chupwalas ('silent fellows'), who prefer to communicate through gesture. The Chupwalas, under thrall to a wicked sorcerer, Khattam Shud ('completely finished'), have declared a war on stories and pleasure, and have begun to pollute the moon's 'Story Sea' with 'anti-stories'. Haroun, in collaboration with the diverse and improbable friends he has made on Kahani, helps end this war when he uses story water to wish that the Moon will once more turn on its axis and so undo a rigid separation enforced by Gup scientists between the realms of darkness and silence inhabited by the Chupwalas and the realms of light and laughter inhabited by the Guppeees. This revolution (a quite literal revolution) causes Khattam Shud's shadow battalions to melt away to nothing; the Wall of Force separating Gup and Chup dissolves; and Guppees and Chupwalas are reminded that despite their cultural differences, they still have a great deal in common with one another.

On one level, this is a narrative designed to appeal to children aged, roughly, eight to twelve: it has an exciting storyline, antic comedy, an electric pace, and vivid characters. Simultaneously, however, *Haroun* is a fiction framed in the allegorical mode to carry levels of meaning that will be understood and appreciated by older readers alone. These second-level meanings are, in part, autobiographical. In the year that Rushdie wrote *Haroun*, he was in hiding, having been sentenced to death for blasphemy by the Ayatollah Khomeini in the wake of the *Satanic Verses* furore. Shuttled from safe house to safe house, fearing for his life and his profession, Rushdie elected to adapt the stories he had told his son during bath-time storytelling sessions in more peaceful times to caricature the illiberalism of Khomeini's Iran, and to mount a potent defence of the storyteller against the forces of silence and oppression (see Teverson 2001 and Gonzalez 2005). *Haroun* is not just about Rushdie's own situation, however, but may also be regarded as an allegorical response to broader political problems current in the revolutionary year in which it was written. In its celebratory depiction of the dismantling of a wall that segregates two communities, it may be seen as an indirect and approving reflection on the levelling of the Berlin Wall dividing East Germany from West that occurred in 1989. Alternatively, it may be seen as an allusive commentary on the dismantling of the apartheid system in South Africa that culminated in the release of Nelson Mandela in 1990. In a less celebratory vein, *Haroun* may also be read as a fiction that warns readers about the dangers of various 'line[s] across the world' (Rushdie 2002: 423) that were gaining in solidity in the late 1980s. Most prominently, it appears to warn against the hardening of hostilities between the now nuclear states of India and Pakistan, manifested most damagingly in Kashmir, which had itself been partitioned in 1972 by a Line of Control (unmistakably echoed in Kahani's Wall of Force). The novel also, more obviously, acts as a commentary upon the growing antagonism between Islam and the West, illustrated, so immediately for Rushdie, by the Ayatollah's *fatwa*.

Diverse as they are, the various real-world scenarios conjured in *Haroun* share a common characteristic that allows Rushdie to express them symbolically in the polarization of Guppees and Chupwalas: they are, in Rushdie's view, expressive of a conflict between a liberal, pluralist and multicultural view of the world that is tolerant of diversity and seeks to overcome the boundaries that segregate peoples, and the view he associates with 'the world's many different kinds of thought policemen' – the Khattam Shuds who seek to enforce boundaries, sediment apartheids and persecute freedom of thought and movement (Rushdie 2002: 434).

Luka and the Fire of Life, written 20 years after *Haroun* for Rushdie's second son Milan (middle name: Luka), extends the Khalifa family saga by narrating the adventures of Haroun's brother, Luka – younger than Haroun by 18 years as Milan is younger than Zafar by 18 years. Luka lives happily in the city of Kahani with his family and with 'a bear named Dog and a dog named Bear' that he has liberated from a circus owned by a piratical villain named Captain Aag ('fire' in Hindi) (Rushdie 2010a: 1). Family happiness is disrupted when Rashid, a latter-day sleeping beauty, falls into a mysterious catatonia from which he cannot be roused, and is visited by a sinister double, Nobodaddy, who has been summoned to devour his life. This event propels Luka on a journey, accompanied by Nobodaddy and a growing cohort of bizarre entities, to a parallel reality – the 'World of Magic' – that resembles the parallel realities found in the computer games he is so fond of. In this 'World of Magic' he must complete a series of 'levels', battling symbolically against time, until he defeats the otherworld apotheosis of Captain Aag ('Granddmaster Flame'), gets past the Aalim ('learned ones' in Islamic tradition) – named Jo-Hua (what was), Jo-Hai (what is) and Jo-Aiga (what will be) – and steals a piece of the 'fire of life'. Once possessed of the fire of life, Luka is able to return home to restore his father to consciousness.

Composed in less-fraught circumstances, *Luka* is a book that, in Rushdie's own words, inhabits a 'very different imaginative milieu' to the earlier children's novel (2010b). *Haroun* is a novel of crisis that seeks, indirectly, to confront the political persecution Rushdie was subjected to in the late 1980s; *Luka* negotiates a more personal anxiety – the fear of the older father that he may not live to see his son grow up (Rushdie 2010b). *Haroun*, because of its rooting in crisis, is an urgent and, for Rushdie at least, relatively streamlined narrative; *Luka*, written in calmer times, returns to the highly digressive, episodic narrative style that characterizes Rushdie's work, especially his later work, for adults. Nevertheless, the two novels share sufficient formal and thematic concerns to bind them together as conceptual as well as narrative counterparts. Both are fantasies that involve quests to alternative realities; both are 'crossover' fictions (Falconer 2009) that aim to demolish 'the boundary between "adult" and "children's" literature' (Rushdie 2010b), and both are fictions about the relationship between fathers and sons that reverse the classic oedipal narrative in which a son must achieve self-definition by over-coming the father and instead depict the son achieving self-definition by rescuing the father. Centrally, however, these fictions are conceptually linked by a desire to use storytelling to celebrate cultural pluralism and condemn cultural segregation. In *Haroun*, as we have seen, this is expressed concisely in the polarization of the Guppees, as a pluralist culture that defends the story sea, and the Chupwalas who, under the sway of Khattam Shud, seek to destroy stories because they represent a world of meaning that cannot be controlled. In *Luka*, comparably, Luka and his eccentric cortege seek to defend the diversity and vitality of the World of Magic against the encroachments of entities such as the Rats from the 'Respectorate of I' who have annexed a portion of magi-cal territory by erecting a barbed wire 'O-Fence' (Rushdie 2010a: 70–1). Here, as in *Haroun*, the ceaselessly metamorphic worlds of storytell-ing and magic embody a richness of culture, a proliferation of mean-ing, that Rushdie associates with cosmopolitan statehood and regards as politically healthy, while the opponents of story and magic exhibit a boundary-drawing, segregationist mentality that Rushdie associates with fundamentalist world views and presents as narrow and authori-tarian. In defending the sea of stories and in defending the world of magic, Rushdie thus seeks to defend, at the symbolic level, cultural values he cares most about, namely 'the values of pluralism and multi-plicity and being many things and not being narrow, not defining your culture or yourself too narrowly' (Reder 2000: 207).

Fairy Tale in *Haroun* and *Luka*

As is characteristic of Rushdie's work, this celebration of the plural quali-ties of storytelling is not just thematic but also formal. In *Haroun*, as adult readers quickly detect, the diversity of the peoples of Kahani is echoed in the flitting presence of a host of narrative allusions drawn freely from east, west, north and south. Likewise, in *Luka*, the imaginative diversity of the World of Magic is expressed, at the level of the text, in a wealth of references, parallels, erudite associations and subcultural name-checks. In the former novel we find, jostling for space in Rushdie's crowded marketplace, references to fantasy films such as Victor Fleming's *The Wizard of Oz* (1939); allusions to narratives of magical transit such as Farid ud-Din Attar's *Conference of the Birds* (1177), Jonathan Swift's *Gulliver's Travels* (1726) and Lewis Carroll's *Alice in Wonderland* (1865); and puns that allude to the lyrics of Beatles songs. In the latter, we find dizzy-ing panoptic surveys of world mythology reminiscent of the extensive comparative surveys of myth to be found in Joseph Campbell's *Hero with a Thousand Faces* (1949), as well as structural borrowings from the elec-tronic games that Luka (and Rushdie's son Milan) are so fond of. As this is a novel about the desire to outwit the tyranny of time, it is also replete with allusions to fictions about time travel including Mark Twain's novel *A Connecticut Yankee in King Arthur's Court* (1889), Jorge Luis Borges's labyrinthine tale 'The Garden of Forking Paths' (1941), Terry Gilliam's cinematic eccentricity *Time Bandits* (1981) and the *Back to the Future* films (1985–90). In each case, Rushdie's use of allusion is profligate and, in generic terms at least, indiscriminate: he draws freely from films, novels, poems, short stories, television programmes and pop songs – and all of these forms of imaginative invention are conscripted to the cause of creating a textual sea of stories that replicates, in the material constitution of the fiction, the symbolic story sea of *Haroun*.

As this profligacy of allusion will suggest, Rushdie has no one genre in mind when he evokes the concept of 'story' in *Haroun* and *Luka*: he means to refer to every form of narration that is to hand – oral or literary, low-tech or high-tech. 'Story', for Rushdie, means the entire, irrepressible and wonderfully various output of the human narrative imagination, and is by no means to be restricted to the classic storytelling genres of fairy tale, legend, myth and saga. That said, however, popular traditions such as the fairy tale, legend, myth and saga come to play an iconic role in Rushdie's writing, partly because they symbolize the idea of the story in concise form, and partly because, as authorless narratives, they embody the idea of circulation, adaptation, transmission and transformation even before they have entered the playful intertextual space of Rushdie's writing. The fairy tale, for Rushdie, is the anonymous migrant text par excellence, and for this reason it becomes, in his work, an over-arching symbol for narrative hybridity and for the capacity of fictions (and the people that carry them) to travel over the boundaries of culture.

Three examples of Rushdie's uses of fairy tales will help illustrate his approaches to the genre. The first concerns his borrowing from the Bengali director Satyajit Ray's film *Goopy Gyne Bagha Byne* (*The Adventures of Goopy and Bagha* 1968); the plot of which, derived from a short story published by Ray's grandfather Upendrakisore Ray, in his magazine for young people *Sandesh* in 1914, is strongly influenced by Indian folktales (as Satyajit later observed, his grandfather specialized in writing 'old legends and folk-tales anew for children'; Robinson 1989: 23). The film centres upon the adventures of the singer Goopy and the drummer Bagha, who are exiled from their respective villages after causing offence because of their inadequate mastery of the musical arts. While wandering in a forest Goopy and Bagha accidentally conjure up the King of the Ghosts who grants them three boons: whenever they clap each other's hand they will get food, whenever they put on a pair of magic slippers they will be able to travel wherever they wish and whenever they sing and drum they will be able to astonish people with their music. Using their newfound powers, Goopy and Bagha travel to Shundi, a kingdom of eccentric music lovers who are unable to speak, but who communicate through music – a language which, as Goopy observes, 'is beyond nation and situation'. The peaceful kingdom of Shundi, however, is threatened with war by the neighbouring Kingdom of Halla, in which the King, an estranged brother of the king of Shundi, is under the sway of a manipulative prime minister and his wicked sorcerer Barfi. Goopy and Bagha visit Halla to try to make peace, but they are captured and imprisoned. During preparations for war, however, they manage to enchant the armies of Halla using their musical powers, and capture the King of Halla. The King of Halla and the King of Shundi are then reunited and reconciled, peace is restored, the wicked prime minister and his magician are overcome and Goopy and Bagha marry the two kings' daughters.

The parallels between this narrative and Rushdie's *Haroun* are plain to see, and Rushdie freely acknowledges his debt in the names of the Plentimaw fishes. What is perhaps less visible is the fact that Rushdie, in revisiting this Bengali fairy tale film is simultaneously revisiting elements of European tradition. This becomes apparent if we compare the plots of *Haroun* and *Goopy and Bagha* with the opening scenario of Marie Catherine d'Aulnoy's fairy tale of 1697, 'La bonne petite souris', translated, and to some extent adapted, in Andrew Lang's *Red Fairy Book* of 1890 as 'The Little Good Mouse'. Here we find depicted a conflict between the 'The Land of Joy' and its hostile neighbour 'The Land of Tears'. The Land of Joy, in which the pursuit of pleasure and happiness is paramount, is ruled over by a king and queen whose 'hearts and inclinations were always in unison' (Zipes 1989: 350). The Land of Tears, by dramatic contrast, is ruled over by a monarch who is a 'declared enemy of pleasure', and who thinks of 'naught but warfare and causing mischief' (350). As is perhaps inevitable, this wicked king prosecutes a war against The Land of Joy and in the course of this war kills its king and abducts its queen. Complicated adventures follow involving a good fairy mouse, but ultimately, the narrative concludes with the defeat of the wicked king and his son in a 'coup d'etat' and the reconciliation of the two kingdoms, easily effected since the subjects of the king of The Land of Tears have, readers learn, only obeyed their wicked leader 'out of terror' (Zipes 1989: 359–60).

The similarities between this plot and the plots of *Haroun* and *Goopy and Bagha* are striking. All three fictions feature the motif of antagonistic lands; in each case, the contentment of a peaceable land is disrupted by the malignant ambitions of a violent aggressor; and in each case harmony between lands is restored when the malignant ruler is defeated. There are also significant thematic parallels between these three stories. In each, the device of the polarized kingdom becomes a tool for analysing admirable and unadmirable social behaviour, and a means of investigating desirable and undesirable political arrangements. In *Haroun*, Guppee society is desirable because it is open, diverse and tolerant, while the political order enforced in Chup by Khattam

Shud is undesirable because it is closed, mono-cultural and repressive. In *Goopy and Bagha*, Shundi is a civilization worth preserving and celebrating because it loves art (specifically music) and shuns war, while Halla, under the influence of the Khattam-Shud-like sorcerer Barfi, is undesirable because it is martial, greedy and philistine. Likewise, in 'The Little Good Mouse', The Land of Joy is admirable because it represents a society that is open to pleasure and the arts, and, importantly for d'Aulnoy, grants women public office, while the Land of Tears is hostile to pleasure and art, and treats women as slaves. In all three fictions, these representations of desirable and undesirable societies have a direct relationship with the political and ideological preferences of their authors as they have been shaped by the political developments of their times. D'Aulnoy was writing in response to a political regime that was increasingly arguing that women should be relegated to the domestic sphere and subordinated to their husbands in marriage, and she used the fairy tale form as a utopian device for imagining more egalitarian socio-political arrangements (Seifert 1996: 84–97). Ray's film, made only 21 years after Indian independence, may be seen as a meditation on both the cultural divisiveness of colonialism (seen in the extraordinary expressionistic dance sequence near the start of the film), and on the fratricidal antagonism between India and Pakistan over Kashmir that was threatening to result in a second conflict even as the film was being made. Rushdie's novel, as we have seen, may also be regarded as an allegorical commentary upon dangerous political antagonisms current in the late 1980s – the ongoing conflict between India and Pakistan over Kashmir foremost among them.

Rushdie's *Haroun and the Sea of Stories* is, thus, firmly rooted in a tradition of allegorical narrative that both protests against contemporary abuses of political power, and, simultaneously, promotes the virtues of tolerance, dialogue and integration over the vices of narrowness, divisiveness and compartmentalization. This tradition of political protest, moreover, is mediated through a fairy-tale narration that not only endorses Rushdie's observation to Günther Grass that the fairy tale is a lie that tells the truth by other means (Reder 2000: 75–6), but also validates the unwritten motto of the story sea: that no story belongs to any one person or culture exclusively.

A second example of Rushdie's uses of fairy tale is supplied by the title of *Luka and the Fire of Life*, in which two traditions are invoked simultaneously: first, the fairy tale 'The Water of Life' (tale type ATU551 in Uther 2004: Part I) in which a son quests for healing water to save his father; second, the international folk tale and myth concerning the fire thief who steals the power to give or restore life from the gods. Together these traditions provide the central narrative mechanism of the novel: like the boy in the fairy tale, Luka quests for a substance that will save his father's life – only in this composite fiction 'water' is translated into 'fire' because, as the Fire Bug tells Luka, 'Life is not a drip. Life is a flame' (Rushdie 2010a: 59). Each of these traditions is known to Europe in variants that have become dominant: 'The Water of Life' is widely familiar because of the popularity of the version published by Grimm in 1815 (tale 97, 'Das Wasser des Lebens') derived from mixed Hessian and Paderbornian sources (Zipes 1992: 732). Likewise, the story of the fire thief is best known in Europe from the classical Greek myth of Prometheus recorded by Hesiod in *Theogony* (ca 700 BCE). Both these narratives, however, have much richer traditions than attention to the European variants alone will reveal. 'The Water of Life' can be found in diverse forms in Scandinavian, British, Caribbean, Mediterranean, Middle Eastern, North African, Russian, Romany and Jewish traditions. It has also been recorded, in what is likely to be one of its oldest variations, as a traditional oral folk-tale in Kashmir (see Thompson and Balys 1958: 243 and Thompson and Roberts 1960: 83), ancestral homeland for Rushdie, and real-world blueprint for the fantasy geography of *Haroun* and *Luka*. The story of Prometheus, similarly, is related to a phenomenally fecund cross-cultural tradition of fire-thievery, referenced directly by Rushdie in *Luka* when he alludes, variously, to the story of the rabbit that steals fire told by the Algonquin Indians, the story of the fire thieving spider told by the Cherokee and the story of Maui-tikitiki-a-Taranga who seized 'Fire from the finger-nails of the fire goddess Mahuika and gave it to the Polynesians' (149–50). In each case, the genealogies of these fictions reinforce Rushdie's view that stories, while they may, in contingent forms, reflect the cultural identities of particular peoples in particular eras, belong ultimately to a vast story sea that is characterized more by interconnection and intersection than by separation and distinction.

This sense of the multiple-belonging of popular traditional narratives also undergirds the iconic presence of *The Thousand and One Nights* in Rushdie's oeuvre – which may stand as our third example of his uses of fairy tale traditions. The *Nights*, as is generally known, derives from the Middle East. It first took shape as a framed collection of narratives in the regions of Egypt, Syria and Iraq between the ninth and thirteenth centuries, and is now familiar to us as a result of the survival of Arabic manuscript versions from the fourteenth or fifteenth centuries (see Haddawy 1992: xii; Irwin 1994: 47–62; and Grotzfeld 2004: 17–18). The history of the *Nights*, however, is not only – or even originally – Middle Eastern. Stories that appear in Arabic manuscripts can also be found in Sanskrit narrative collections, such as the collection that Rushdie alludes to repeatedly in *Haroun*: the *Katha Sarit Sagara* (*Ocean of Streams of Story*) written by the Kashmiri court poet Bhatta Somadeva in the eleventh century. Tales that appear in the *Nights* may also be found in numerous works of early European literature, including, but not limited to, Boccaccio's *Decameron* (1353), Ariosto's *Orlando Furioso* (1516–32), Giovan Francesco Straparola's *Le piacevoli notti* (1550–3) and Cervantes's *Don Quixote* (1605–15). We might speculate that these narratives travelled to Europe along the complex paths of exchange and interaction that were opened up by Roman imperial expansion during the first century BCE, the Moorish conquest of Southern Spain from the eighth century and European crusades in the 'holy land' from the tenth century. Ultimately, however, it is now, as Robert Irwin observes, 'almost always impossible to tell' when a story from *The Nights* 'was first told and when it was first written down, or how it was transmitted': these stories 'pay little attention to cultural or linguistic frontiers' and so the student of such collections 'finds himself adrift on an ocean of stories, an ocean which is boundless, deep and ceaselessly in motion' (Irwin 1994: 64–5).

To further complicate this textual history, the East/West genealogy of the *Nights* becomes even more convoluted after its official arrival in Europe in the shape of Antoine Galland's French translation made between 1704 and 1717. Galland used, as a basis for his translation, a fourteenth- or fifteenth-century Syrian manuscript, and in this respect, he was the first to convey, in substantial form, the Arabic *Nights* to the West. But he also transformed the *Nights* significantly for his European audience, adapting the language of the stories so that they would appeal to readers of the French court in the era of Enlightenment, and adding stories from other sources (such as 'Aladdin') in order to create a more substantial work (see Irwin 1994: 14–18; and Kabbani 2004: 26). For the literary critic Rana Kabbani it naturally follows that Galland used the *Nights* to falsify the orient for the West, mounting, on the slim foundation of an obscure collection of tales, an edifice of exotic, orientalist fictions that could be used to position the East in ways that were politically advantageous for an expansionist, imperially rapacious colonial power (1986: 23–4; 2004: 25–6). Recently, however, Madeleine Dobie has argued for a more nuanced understanding of Galland's achievement. In Dobie's view, it is better to see Galland's collection neither as an innocent engagement with the 'East' nor as a straightforward manifestation of 'the lurking spectre of Eurocentrism', but as a complex and pioneering work that 'navigate[s] the interface between Arabic and French literary traditions' by demonstrating the *departures* and 'the still deeper continuities* that bind these traditions together (2008: 47). Galland's *Nights* is thus, for Dobie, a fiction forged in the 'contact zone' between cultures, and is culturally significant for both regions because it enables readers and scholars to better understand the East/West encounter 'as a layered, discontinuous, and elusive process of cultural exchange' (2008: 29).

The *Arabian Nights* is referenced extensively by Rushdie in *Haroun* and *Luka*. It is present implicitly in the structure of the storytelling; it is also alluded to repeatedly in the course of narration. In *Haroun*, it emerges in the name of the houseboat that Haroun and Rashid stay on ('Arabian Night Plus One'); in the reference made in the names of the protagonists to the Caliph that features prominently in the *Nights*, Haroun al Rashid; and in the reworking of a frame narrative concerning female infidelity (see Bacchilega 2004: 182–3). In *Luka*, it emerges in references

to the 'roc' that swoops out of the pages of *Sinbad the Sailor* (147), and in
the identification of Nobodaddy as a kind of genie (as well as a German
doppelganger, a Norse Loki and a medieval European figuration of
Death, 46–7). It would be misleading to claim that Rushdie's interest in
the *Nights* does not stem, at least in part, from the idea that the narrative cycle is 'eastern' in origin and may supply an alternative to 'western' models of narration. Rushdie, however, is simultaneously aware
that the *Nights* is a body of fiction that has been shaped by a complex
history of international exchange: it has roots in India (most especially
in Kashmir) and later travelled back to India with Mughal conquer-
ors in the sixteenth century; it went to Spain with Moorish invaders,
where, in course of time, it became a vital influence upon the European
novel; then, in the eighteenth century, following Galland's translation, it
became a focal point for enlightenment and post-enlightenment intersections of East and West (see Reder 2000: 111, 150). The processes of
exchange that have produced these interrelations are rarely peaceable
or equitable. More often than not they are a consequence of violence
and cultural appropriation (an aspect of the process of exchange that the
utopian image of *Haroun*'s story sea elides). Violent or otherwise, however, they have resulted in a textual tradition that records culture as a
historical complexity, and that embodies intersections between East and
West even as it bears the traces of discursive efforts to polarize the two
regions. The *Nights*, in this sense, is meaningful for Rushdie not only as
an Eastern fiction, but also as a fiction that validates his vision of culture
as a process of cross-fertilization – sometimes violent and appropriative,
sometimes peaceable and dialogic – but always hybridizing.

   In the approaches to fairy tale outlined above, Rushdie departs significantly from the understanding of story and culture advanced by
earlier, anti-colonial nationalist writers. His anti-colonial predecessors
tend to draw upon traditions that are easily identified with specific cultural groups; they also sought to use stories to root their communities in
a known soil and a long history (see for instance Raja Rao's *Kanthapura*
(1938) and the discussion of this in Kumar 2007). Rushdie's preference
is for narrative traditions that are more obviously formed in the contact
zones between cultures. When he uses these traditions, moreover, he
seeks to foreground the idea that the territories of tradition are never
untrammelled, but have been marked by the footprints of diverse trav-
ellers. In so doing, Rushdie does not seek to deny that cultural traditions
help to bond a community and to tell that community about its cultural past – stories, he affirms, are the glue that holds families and tribes
together (Rushdie 1998) – he does, however, seek to resist the nationalist assumption that any given story is the exclusive possession of a
national culture, or that it is capable of defining that culture in absolute
distinction to other cultures. Stories tell us who we are, for Rushdie, but
one of the things they tell us about who we are is that our belonging is
never singular. Like the stories we tell, our culture has come to us from

many places and many times, and our understanding of community, of nation, ought to reflect this narratological truth.

Rushdie, in this sense, has broken the bond between traditional story and the nation by making traditional story stand for plurality of inter-cultural contact and dialogue between sites of difference. Ironically, this means that the very medium that became so potent an agent of national self definition in the Romantic movement of the eighteenth and nine-teenth centuries, becomes the vehicle by which Rushdie seeks to contest and disrupt singular conceptions of nation and identity in the late twen-tieth and twenty-first centuries: the narrative agents of nationhood in the hands of the Romantic Nationalists have become the agents of cos-mopolitanism in the hands of Rushdie. As suggested at the start of this chapter, however, the rejection of the alliance between nationalism and the traditional tale engineered by Rushdie does not sever him absolutely from the conception of culture proposed by Herder and the Grimms but aligns him, distantly, with what may be regarded as the higher goal of Romantic Nationalism: the possibility of conceiving a *perfect cosmo-politanism* in which links are formed between 'man as a member of a nation and of humanity at large' (Barnard 1965: 94). For Herder, this utopian possibility was called *humanität* – a form of internationalism that involves recognition of human commonalities across the borders of nation and clan. In Rushdie's fiction, the story sea becomes a modern vehicle for this old idea: it is a vision of oceanic plurality in which every narrative flows into every other narrative, and the walls that hold cul-tures apart dissolve in a fluid *mêlée* of fictions.

CHAPTER SEVEN

'Illuminated by a ray of the sun at midnight': *The Enchantress of Florence*

MARTIN MCQUILLAN

The story was completely untrue but the untruth of untrue stories could sometimes be of service in the real world.

Rushdie 2008: 211

Let us begin with a grand proposition: every text (literary, filmic, cultural or historic) contains within itself an instance of figurative self-referentiality in which it thematizes its own textuality. That is to say, every text always refers to itself as a text and puts on display means through which it produced itself. This is true whether the text is a medieval Romance, an Epic poem, a Realist novel, a biography, a work of History or Philosophy, or the daily news. It is not always the case that such moments of textual self-awareness are the most prominent components of a text. Rather, the alert reader will often have to seek them out in an attempt to recover what is lost when a text presents itself to be analysed in terms of 'what's being said', 'what the author meant', immediate legibility and representational common sense. As Barbara Johnson puts it in her essay 'Rigorous Unreliability':

[By] shifting the attention from intentional meaning to writing as such, deconstruction has enabled readers to become sensitive to a number of recurrent literary topoi in a new way. Texts have been seen as commentaries on their own production or reception through their pervasive thematizations of textuality – the myriad letters, books, tombstones, wills, inscriptions, road signs, maps, birthmarks, tracks, footprints, textiles, tapestries, veils, sheets, brown stockings, and self-abolishing laces that serve in one way or another as figures for the text to be deciphered or unravelled or embroidered upon. (1987: 18)

Johnson's work and those of her 'Yale School' colleagues tends to focus on eighteenth- and nineteenth-century literature in which the relation between the representative system of a text and textual self-referentiality as a discordant signifying element is not always so clear, requiring the deconstructive reader to illuminate the text through their imaginative unravelling or re-embroidering of the text. However, the question that a novel such as Salman Rushdie's *The Enchantress of Florence* (2008) gives us to think is what should the reader make of a text in which such moments of textual self-awareness appear on every page and are clearly part of the authorial intention and representative system of the novel itself? Can we be content to put this reversal of values down to the knowing, even cynical, stylistic parameters of literary postmodernism, or is there something more complex at play in this book and by extension in all and every so-called postmodern text? Leaving to the side the vexed question of what might constitute a postmodern text, this chapter will read Rushdie's novel in terms of its own strategy for textual self-referentiality as a means of simultaneously positing an idea of textual sovereignty and undoing it by turns in order to render itself ever more unreadable and so require the reader to affirm this unreadability as the condition for continued critical reading in the world beyond the border of the book itself.

This novel, like much of Rushdie's work is replete with the instance of narrativizing, fabrication, letter writing, rumour mongering, archiving, publication, mirroring and reflection. The plot of the novel concerns the unfolding of a double plot, a story about storytelling and the intrigue it engenders. A blonde-haired traveller, Niccolò Vespucci, arrives at the court of the Grand Mughal, Emperor Akbar, determined to tell the tale of 'a secret so astonishing that it could shake the dynasty itself' (105). The novel unfolds as Vespucci, the self-proclaimed Mogor dell'Amore, tells his story to the Mughal, constantly interrupted by the manoeuvring of the court, the politics of the empire and the civil culture of the city. As the novel progresses we flip between two worlds and two stories: that of the Mughal Empire, the present of Vespucci and Akbar and that of Florence under the Medicis, the past of three friends whose history leads back to the Mughal present via the introduction of a third, new world. In the telling of this serpentine tale, the importance of the theatrical and dashing Vespucci as a character recedes as the story of Qara Koz, the lost Mughal princess, who he believes to be his mother, is told. The novel flips to be no longer Vespucci's story but the story of Qara Koz and Akbar, who must, in the end, decide whether Vespucci's narrative is true or false. At the end Vespucci slips away and Akbar is left in a world of doubt and recrimination, uncertain as to what remains at the end of this narrative marathon. Layer upon layer of storytelling sits embedded within each other in a labyrinthine tale of referential excess in which impossible historical conjunctions (Genghis Khan, Lorenzo de Medici, Vlad the Impaler, Machiavelli, Amerigo Vespucci, Christopher Columbus, Botticelli and Elizabeth I) are drawn together in the timeline of Qara Koz and her uncertain offspring; as both bricolage and hybrid, the novel's narrative acts as story-funnel for the history of two worlds. At every turn the story and its teller are at risk as his plot bewitches the city, leading to counter-plots against him, and from time to time the Mughal's own suspicions of this unreliable narrator. From the land of the *Decameron*, Vespucci, must survive to tell his tale but is not adverse to the deferred gratification of its ending. In the end it is not concluded by Vespucci but by Qara Koz herself ('the hidden chapter' 137), returned from the dead, to tell her tale aright to supplement the Mogor dell'Amore who ultimately proves to have been an unknowing vessel for her story. The novel works on a high level of narrative sophistication but its structural intricacies are probably the least interesting thing it has to say about storytelling.

At the heart of the story that Vespucci tells Akbar, sits the tale of Qara Koz's marriage to the Florentine Argalia. 'In the beginning were three friends Niccolò 'il Machia' [Machiavelli, author of *The Prince*], Agostino Vespucci [cousin of Amerigo], and Antonio Argalia' (200) who leaves Florence to fight as a mercenary and who wins Qara Koz in battle later converting to Islam. The story of Argalia's adventures is recounted through the textual device of 'The Memory Palace', a slave girl sent by Agralia to his friends in Florence to report his story. The Memory Palace is a mnemonic device who serves only to record and relay the message of Agralia's narrative and who will only tell it to one of the other two friends. She arrives at the brothel of Alessandra Fiorentina (one of many enchantresses) in a catatonic state, repeating '*Je suis le palais des souvenirs*' (203). With the mention of the keyword 'Florence' ('there is a room in this palace containing that name', 203) she begins to slowly recover mobility in direct relation to the progress she makes in telling the story recorded within her. Machiavelli explains to Agostino:

> According to Cicero . . . this technique was invented by a Greek, Simonides of Ceos, who had just left a dinner party full of important men when the roof fell in and killed everyone. When he was asked who was there he managed to identify all the dead by remembering where they had sat at the dinner table. . . In the *Rhetorica* it's called by the same name, the memory palace . . . You build a building in your head, you learn your way around it, and then you start attaching memories to its various features, its furniture, its decorations, whatever you choose. If you attach a memory to a particular location you can remember an enormous amount by walking around the place in your head. (204–5)

But *le palais des souvenirs* takes this architectonic principle to a new height, making her body the warehouse of Argalia's *memoires*: 'somebody has gone to a great deal of trouble . . . to build a memory palace the size of an entire human brain. This young woman has had her own memories removed, or consigned to some high attic of the palace of memory which has been erected in her mind, and she has become the repository of everything her master needed to have remembered' (205). She is

Polenta, the girl the three friends sing of in the forest outside Florence in their youth: 'if she was a message I would have sent her. If she was a meaning I would have meant her' (172).

The girl releases a new stretch of the recording night after night, like an automated Scheherazade, with each chapter returning closer to consciousness of herself, telling of Argalia's own 1,001 nights against the backdrop of Machiavelli's libidinal interest in her somnambulant body: 'tell me your secret, my little snackerel, and I promise I won't eat you until it's told' (209) as a giant tells the young Argalia in an early adventure of a 'story-filled boy' who through his invention 'lived to tell another tale another day' (215) only to rise to become the stuff of legend and epic narratives himself. The Florentine friends are disconcerted by Argalia's use of the girl in this way but Machiavelli is not adverse to fondling her stationary body as 'the rote-learned words poured out' (231) promising himself that he will not have her until her story is complete:

> He whispered in her ear, '*This is the last time you will ever tell this story. As you tell it let it go'*. Slowly, phrase by phrase, episode by episode, he would unbuild the palace of memories and release a human being. He bit her ear and saw a tiny answering tilt of the head. He pressed her foot and a toe moved gratefully. He caressed her breast and faintly, so faintly that only a man looking for the deeper truth would have seen it, her back arched in return. There was nothing wrong in what he did. He was her rescuer. She would thank him in time. (232)

Scheherazade, Pygmalion and Coppelia in one, to Machiavelli's lecherous Orpheus, the memory palace unspools her data towards the last story that 'colonized her brain' and 'had to be told as she passed out through that doorway and reawakened to ordinary life' (236). Her last story is of herself, revealing her true identity as 'Angélique and I am the daughter of Jacques' (237), Jacques Coeur a merchant of Montpellier. Abducted by pirates she had by turns become the recorder of Argalia's epic story. Having told her final tale she awakes in the night and throws herself through a window to her death:

> While you were anaesthetized to the tragedy of your life you were able to survive. When clarity was returned to you, when it was painstakingly restored, it could drive you mad. Your reawakened memory could derange you, the memory of humiliation, of so much handling, of so many intrusions, the memory of men. Not a palace but a brothel of memories . . . It was necessary that you run as fast as possible until you reached the edge between the worlds and then you didn't stop you ran across the border as if it wasn't there as if glass was air and air was glass, the air shattering around you like glass as you fell. The air slicing you to pieces as if it were a blade. It was good to fall. It was good to fall out of life. It was good. (240–1)

The mnemonic daughter of Jacques, at the heart of this narrative, driven mad by the consciousness of the terms of her own storytelling falls out of life from a brothel window, inglorious and tawdry, between two worlds and beyond reason.

The rebooted Angélique cannot bear the truth of storytelling. This is not a sovereign narrator in command of her destiny, writing her own story. She is rather a gramophone, written upon and repeating a terrible inscription, grammar phonē. She reports to Machiavelli, who is himself referred to as 'Mr Secretary' (240), the Florentine bureaucrat whose life is spent in the service of the rule of paper. He is the recorder of Florence, the keeper of secrets. Machiavelli in turn becomes another copy of the house of memories, having downloaded the data and accidentally wiped clean the source. Just as Niccolò Vespucci becomes another recording device ('delivering a dead man's mail', 117) sent to play himself in front of the Mughal Akbar, who having vanquished his friend becomes the repository of the tale, the data bank and memory. The novel itself is the hardware that holds this recording, full of back ups and mirror sites, iterations of a logic of inscription that is the truth of storytelling. Narrative is not, as one might presuppose, a mimetic art in which a copy of an original ideal is represented in its exactitude. There is no original Akbar, Vespucci or Qara Koz to present. They are the iterations of the non-original, other traces of a storytelling machine. Storytelling is what Tom Cohen calls a 'mnemotechnics', not a system of reference and representation accessible to a hermeneutics of interpretation but rather it is the phenomenalization of inscription that is never brought to presence but which names the simultaneous constitution and making unpresentable of a field of meaning it cannot master. In this sense storytelling is always removed from the *autos* of the storyteller. Like 'Angélique, daughter of Jacques', it is a grammar of phones, out of which narrative is generated, with machinelike rigour: independent and random. Angélique is the real 'il Machia', il macchina, her machinations produce her plots beyond the control of her audience who in turn are transformed in their listening, reinscribing the memories she spews out. As an automaton she runs towards death, free of the life-giving maker of her author or user, driven only by the *thanatos* of her own desire to end her story. This is why as a textual system, postmodern narratives at once generate their own self-referential thematization of textuality but cannot reduce those moments to questions of authorial intention or style. *The Enchantress of Florence* is a book full of self-conscious reference, letters, storytellers and messengers, as are many other earlier metafiction of the eighteenth century. However, the truth about storytelling that these texts tell lies not in their overt display of textual self-consciousness but in the irreducible discordance of the machinic inscription of meaning that interrupts and undoes all self-consciousness and which can never be suppressed or erased.

In terms of the novel, Angélique acts as a plot device, another pocket within a pocket, by which to progress the story that connects the two worlds of the Mughal and the Medicis, traded and exchanged as the daughter of a merchant, pirated and copied. She shares the name taken by Qara Koz and her Mirror as they cross over into Europe, Angelica: non-human but not quite divine, of the *Paradiso* promised by Beatrice, the first enchantress of Florence. She dies in a Florentine brothel that mirrors the House of Skanda where Vespucci lives in the Mughal's city. The memory palace is the bridge that joins an architectonic chain that connects palaces and places from the House of Skanda to the House of Mars (the Florentine brothel where she dies), the 'Tent of the New Worship' (the house of disputation set up by Akbar for philosophical debate) to Machiavelli's study, the Imperial Palace to the Medici palace and the 'Abode of Bliss' (the garden from which Qara Koz and Argalia run for their lives, 284) to the Mughal himself 'Shelter of the World' (54). Like Qara Koz and her Mirror, each world reflects the other but not as equals. They are alike in beauty but not the same, one slightly imperfect in relation to the other, not a pure mimesis but an architectonics of difference in which the memory palace is the tain of the mirror, that which in its opacity makes reflection possible. Qara Koz believes that 'the house of defeat was no place for her . . . She was meant for palaces and kings' (326–7) but ends her mortal life in a wooden shelter in the new world. Akbar's palace has to be abandoned when, after Vespucci's departure, the river that supports life there runs dry; on the last carnivalesque evening 'a peasant could sit in the highest storey of the Panch Mahal and be monarch of all he surveyed' (439). Just as the highest storey of the Mughal palace is overrun and left in Ozymadian ruin, so Angélique is the highest story of this architectonic principle. It is a narrative architecture produced by a mad mnemotechnic bridge as the defective keystone of an impossible Mobius narrative arch. Her presentation of her story joins the timelines of the novel together, while her death and ruin removes the support to any attempt to master the unpresentable whole. Finally even the Mogor dell'Amore does not know everything (his mother was not Qara Koz but the daughter of her Mirror) and Akbar is left to reside in a glass darkly: 'all our certainties are being blown away and we must live in [a] universe of mystery and doubt' (131).

The doubt that Akbar lives with is the effect of the building programme that the architectonics and mnemotechnics of this novel put in place. Akbar has ambitions to be 'a philosopher-king: a contradiction in terms' (41) but may have to settle for being 'a poet with a barbarian's history and a barbarian's prowess in war' (43). He establishes 'a house of adoration, a place of disputation where everything could be said to everyone by anyone on any subject, including the non-existence of God and the abolition of kings' (45). In his commitment to freethinking, Akbar is every bit the Enlightenment monarch and centuries in advance of his visitors from Renaissance Europe. For his reward, his people say 'the king is mad' (45): a sovereign who allows the disputation of sovereignty, a divine ruler who challenges the existence of God. The worldly-wise Akbar is said to be 'losing confidence in . . . religious faith' (72) but as Universal Ruler must submit himself to the Royal protocols whereby he cannot allow himself to be surprised:

> As regarded books, however, Akbar had changed the protocol. According to the old ways, any book that reached the imperial presence had to be read by three different commentators and pronounced free of sedition, obscenity and lies. 'In other words', the young king had said on ascending the throne, 'we are only to read the most boring books ever written. Well, that won't do at all'. Nowadays all sorts of books are permitted, but the three commentator's reviews were relayed to the emperor before he opened them, because of the overarching, supreme protocol regarding the inappropriateness of royal surprise. (107)

For Akbar 'the absence of surprise is the necessary penalty of the life of power' (89) but the story told by Vespucci evades the elaborate hermeneutic systems designed to protect kingship. It begins as a plot that ensnares him and ends by casting him out into the old story of endless unease. Unmediated by the scholars and the critics, Vespucci's story surprises Akbar and puts at risk the foundations, supreme protocol and overarching architectonics of his sovereignty. And yet, Akbar and Vespucci, Muslim and Christian, share the same Abrahamic legacy: they are both followers of the book. For Akbar the book need not be without interest but without revelation. Nothing can come into his presence unmediated. The sovereign must sit above all and have purview of all, without blind spot or the possibility of surprise: the Universal Ruler must be all seeing and so all knowing. In this way revelation is at once reserved for the sovereign as the divine right of kingship and denied him as the *telos* of the operation of the court. Surprise puts the principles of sovereignty at risk and this is why the courtiers view the unknown Vespucci with suspicion.

For those with a vested interest in maintaining the status quo of sovereignty, Vespucci is 'a sleight-of-hand-artist' (89), a 'shameless lying thief' (117) and a 'confidence man' (254). He is, of course, all three: he is a storyteller who presents appearance from what merely seems on the basis of the credulity of others in his unassured self, who shows with one hand and steals with the other. It is Vespucci who is the most subversive man in the tent of philosophers and who states openly that it is here 'reason, not the king, that ruled' (100). The courtiers are appalled, but not by Vespucci's rationalism that he throws in the Mughal's face but 'to do it in public, which was worse' (101). For Akbar, Vespucci among the philosophers is 'a man of reason who in reason's name took unreasonable risks. A paradoxical fellow' (102). For Derrida, it is 'the principal right to say everything . . . and the right to say it publicly' that connects the Humanities, such as philosophy, to the age of Enlightenment. In particular, the right to public declaration is affiliated, for Derrida, with literature and 'the form of fiction' (Derrida 2002: 205), that public avowal that presents a secret while forever rendering it unreadable. Vespucci's fiction occupies the public space of Akbar's city: it is on everyone's lips and the cause of continued speculation about his regime. It is Akbar who must decide if Vespucci's story is reasonable, he must take responsibility for it and respond to it because it puts at risk his sovereignty and Empire. It falls to Akbar to make the sovereign decision, to offer the definitive reading of Vespucci's story, without the Talmudic mediation of scholar or critic. However, in contrast to the surprising storyteller 'the emperor wanted to confess his secret disappointment in all mystics and philosophers' (103). The exchange of divine revelation for reason is merely the exchange of one form of sovereignty for another. Vespucci's story challenges everything Akbar knows and has always thought about the world. In its powerlessness, it undoes his power. It eludes his mastery and has the potential to topple his throne. While others warn him of the dangers and of the corruption of storytelling (253, 255) the Mughal is drawn in and on by the story at once frustrated by its delay ('a curse on all storytellers', 262) and dismissive of its potential, calling its author a mere 'creature of fables, and a good *afsanah* never did anybody any real damage' (256). But Akbar, like the opium smokers in his family he abjures, is hooked on this tale, caught in its 'webs of paradox' (390) far more taxing to the mind than any philosophy. As the story infests the public realm, the wise councillor Abul Fazl notes: 'the king's belief in the alleged harmlessness of stories was becoming a more embattled position to defend' (257).

In the exercise of the sovereign decision that Akbar must make lies the mutability and ruin of his sovereignty. Vespucci's tale is unreadable, rigorously unreliable, as Barbara Johnson would have it, and Akbar, 'Very God . . . Absolute Doer!' (273–4), can achieve no point of anteriority or transcendence from which to comprehend and judge it. The all-powerful powerlessness of alterity, what Hélène Cixous calls '*le toute-puissance autre*' (Cixous 2006: 47) of literature, cannot be mastered by the sovereign Akbar:

> He was the Universal Ruler, king of a world without frontiers or ideological limitations. What followed from this was that human nature, not divine will, was the great force that moved history. He, Akbar, the perfect man, was the engine of time. (387)

When he makes a final sovereign decision to marginalize Vespucci for the good of the Empire, he realizes his error and restores him to favour only to recant his own recantation and again dismisses Niccolò this time for good, resulting in the ruin of his palace and city. However, it is not Vespucci himself that corrupts the city but the magic of the story, the powerful magic that accompanies Vespucci and is reserved for those who do not assist him in the telling of his tale. When challenged by Vespucci's story, the Mughal's sovereignty is not pitted against an equal strength; he has no arsenal or army that can counter its force. The story has no sovereignty of its own. It is, rather, the mnemotechnic ruin of a making present that cannot be overcome because it has already undone itself in advance. It is at once the story of an immutable royal dynasty brought into being by conquest, kingship and reason, and the seed of doubt planted at the heart of that monarchy that corrupts it and unravels it from inside out.

Storytelling in this novel is then a form of enchantment: both a bewitching and a sense of wonder or delight. The enchantment of Akbar leaves him spellbound and incapable of reason. As with the rest of this novel, it is only possible to be enchanted in one of two ways: either by stories or by love. Something of the novelistic core of magic and love has always been present in the words 'Necromancy' and 'Romance'. When freed from the enchantment, at the expense of his dominion, he understands that one can never be reasonable enough in the face of that which knows no reason. Narrative is that which both makes sovereignty and begins its slow inevitable unravelling from the very point at which it feels most secure. Akbar, the all-powerful and the bewitched, through the exercise of his will, and beyond all reason, conjures into being Qara Koz and takes her as his queen. Despite the divine powers credited to the Mughal, this episode is unreasonable, the court and the city are scandalized ('in the streets of monotheism . . . there was some shock', 410). Again Akbar's sanity is called into question:

> A low murmur had begun, a murmur that only the most finely tuned ears could detect, concerning the emperor's mental well-being . . . Only the Almighty had power over the living and the dead, and to bring a woman back from the afterlife just for one's personal enjoyment was to go much, much too far, and there was no excuse for it. (411)

At the height of the exercise of his absolute power Akbar is at his most vulnerable. By genealogy, Qara Koz would be his grandaunt, and word gets around; a 'word so powerful it could severely damage the esteem in which the emperor was held, and maybe even rock his throne . . . The word was *incest*' (411). This line seems curious, it would appear to be a more or less oblique reference to Nabokov's *Lolita* when Humbert and Lolita stay at the Enchanted Hunters Hotel; Humbert tells Lolita disingenuously 'two people sharing one room, inevitably enter into a kind – how shall I say – a kind . . .' only for the knowing Lolita to fire back: 'The word is incest' (Nabokov 1955: 119). Humbert's enchantments take the form of darkness and drugs, Akbar's enchantment is done through will and magic in an age 'before the real and unreal were segregated

for ever and doomed to live apart under different monarchs and separate legal systems' (409). But what is Rushdie trying to suggest with
this reference to another master storyteller and émigré to the United
States? Is it merely a treasure buried from the scholar longing to connect Rushdie to his literary forebear, or, is the comparison of Akbar to
Humbert more sustained: a literate seducer and corruptor of innocence,
whose fate is sealed by his owed dreams and enchantments? Not the
master of all he surveys but 'the emperor of dreams', a madman caught
in the unfolding of this plot that 'was his story now' (427). Not Akbar
the Great, 'the Prince' of Machiavelli's discourse, an enchanted hunter,
but Humbert Humbert, deceiving and deluded, just another corrupt
record in an unreliable mnemotechnic chain, the architect of his own
downfall, careering out of control, pursued by sirens.

Such is the madness of sovereignty and storytelling. Both narrative
and sovereignty share a similar responsibility and fate. It is the right of
the sovereign, and only the sovereign, to decide. The sovereign has the
right to decide who should be put to death, the right to decide which
life shall be sacrificed, who shall be killed and it not be named murder.
The right and rite of sacrifice belongs to the sovereign, as it does to the
storyteller who must choose which elements of their story to include
and exclude, or sacrifice for the good of the whole. The Abrahamic tradition initiates a sacrificial culture when God stays Abraham's hand and
accepts the ablation of the ram caught in thorns. This culture begins in
narrative, with the story of Abraham and Isaac on Mount Moriah. The
story of sacrifice is also the sacrifice of story. The Abrahamic Akbar,
father of the nation, comes to a decision concerning Vespucci, his
would-be adopted son in favour of his legitimate heir, his own son the
crown prince Salim:

> To give him [Vespucci] official standing would be, in effect. To say that the
> truth was no longer considered significant, that it no longer mattered if his
> tale was just a clever lie. Should not a prince avoid making his contempt
> for the truth so clear? Should he not defend that value, and then lie when
> it suited him under cover of that defence? Should not a prince, in short, be
> colder, less susceptible to fantasies and visions? Perhaps the only vision he
> should allow himself was power. Did the elevation of the foreigner serve the
> emperor's power? Maybe it did. And maybe not. (401)

What should be sacrificed in order to preserve the power of the dynasty:
stories and Vespucci, or truth and his opium-smoking son? Akbar will
not be like his drug-addled father who died falling down the steps of
a library (46). Vespucci is sacrificed, as he has been twice already in
the novel (once to the mad elephant's judgement, once on the advice of
courtiers), as Argalia the storytelling boy was sacrificed by the Venetian
pirates to escape the Ottoman fleet, and as the memory palace was to

report Argalia's sovereign tale. Qara Koz survives and moves around the world through a chain of sacrifice and exchange, swapping the protection of one great man for another, giving up the life of her husband and her own life as a consort whenever a 'survivor's choice' (325) has to be made 'she became a sacrificial offering' (155). In the moment of sovereign decision-making we experience the madness of narrative mutability. The decision is never derived from knowing what to do when presented with facts and evidence that make up one's mind for you. This would not be a decision; it would be the programmed effect of those irrefutable facts. Decision happens when the outcome of those facts is unknown or uncertain, only then is decision required and it must be based on something other than fact. Decisions are then made on the basis of faith, belief in the extra-factual, something beyond reason that both grounds the decision and gives no reliable base for it. Beyond reason the decision is always a moment of madness and of the impossible, a cloud of unknowing 'illuminated by the ray of the sun at midnight' (198). It may as well be magic. Akbar ultimately believes in the dynasty, or at least prioritizes his responsibility to the dynasty, but it is the wrong choice that brings ruin on his city. In the moment of decision, the choice to sacrifice one thing for the other, the singular (Vespucci) for the general (the dynasty), or the general for the singular, there resides the moment of mutability that will corrupt the outcome of the decision from within. What remains (the outcome of the decision) is the result of sacrifice, it is ashes and cinders, like the charred remains of the numerous public burnings that litter the Florentine scene in the novel, or the spiked remains of villagers left behind by Vlad the Impaler's retreat. The decision can only ever leave behind its own ruin. Similarly, narrative, which is nothing other than a chain of decisions, made in turn to choose one possible outcome from another, contains within itself the seeds of its own auto-immunity: those discordant signifying elements that although sacrificed and repressed in the name of intelligibility and representativity cannot be contained and return to disrupt the coherent operation of the text. This is something beyond the control of any sovereign author or storyteller, it is the result of the mnemotechnic grammar of narrative in which epistemology and figurality combine and interfere with one another to render the onto-theological truth of princes and sovereigns forever undecidable. Like Dashwanth the court painter who succumbs 'to the final madness of the artist' (157–8) by painting himself into his own picture and Vespucci who at the conclusion of his tale similarly 'had crossed over into the empty page after the last page' (435), the work of narrative is to render the choices between the sovereign and the textual unreadable and to impress upon the reader the need to reaffirm this unreliability as the condition for reading as such.

Akbar is prepared to give up Vespucci but he will not renounce the subject of his narrative, Qara Koz. In sacrificing the storyteller but not his lover, the Mughal seals the fate of his city. He is only prepared to give up on stories when it suits him, ultimately stories make power and the sovereign has the power to make stories real. When no one is prepared to question the truth of a narrative that is when we have entered into the phenomenalization of reference, like Qara Koz a 'dream made flesh' (388). Stories can become fact not because stories make them so but because power has used them thus. This is real magic or the magic of the real. In the modern era 'the real and unreal [are] segregated for ever and doomed to live apart under different monarchs and separate legal systems', with the exception of one place: the space of literature. Here fact and fiction, epistemology and rhetoric, Botticelli, Machiavelli, Akbar and Qara Koz coexist as the basis for a performativity that the reader takes for granted as a condition of reading. This is not to propose that literature, fiction or narrative are the irresponsible collapse of categories that would otherwise separate our dreams from reality. Rather, literature is the space in which the tension between real and unreal remains as a constant question that predicates reading. Literature, as a figurative text among others (and all texts are figurative), is the one responsible arena in which the difference between fact and fiction is the basis for an irreducible and interminable interrogation of meaning. As long as we have literature we will always have leverage over the phenomenalization of reference by power, over how power uses stories for its own ends.

There may be those literalists among us who might want to see something like a more overtly political reading of this novel, written by Rushdie seven years into the Bush administration's so-called War on Terror and almost two decades after the first issue of the *fatwa*. Such readers might see Rushdie in this novel as like Qara Koz arriving in Florence, 'in the hope of forging a union between the great cultures of Europe and the East, knowing she has much to learn from us and believing, too, that she has much to teach' (348). However, if pedagogy were all that this novel had to offer us then it would be of little effect as a novel. Rushdie has his own answer to those literalists. The narrator (an omniscience that sits beyond the Universal Ruler, reading his mind) having offered an account of the belief in the mystical powers of Qara Koz, the enchantress of Florence, talks of 'those sceptics who by virtue of their sour temperament resist a supernatural account of events' and who 'prefer more conventional explanations for the time of golden contentment and material prosperity that Florence enjoyed in those days' (352–3). Those 'dry-as-dust quibblers' (353) would be correct in attributing the powers of Florence and the Medicis to the might of the papacy, wars of subjugation and the value of its trade, just as one might wish to identify Rushdie's novel as the product of a Western, specifically American, capitalism that the story may or may not take allegorical aim at: 'servants who believed themselves to be masters until they were shown the bitter truth' (334). However, to draw such literal lines between Rushdie's fiction and the world at large would be to inverse and repeat the phenomenalization of reference, as if those lines were in any way secure or tethered to a ground that was in any way reliable at either end. There is no counter-magic that is not also itself a form of magic. *The Enchantress of Florence* is no doubt a political book but it is also a story about storytelling and in the truth it tells about narrative lies its most political statements.

CHAPTER EIGHT

Rushdie's Non-Fiction

DANIEL O'GORMAN

I am arriving by degrees at my point: which is that the great issue facing both writers of journalism and of novels is that of determining, and then publishing, the truth. For the ultimate goal of both factual and fictional writing is the truth, however paradoxical that may sound. And truth is slippery, and hard to establish.

Rushdie 2003: 141

The most immediately noticeable thing about Rushdie's journalism, for readers already familiar with his fiction, is that it is for the most part highly 'journalistic'. If the term 'Rushdie-esque' initially conjures a sense of the effusive, heavily self-reflexive style that he frequently employs in his novels, then the short, direct sentences of his non-fictional writing can be seen to take precisely the opposite approach. While a superficial reading might ascribe the reasons for this rift to an acknowledgement on Rushdie's part of a disparity between each style's respective access to a notional authentic 'truth', the quotation above shows that his thinking is actually considerably more sophisticated: the key is in the verb 'determining'. To 'determine' the truth is, evidently, a process subtly different to that of simply 'revealing' or 'unveiling' it. The dictionary lists a number of definitions for the word: 'cause to occur in a particular way; be the decisive factor in'; 'ascertain or establish by research or calculation'; 'firmly decide' (Pearsall 2001: 390). This last definition in particular confers a degree of subjectivity upon Rushdie's use of the word 'truth' that renders it, at least after a moment's thought, perhaps slightly less paradoxical than he at first seems to suggest. Moreover, it reaffirms the contention that he puts forward in his 1983 essay, '"Errata": Or, Unreliable Narration in *Midnight's Children*', that '[r]eality is built on our prejudices, misconceptions and ignorance as well as on our perceptiveness and knowledge' (Rushdie 1992: 25). In this chapter, I argue that Rushdie's non-fictional writing is neither more nor less 'truthful' than his fiction, but that it simply goes about 'determining' the truth in a different way; that is, by acknowledging that his shift between fiction and non-fiction is also one between the 'jostling crowd of "I"s' which he elsewhere describes as being constitutive of the contemporary self

(Rushdie 2003: 179). It is this 'determining' of truth through a comingling of voices that, as in his fiction, constitutes the central theme of his journalism. To paraphrase a key sentence from *The Satanic* Verses, I will attempt to demonstrate that this comingling has a fundamental bearing upon the question of 'what kind of idea' it is to be human in today's world.

Rushdie's non-fiction has so far been collected in four volumes: *The Jaguar Smile: A Nicaraguan Journey* (1987), *Imaginary Homelands: Essays and Criticism 1981–1991* (1991), *Step across This Line: Collected Non-Fiction 1992–2002* (2002) and *The Wizard of Oz* (2002). His long-awaited *'fatwa* memoir', *Joseph Anton*, is also to be published shortly before this book goes to press (and is discussed at length in Chapter Nine). *Imaginary Homelands* and *Step across This Line* are, as their subtitles suggest, lengthy anthologies collating the many essays, articles and reviews that Rushdie published in various newspapers, journals and magazines during the 1980s, 1990s and early 2000s. *The Jaguar Smile* is a 137-page extended report on a journalistic excursion that Rushdie made to Nicaragua at the height of the civil war in 1986, while *The Wizard of Oz* is a pamphlet-length essay on the film of the same name written for the British Film Institute, and then republished as 'Out of Kansas' in *Step across This Line*, of which it is the opening piece.

While it is tempting to sift through these dense and richly eclectic publications one by one, this might not be the most useful approach for this chapter to take. The books – and the two anthologies in particular – are carefully structured in a way that, on the whole, favours topic and theme over chronology, so a book-by-book 'guide' may not be the most appropriate format. Rather, it is important to acknowledge the meticulous ordering of the articles (at least in the two big anthologies) as part of Rushdie's journalistic aim to show how truth is 'determined', as opposed to simply 'unveiled', through the act of writing. In turn, this chapter has also been structured by theme. It begins with an examination of Rushdie's writing on the *fatwa* and its implications for secular democracy. It then goes on to briefly look at his early political writing, seeking in particular to identify the extent to which his politics have been affected by the *fatwa* (and later by 9/11). The chapter will then culminate in an analysis of the ways in which Rushdie's non-fiction can be seen to simultaneously critique and endorse an impulse to turn consensus logic 'upside down' by 'stepping across' the line between the worlds of the factual and the literary.

Secularism and the *Fatwa*

'I never thought of myself as a writer about religion until religion came after me': this is the opening sentence of 'Coming After Us', Rushdie's contribution to the 2005 English PEN-commissioned collection *Free Expression Is No Offence* (Appignanesi 2005: 21). He continues:

> Religion was a part of my subject, of course; for a novelist from the Indian subcontinent, where the supernatural and the mundane coexist in the streets and are considered as being of the same order of reality, how could it not have been? But in my opinion I also had other, larger, tastier fish to fry. Nevertheless, when the attack came, I had to confront what was confronting me, and to decide what I wanted to stand up for in the face of what so vociferously, repressively, and violently stood against me. At that time it was often difficult to persuade people that the attack on *The Satanic Verses* was part of a broader, global assault on writers, artists, and fundamental freedoms. (Appignanesi 2005: 21)

In 1989, the *fatwa* brought politics and religion into collision in a way that, as Rushdie argues above, reconfigured not only his own reality, but also, to an extent, that of democratic society itself. In a manner that clearly foreshadowed the paradigmatic reframing of global debate around religious 'fundamentalism' that has taken place since 9/11, Ayatollah Khomeini's call for Rushdie to be killed in the name of Islam made it impossible for the novelist to speak or write about politics without also passing comment on religion, and vice versa. (The journalist Christopher Hitchens, a long-time supporter and friend of Rushdie – and the person to whom *Step across This Line* is (perhaps quite tellingly) dedicated – stated in a 2010 BBC Radio interview that 'It was rather the same feeling as I later had on the 11th of September 2001: a direct confrontation between everything I love and everything I hate'; Hitchens 2010.) The controversy surrounding *The Satanic Verses'* engagement with Islam is itself one about the point at which religion ends and politics begins. As Kenan Malik suggests in *From Fatwa to Jihad: The Rushdie Affair and Its Legacy*, it signalled 'the moment when Britain realized it was facing a new kind of social conflict' (Malik 2009: xvii). The conflict that the novel ignited is not so much one between two opposing ways of 'determining' truth, but, rather, one about whether truth is something that can – or, more specifically, should – even be considered 'determinable' at all. In light of this, three main driving forces can be seen to underlie Rushdie's non-fictional writing on the *fatwa*: (1) an urgent need to *persuade* his reader of the scale that the implications of his individual persecution hold for democratic society at large (the quotation above would fall into this category); (2) a *challenging* of conservatism and complacency among the British public regarding its political involvement in both the 'Rushdie Affair' and with reactionary Islam (a challenge that, interestingly, becomes more international after 9/11); and (3) a challenge to Islam itself, *questioning* Muslims about their sense of identity.

This third driving force is closely tied with the first: it is clear from Rushdie's writing on the *fatwa* that he sees it as not merely a personal attack on himself, but rather the violent frontier in a clash between secular and theocratic understandings of civilization. Prior to the publication of *Joseph Anton*, details of his life in hiding are less extensive in his non-fiction than one might think, although what he does reveal is often insightful: in a 1993 article entitled 'The Last Hostage', for instance, he writes that '[a] police officer had to distract the plumber's attention so that I could slip past him when his head was turned away. Once . . . a neighbour turned up unexpectedly. I had to dive down behind a kitchen unit and remain there, crouching, until he left' (Rushdie 2003: 240). It is, rather, mainly upon the *implications* of the *fatwa* for both secularism and Islam that Rushdie lays his journalistic focus. Some of his most visceral – and at times desperate – thoughts on the topic appear in the numerous letters and articles published in national and international newspapers during the early 1990s (reprinted collectively in *Step across This Line* as 'Messages from the Plague Years'). In a 1993 *New York Times* article entitled 'The Struggle for the Soul of Islam', he writes the following:

> We should understand that secularism is now the fanatics' Enemy Number One, and its most important target. Why? Because secularism demands a total separation between Church and State; philosophers such as the Egyptian Fouad Zakaria argue that free Muslim societies can exist only if this principle is adhered to. And because secularism rejects the idea that any society of the late twentieth century can be thought of as 'pure', and argues that the attempt to purify the modern Muslim world of its inevitable hybridities will lead to equally inevitable tyrannies . . . [It] sees Islam as an event within history, not outside it.' (Rushdie 2003: 260)

The threat posed to secularism by the *fatwa* is not simply one of religion (or even 'fundamentalist' religion) attacking irreligion: more than this, it is a threat that pits an understanding of humanity as fundamentally homogeneous against one that is fundamentally heterogeneous. It is for this reason that, for Rushdie, secularism should not be viewed as being straightforwardly at odds with religion, nor should it be lazily equated with atheism. Instead, as he suggests above, it is a system founded in 'hybridity', locating religious belief in a historical context: faith is understood as a plural phenomenon, existing alongside a multiplicity of other beliefs. Moreover, it is important to note the easily overlooked – but nonetheless key – emphasis that Rushdie places on the argument that this struggle is not so much a Huntingtonian 'clash of civilizations', but instead a clash *about* civilization, the most consequential battle of which is being fought within Islam itself (Rushdie 2003: 395). The *fatwa* must not, he argues, be seen as 'an isolated act', but rather as 'part of a deliberate, lethal programme, whose purpose is to criminalize, denigrate and even to assassinate the Muslim world's best, most honourable voices: its voices of dissent. And remember that those dissidents need your support. More than anything, they need your attention' (Rushdie 2003: 261).

As is the case throughout much of Rushdie's fiction, in his journalism the political and the personal are intimately entwined. This emphasis on viewing the *fatwa* as more than an isolated act signals a deep frustration at the accusations that he has received, at various points in his post–*Satanic Verses* career, about cultural insensitivity and deliberate provocation, and he has evidently often found himself at a loss when in need of support from those – fellow writers, democrats, secularists – who might perhaps have been more outspoken in his defence. Rushdie's list of detractors on both the left and right is a long one, but those from the literary world could count among their number Roald Dahl (who called Rushdie 'a dangerous opportunist'); John Berger (who wondered whether Rushdie 'might, by now, be ready to consider asking his world publishers to stop producing more or new editions . . . Not because of the threat of his own life, but because of the threat to the lives of those who are innocent of either writing or reading the book'); and John Le Carré (who wrote: 'It seems to me he has nothing more to prove except his own insensitivity') (See Donadio 2007, and Rushdie 2012). Such was Rushdie's apparent desperation at the height of the initial *fatwa* period that, in 1990, he published a lengthy essay entitled 'In Good Faith', an ostensible attempt at reconciliation in which he attempts to explain his thinking behind the novel. The essay contains some of his clearest and most explicit writing on the kind of pluralistic secularism that he personally espouses, but it is arguably also marred by an overly capitulatory attempt to deconstruct – almost in the style of a step-by-step guide for his less literary opponents – some of the novel's more controversial passages. It goes slightly against the spirit in which, elsewhere in the same essay, he suggests the novel was initially written: namely that 'Central to the purposes of *The Satanic Verses* is the process of reclaiming language from one's opponents' (Rushdie 1992: 402). If this is the case, then his extensive endeavour to explain is rendered somewhat pointless, as it concedes that either the novel's attempt to reclaim language has failed, or – more likely – it has been wilfully ignored (there is no evidence that Khomeini ever read the novel, so the *fatwa* cannot in any way be said to have been about its literary merit). On the one hand, Rushdie writes: 'There are times when I feel that the original intentions of *The Satanic Verses* have been so thoroughly scrambled by events as to be lost forever' (Rushdie 1992: 403), but on the other, the novel itself seems so strongly to advocate an understanding of textual interpretation as being fissiparous and disconnected from authorial intention that this complaint about the 'scrambling' of meaning ultimately comes across as a little redundant.

Indeed, the final irony of the 'In Good Faith' article (which in hindsight should have been obvious at the time) is that despite its measured and carefully worded argumentation, the 'intention' behind it was ultimately ignored in much the same way as that of the novel (the *fatwa* remained in place, and was officially supported by the Iranian government until 1998). Perhaps it is possible to see in this essay the beginnings of the desperate thinking to which Rushdie briefly acceded in 1990, when, following the advice of a group of British Muslim scholars, he put his name to a short document entitled 'Why I Have Embraced Islam'. The statement formed the closing piece of the hardback edition of *Imaginary Homelands*, but he later came to repudiate it, describing it as 'a crime against himself' (Rushdie 2012: 276), and replaced it in the paperback edition with the longer 1991 essay 'One Thousand Days in a Balloon'. In this latter article, Rushdie himself goes some way towards acknowledging the futility of his initial attempt to explain his intentions:

> In 'In Good Faith' I wrote: 'Perhaps a way forward might be found through the mutual recognition of [our] mutual pain', but even moderate Muslims had trouble with this notion: what pain, they asked, could I possibly have suffered? *What was I talking about?* As a result, the really important conversations I had were with myself. (Rushdie 1992: 435)

Elsewhere in the essay, he writes: 'For many people, I've ceased to be a human being. I've become an issue, a bother, an "affair"' (Rushdie 1992: 431). In light of these comments (as well as their placing at the conclusion of the anthology), Rushdie's non-fictional writing takes on an extra degree of personal importance, providing him with the only platform by which he can communicate across the restricting lines of identity and caricature that have been imposed upon him by a rampantly domineering political media discourse. However, while his articles do fulfil this function to an extent, I would argue that they are also important in a more sophisticated way. It is clear that sometimes, as in the case of 'In Good Faith', no amount of considered argumentation is enough to win over those whose minds are closed off to reason. Nevertheless, if we view Rushdie's non-fiction not so much in terms of its comparative 'directness', 'factuality' or apparent lack or artifice, but rather as constituting a different *kind* of textuality, then we can perhaps begin to see it as being on a continuum with his novels, employing rhetorical techniques to similar effect but in a much subtler way. It does not provide a counterpoint to his fiction so much as a closely interwoven supplement, blurring the line between the two. Indeed, it is arguably because 'In Good Faith' attempts a degree of directness which his other non-fiction only simulates that it ironically becomes a somewhat *less* direct, or honest, piece of writing.

Rushdie's Political Journalism

The rhetorical or 'literary' quality of Rushdie's non-fiction is significant on more than just an aesthetic level. It is fundamentally tied up with the anti-conservative, pluralistic politics that he figuratively gestures towards in his fiction. This can perhaps be seen most clearly in *The Jaguar Smile*, the 1987 book-length account of his travels in Nicaragua. Arguably the most 'left-wing' (at least ostensibly) of his journalistic works, the book takes a highly critical view of the US-backed conservative Contra government, showing a degree of sympathy for the leftist Sandinista cause (albeit not always for its strategies). However, even this sympathy is tempered with recognition of the 'small c' conservatism and ignorance that he identifies in some of the attitudes propagated by a number of the Sandinista sympathizers he encounters. At one point, Rushdie recalls a conversation with a woman who refuses to acknowledge the existence of labour camps in the USSR on account of the Soviet Union being 'so helpful to third world countries' (Rushdie 2007: 77). He writes:

> [t]here is a kind of innocence abroad in Nicaragua. One of the problems with the romance of the word 'revolution' is that it can carry with it a sort of blanket approval of all self-professed revolutionary movements. Donald Altamirano told me how deeply he felt in solidarity with the Provisional IRA. (Rushdie 2007: 77–8)

It is this purism of thought – or the reduction of the world's hybrid complexity to a simple, self-gratifying version of reality – which is the real conservatism that Rushdie sets himself against throughout the book, and indeed throughout most of his writing, both fictional and non-fictional. Moreover, it is specifically in the *literary* aspect of his writing (in his fiction, explicitly; in his non-fiction, often subtly) that he locates the potential for a 'nuancing' of thought: that is, for a prompting of his reader to recognize the possibility of alternative points of view or versions of reality. Indeed, *The Jaguar Smile's* title is itself taken from a local anecdote that Rushdie hears about on his travels, and to which he returns at a key point in the text:

> [t]hroughout my visit to Nicaragua, amidst all the songs and poetry and prose, I had been plagued by the limerick about the young girl from Nic'ragua, her jaguar ride, and the transferred smile. It had been infuriating, at times, like a jingle that refused to be forgotten. That last night, the thing invaded my dreams; or, rather, the smile did, the smile on the face of the jaguar, except that there wasn't any face. I was pursued across an amorphous, shifting landscape by that lethal rictus which one might have likened to the grin of the Cheshire Cat had it not been for the teeth, which were long,

curved and melodramatically dripping with blood. I ran for my life across the dream, chased by the jaguar smile. (Rushdie 2007: 128–9)

The recollection is then immediately followed by a passage that explicitly explores the links between narrative and politics, and the ambiguity with which the act of reading can potentially imbue each:

> I woke up in a jumble of nightmare, limerick and sweat. As I lay awake and calmed down, it occurred to me that the limerick, when applied to contemporary Nicaragua, was capable of both a conservative and a radical reading, that there were, so to speak, two limericks, two Misses Nicaragua riding two jaguars, and it was necessary to vote for the version one preferred. If the young girl was taken to be the revolution, seven years old, fresh, still full of the idealism of youth, then the jaguar was geopolitics, or the United States; after all, an attempt to create a free country where there had been, for half a century, a colonized 'back yard', and to do so when you were weak and the enemy close to omnipotent, was indeed to ride a jaguar. That was the 'leftist' interpretation; but what if the young girl were Nicaragua itself, and the jaguar was the revolution? Eh? What about that? (Rushdie 2007: 129)

The deconstruction of the jaguar limerick here plays a doubly self-reflexive role. On one level, it draws attention to the ability of narrative art, even if only in the form of a simple limerick, to render ambiguous the rigid, purist realities that can easily take hold in the context of a political discourse as antagonistically dialectical as that of late 1980s Nicaragua. It attempts, moreover, to show how the act of reading and interpreting such a narrative can help to open up the space for new, fresh and nuanced realities to materialize in their place; precisely the kind of realities that Rushdie is getting at earlier in the book when he writes: 'I left the Assembly building feeling genuinely angry. At the Enrique Acuña co-operative, and again today, I had seen a new reality, a reality that the external pressure might crush before construction work had even been completed' (Rushdie 2007: 74). On another, slightly more complex level, the self-reflexivity of the jaguar passage brings to a head the 'literary' quality of Rushdie's own non-fictional narrative, raising questions about the extent to which political journalism is able, in actuality, to grasp a firm sense of truth, and the extent to which it can (or even should) aid in the construction of a new one. The anecdote foregrounds the sense of ambiguity that, for readers outside of Nicaragua, will constitute the basis of any journalistic writing on a place or situation other than their own: it aims at an already existing, hidden truth, and yet in doing so necessarily, through something like what Homi Bhabha describes as 'a sudden disjunction of the present', brings a new one into being (Bhabha 1994: 310).

The views that Rushdie expresses in early journalistic pieces such as *The Jaguar Smile* gave him a reputation, throughout much of the 1980s, as a firm (if by no means uncritical) 'man of the left' (as recently as 2004, the American conservative pundit Daniel Pipes ridiculed Rushdie's pre-*fatwa* politics as 'vapid leftism'; Pipes 2004). However, with the issuing of the *fatwa* in 1989, questions started to be raised about whether his vocal critique of the more hardline elements of Islamic culture and theology constituted a rightwards shift; a feeling that has been aired once again since 9/11 in response to his continued critique of worldwide Islamism (in the introduction to a special issue of *Twentieth Century Literature* on Rushdie's work, Sabina Sawhney and Simona Sawhney suggest that '[w]hile most of his earlier political essays . . . come from a recognizable liberal-left position, these new [post-9/11] articles are surprisingly indistinguishable, in their tone and argument, from many mainstream media responses to the events of September 11'; Sawhney and Sawhney 2001). In 2006, for instance, Rushdie was a signatory of an open letter entitled 'Manifesto: Together Facing the New Totalitarianism', which expressed strong support for the publication, in the Danish satirical paper *Jyllands-Posten*, of a series of extremely controversial cartoons depicting the Islamic Prophet Mohammed. (The 'Manifesto', originally published in the French magazine *Charlie Hebdo*, on 1 March 2006, is available to be read in full on the BBC website). Other post-9/11 articles have taken strong issue with what he sees as the kind of anti-American 'sanctimonious relativisms' generally associated with the political left (Rushdie 2003: 392). 'Let's be clear about why this *bien-pensant* anti-American onslaught is such rubbish', he writes in 'The Attacks on America', 'Terrorism is the murder of the innocent; this time, it was mass murder. To excuse such an atrocity by blaming US-government politics is to deny the basic idea of all morality: that individuals are responsible for their actions' (Rushdie 2003: 392). Such positions have led some formerly sympathetic leftist commentators to turn on him in disgust: Tariq Ali, for example, has described him, along with Martin Amis, as a member of an Islamophobic 'belligerati' (Ali 2002), while the *New Statesman* columnist Ziauddin Sardar has labelled him – as well as both Amis and Ian McEwan – as a 'Blitcon', or 'British literary neoconservative' (Sardar 2006).

However, I would argue that Rushdie's politics have been more consistent than some of his critics – post-*fatwa* and post-9/11 – allow for, and that the changing attitudes towards him from some corners are closer to evidencing a shift in the political discourse in which he is located. His sceptical views on relativism have not developed in reaction to the *fatwa* or 9/11, but are evident, to varying degrees, throughout his career. For instance, in a 1982 response to the Brixton Riots in London titled 'The New Empire within Britain' (adapted from his documentary film of the same name), he harshly critiques what he sees as the superficiality of British government–sponsored diversity policies:

> The call for 'racial harmony' was simply an invitation to shut up and smile about our grievances. And now there's a new catchword: 'multiculturalism'.

In our schools, this means little more than teaching the kids a few bongo rhythms, how to tie a sari and so forth. In the police training programme, it means telling cadets that black people are so 'culturally different' that they can't help making trouble. Multiculturalism is the latest token gesture towards Britain's blacks, and it ought to be exposed, like 'integration' and 'racial harmony', for the sham that it is. (Rushdie 1992: 138)

Reading this passage three decades later, the viciousness of its tone might initially come across as shocking, or even somewhat right wing, but it is taken from one of the most overtly and angrily anti-conservative pieces of writing that Rushdie has published to date. Exploring the problem of racism in Britain under the Thatcher government, he asks his reader to 'think about [the] word "immigrant", because it seems to me to demonstrate the extent to which racist concepts have been allowed to seize the central ground, and to shape the whole nature of the debate' (Rushdie 1992: 132). Already, at this early stage in his career, it is clear that Rushdie is starting to become wary of a certain potentially dangerous kind of relativistic thinking encroaching upon the 'centre ground'. This cautioning quickly crystallizes into outrage in 'An Unimportant Fire', the article that immediately follows in *Imaginary Homelands*. In perhaps the most scathing of all his non-fictional pieces, Rushdie responds in uncompromising terms to the recent deaths of a Pakistani family in a domestic fire caused by the substandard temporary accommodation that they were placed in by London's Camden council: 'If the deaths of Mrs Karim and her children are to be treated as murders', he writes, 'then many of us would say that the murderers are to be found in Camden Town Hall' (Rushdie 1992: 142). It is this attempt to upturn the consensus reality of the 'centre ground', re-determining his reader's understanding of truth by exposing hypocrisy and corruption where it is going unaddressed that constitutes the primary drive of Rushdie's non-fiction throughout his career, and to which this chapter will now turn for a more detailed analysis.

Turning Logic Upside Down

As I have already suggested, there is little to distinguish the anti-conservatism of Rushdie's early articles from that of his later, more controversial arguments on Islam and anti-Americanism: the difference, I would suggest, is primarily in the increasing number of places in which he begins to identify conservative thinking and practice. As I have attempted to show, the early political pieces become particularly interesting after the *fatwa* not so much because they draw attention to a change in Rushdie's politics, but because of the way they foreground what he sees as a political paradigm shift taking place around him in 'the crazy, upside-down logic of the post-*fatwa* world' (Rushdie 1992: 431).

Referring, in 'One Thousand Days in a Balloon', to the apparent endorsement of his death sentence by the British folk singer Yusuf Islam on a television talk show, he asks of his reader the following question: 'When a white pop-star-turned-Islamic-fanatic speaks approvingly about killing an Indian immigrant, how does the Indian immigrant end up being called the racist?' (Rushdie 1992: 431). This kind of 'upside-down logic' constitutes the target, both explicitly and implicitly, of much of his non-fiction throughout his career. However, it is also very often his purpose to effectively turn this 'upside down logic' itself upside down, not so much in order to put it back 'the right way up', so to speak, but rather to unsettle and dislodge the potential establishment of any kind of unthinking consensus logic in the first place. This 'unsettling' of consensus logic has perhaps most recently been evident in an article titled 'Is It Time to Declare Pakistan a Terrorist State?', which Rushdie wrote for the American *Daily Beast* website in response to the death of Osama Bin Laden in May 2011:

> This time the facts speak too loudly to be hushed up. Osama bin Laden, the world's most wanted man, was found living at the end of a dirt road 800 yards from the Abbottabad military academy, Pakistan's equivalent of West Point or Sandhurst, in a military cantonment where soldiers are on every street corner, just about 80 miles from the Pakistani capital Islamabad. This extremely large house had neither a telephone nor an Internet connection. And in spite of this we are supposed to believe that Pakistan didn't know he was there, and that the Pakistani intelligence, and/or military, and/or civilian authorities did nothing to facilitate his presence in Abbottabad, while he ran al Qaeda, with couriers coming and going, *for five years*? (Rushdie 2011)

The piece takes a position of qualified support for an American military intervention into Pakistan that has left a number people on the left feeling uncomfortable. (The most prominent of these voices in Britain was that of the Archbishop of Canterbury, Rowan Williams, who said that the killing of bin Laden left him 'feeling uncomfortable', and that it '[didn't] serve justice'; see Boycott 2011). From one angle, it might be seen to reflect, at least at first, the kind of support for US imperialism that Sardar accuses him of displaying in his post-9/11 non-fiction:

> The main two-part essay in *Step across This Line* argues that the US is a frontier civilisation. But at the beginning of the 21st century, the frontier has become the whole world and America can legitimately lay claim to any part of the globe. The irony that the disparity of power now permits the US to do to the world what it did to the Native Americans is totally lost. In the defence of American liberties, Rushdie declares, 'we must send our shadow warriors against their shadow warriors'. (Sardar 2006)

I would suggest, however, that this is a rather superficial reading of both the essay in question and Rushdie's politics more broadly. Indeed, I would go along with Ana Christina Mendes, who, in her contribution to Cara Cilano's edited volume *From Solidarity to Schisms: 9/11 and after in Fiction and Film from Outside the US*, seeks 'to undermine the idea that the writer manifests, or did indeed manifest, a clear-cut pro-US government position in support of the "war on terror"' (Cilano 2009: 96). As with his allegations about the West wilfully ignoring possible Pakistani collusion with al-Qaeda ('facts [which] speak too loudly to be hushed up'), the notion of the United States being an imperialist frontier state is, for Rushdie, an *observation* rather than a straightforward endorsement. Moreover, Sardar ignores the key question that this observation raises at the essay's conclusion: namely that '[t]he struggle for artistic freedom serves to crystallize the larger question which we were all asked when the planes hit the buildings: how should we live now? How uncivilized are we going to allow our own world to become in response to so barbaric an assault?' (Rushdie 2003: 442). It is a question not about the moral rights or wrongs surrounding the global 'disparity of power' per se, but rather about how, given that this disparity ineluctably exists, those who wield it should respond to the ethical dilemmas thrown up by an event on the scale of 9/11.

A similar attack on 'upside down logic' is evident in Rushdie's 2002 article, 'Anti-Americanism', in which he argues that '[w]hat America is accused of – closed-mindedness, stereotyping, ignorance – is also what its accusers would see if they looked into a mirror' (Rushdie 2003: 400). Moreover, he contends that 'America did, in Afghanistan, what had to be done, and did it well' (Rushdie 2003: 399), a statement that has been sharply criticized by Rushdie's post-9/11 critics as an example of his apparent 'support for the war on Afghanistan' (Sawhney and Sawhney 2001). I would argue that Sawhney and Sawhney's heavily loaded use here of the preposition 'on' (as opposed to the technically correct 'in') is problematic in itself, but their suggestion that Rushdie's initial support for Operation Enduring Freedom in Afghanistan somehow belies a new, unquestioning espousal of US global hegemony is also both reductive and patronizing: his defence of the intervention's first phase (which aimed to weaken al-Qaeda networks in the region and to topple the Taliban regime) is by no means equivalent to 'uncritically accept[ing] the terms and narratives generated by the American media' (Sawhney and Sawhney 2001). As Rushdie clearly warns at his article's conclusion, '[i]t would be easy for America, in the present climate of hostility, to fail to respond to constructive criticism' (Rushdie 2003: 400). Highlighting '[t]he treatment of the Camp X-Ray detainees [as] a case in point', he distances himself from 'President Bush and Mr Rumsfeld' and, rather than uncritically endorsing US imperialism, goes on to emphasize that 'more than ever, we need the United States to exercise its power and economic might responsibly. *This is not the time to ignore the rest of the world and decide to go it alone'* (Rushdie 2003: 400; emphasis added). (See also Mendes in Cilano 2009.)

Sardar's critique: also overlooks the emphasis that Rushdie places on the transformative nature of existence on a frontier: the act of crossing a border is one that catalyzes 'an opening in the self, an increase in what it is possible for the voyager to be' (Rushdie 2003: 409). Indeed, it is precisely by *ignoring* this transformative quality of borderline existence that, according to Rushdie, the very imperialistic exceptionality that Sardar accuses him of supporting can potentially be given a free rein. As he puts it in a passage comparable to the jaguar limerick for its ebulliently 'literary' non-fictional style:

> The frontier is a wake-up call. At the frontier we can't avoid the truth; the comforting layers of the quotidian, which insulate us against the world's harsher realities, are stripped away, and, wide-eyed in the harsh fluorescent light of the frontier's windowless halls, we see things as they are. The frontier is physical proof of the human race's divided self. (Rushdie 2003: 412)

One might argue that the emphasis in this passage on realities being 'stripped away' to reveal an unavoidable truth actually contradicts the notion – articulated elsewhere in the same essay – of truth being 'determined'. However, any reading of the passage is, once again, necessarily dependent upon the reader making a decision about how to interpret the idea that truth is something that 'we can't avoid'. As with the jaguar segment, a close reading of the passage reveals it to be more ambiguous than it might at first appear: truth is by definition universal, but simultaneously it is bound up with the notion of 'the human race's divided self'. Truth is necessarily both singular and plural: it is the point – or borderline – at which different realities meet. Moreover, it is also the point at which fiction and non-fiction meet, and this, for Rushdie, has a crucial bearing on the role of the writer, whose job, he argues, lies in 'the examination of the permeable frontier between the universe of things and deeds and the universe of the imagination' (Rushdie 2003: 434).

There is a degree of transcendentalism to this sentiment that one might consider unusual coming from the pen of a professed atheist. Arthur Bradley and Andrew Tate have picked up on something similar in their recent study *The New Atheist Novel: Fiction, Philosophy and Polemic after 9/11*. They argue that, for Rushdie,

> [l]iterature, and the novel in particular, transcends the limits of the everyday – including the excessive rules and regulations of publishing – and speaks to readers, prophet-like, with a unique voice. But how does this voice – one that must pursue true 'intellectual liberty', argues Rushdie, with reference to Orwell – gain such autonomy? And why does he believe that 'what one writer can make in the solitude of one room is something no power can easily destroy' . . . ? Whether he intends to or not, this

defence of creativity imbues writing with a quasi-transcendental quality, giving fiction, in particular, an aura of eternal durability. (Bradley and Tate 2010: 97)

Bradley and Tate are right to draw attention to this element of transcendentalism in Rushdie's writing (and commendable for doing so without recourse to the clichéd accusations of secular fundamentalism sometimes put forward by his other critics; see e.g. Guldberg 2008). However, I would hesitate to agree with their implication that the apparent contradiction inherent in this 'prophet-like' idealism is necessarily problematic, or at least not disparagingly so. On the contrary, Rushdie's transcendentalism – at least as it comes across in his non-fiction – is not unlike that which Derrida describes in *Specters of Marx* as a '*socius* . . . which binds "men" who are first of all experiences of time, existences determined by this relation to time which itself would not be possible without surviving and returning, without that being "out of joint" that dislocates the self-presence of the living present and installs thereby the relation to the other' (Derrida 1994: 193). Literature is not so much a conduit for an ethical relationality between the self and the other, but rather a dream-like border zone in which the limits of the self and of the other, and between the real and the unreal, are continually put 'out of joint'; in other words, they are deconstructed and reconfigured – or *re-determined* – in new and sometimes quite unsettling ways. As Rushdie writes in 'Step across This Line':

> [i]n dreams begin responsibilities. The way we see the world affects the world we see . . . Our dreams of our own and our children's future shape the everyday judgements we make, about work, about people, about the world that either enables or obstructs those dreams. Daily life in the real world is also an imagined life. The creatures of our imagination crawl out from our heads, cross the frontier between dream and reality, between shadow and act, and become actual. (Rushdie 2003: 436)

A few sentences later, Rushdie explicitly politicizes this idea of literature as a forum for the determination of truth by placing it in the context of a post-9/11 ideological conflict between not only (as Sardar suggests) US-style democracy and fundamentalist Islam, but also, on a deeper level, between dialectically opposed and incommensurable understandings of what it means to 'determine' truth at all. 'It may seem unimaginable to us', he writes, 'but to those who perpetrated this crime, the deaths of many thousands of innocent people were a side issue. Murder was not the point. The creation of meaning was the point' (Rushdie 2003: 436).

(Rushdie touches on a similarly 'out of joint' experience of transcendentalism in *Joseph Anton*: 'The soul had many dark corners and books sometimes illuminated them. But what did he, an atheist, mean when he used the word "soul"? Was it just poetry? Or was there something non-corporeal in us, something more than flesh, blood and bone, the thing that Koestler called the ghost in the machine? He toyed with the notion that we might have a mortal soul instead of an immortal one; a spirit housed in the body that died when the body died. A spirit that might be what we meant when we spoke of *das Ich*, the I'; Rushdie 2012: 107.)

The role of literature in this ideological struggle is, for Rushdie, one that is aggressively anti-fundamentalist: by bringing the knowable into contact with the unknowable, it creates an aporetic tension in which certainty and uncertainty are merged into one. This politicization of literature, and particularly the novel, can be traced back to Rushdie's 1990 essay 'Is Nothing Sacred?', in which he argues the following:

> What is forged, in the secret act of reading, is a different kind of identity, as the reader and writer merge, through the medium of the text, to become a collective being that both writes as it reads and reads as it writes, and creates, jointly, that unique work, 'their' novel. This 'secret identity' of writer and reader is the novel form's greatest and most subversive gift.
>
> And this, finally, is why I elevate the novel above other forms, why it has always been, and remains, my first love: not only is it the art involving least compromises, but it is also the only one that takes the 'privileged arena' of conflicting discourses *right inside our heads*. The interior space of our imagination is a theatre that can never be closed down; the images created there make up a movie that can never be destroyed. (Rushdie 1992: 426)

This combining of reader and writer is nowhere more evident than in the numerous articles *about* literature and literary authors that are collected in both of the anthologies (but especially in *Imaginary Homelands*). Apart from providing strong evidence of the 'love' for the novel that he proclaims in the passage above, Rushdie's literature essays are notable for the ways in which his reading of the work of others helps him, like Saleem Sinai, the protagonist of *Midnight's Children*, to 'write himself, in the hope that by doing so he may achieve the significance that the events of his adulthood have drained from him' (Rushdie 1992: 24). The 'merging' experience itself is evident as early as 1981, in a piece on Italo Calvino: 'although the reader . . . will be taken further out of himself than most readers, he will also discover that the experience is not a flight from, but an enrichment of himself' (Rushdie 1992: 261). In a 1989 essay on Philip Roth, he responds to the latter's use of fiction to explore his own vilification by some Orthodox Jewish critics as an 'anti-Semitic, . . . self-hating Jew' by stating that '[Roth] seems to speak directly, profoundly, not only to, but *for* me' (Rushdie 1992: 347). However, perhaps the most tellingly self-referential example of Rushdie's non-fictional engagement with fiction can be found in a 1984 essay on Günter Grass, which could just as easily be read as a description of Rushdie's own writing about literature, as well as of the permeable border between his fiction and his non-fiction:

> A writer who understands the artificial nature of reality is more or less obliged to enter the process of making it. This is perhaps why Grass has so determinedly sought a public role, why he has used his great fame as a novelist as a platform from which to speak on the many issues . . . which concern him. And since to argue about reality is to be at once creative and political, it is not surprising that when Grass writes about literature he finds himself writing about politics, and when he discusses political issues, the quirky perspectives of literature have a habit of creeping in. (Rushdie 1992: 281)

This chapter has aimed to explore the multiple ways in which precisely these 'quirky perspectives of literature' persistently creep into Rushdie's own non-fiction, helping it to 'determine' truth by stepping across the lines between fiction and journalism, the self and the other, the knowable and the unknowable. It has done so by looking in turn at the developments (or, more accurately, resolute consistencies) in his views on religion, politics and literature over the course of his career, identifying the *fatwa* and 9/11 as the two key influences on his attitudes toward all three. Ultimately, it has attempted to show that religion, politics and literature are impossible for Rushdie to discuss in isolation from one another, and that his non-fiction reflects the way in which his career has raised a mirror to a similar merging of the three topics in a global political discourse perpetually challenged by the twin forces of fundamentalism and terror.

CHAPTER NINE

Po-fa: *Joseph Anton*

ROBERT EAGLESTONE

> He had always been post-something according to that mandarin liter-
> ary discourse in which all contemporary writing was mere aftermath –
> post-colonial, post-modern, post-secular, post-intellectual, post-literate.
> Now he would add his own category, post-fatwa, to that dusty post office,
> and would end up not just po-co and po-mo but po-fa as well.
>
> *Joseph Anton* 442

The aim of this chapter, taking Rushdie at his word, is to examine Salman
Rushdie's 2012 memoir *Joseph Anton* as 'post-*fatwa*' writing, po-fa, and to
explore how the memoir relates to the rest of his corpus. I suggest that
Joseph Anton is a special form of memoir, an *archive*, which demonstrates
the development of Rushdie's thought and novelistic practice.

Names

Joseph Anton, which is centrally about the years during which Rushdie's
life was under threat because of the *fatwa*, was published in September
2012 to fairly general critical acclaim from the serious press, although
a few reviewers expressed reservations. The title stems from the alias
that Rushdie took as part of his protection: he chose it, under duress,
by combining the names of two of his favourite writers, Joseph Conrad
and Anton Chekov: he 'had spent his life naming fictional characters.
Now by naming himself he had turned himself into a sort of fictional
character as well' (165). If the book was a novel, the names would have
a literary significance: Conrad, the great writer not only of adventure
but of the internal psychological impact of adventure (the real adventures in Conrad happen within); Chekov, the writer whose plays and
short stories explore failure and disappointment in the domestic and the
day-to-day. Thus, from the name alone *Joseph Anton* is a realistic, bitter
adventure (indeed there are the trappings of a thriller: presidents, prime
minsters, armed police, spies and armoured cars) but with the emphasis on the protagonist's internal life, his weaknesses, his successes, his
anger, his battles with himself. And while the book is not a novel, it is
written, unconventionally for a memoir, in the third person: as if the

events happened not to Salman Rushdie, but to the third person Joseph Anton.

The book is about naming, about the control of names. The name 'Rushdie', in what can only be described as a Rushdie-esque kind of way, was invented by Salman's father: he chose it in 'admiration for Ibn Rushd' (22) the twelfth-century philosopher known in the West as 'Averroës' and one of the most important commentators on Aristotle. In Rushd's opposition to the 'Islamic literalism' (23) of his own age, Rushdie finds an echo of his yet-to-come predicament. As the chaos of the *fatwa* begins, he sees and hears his name everywhere and the 'gulf between the private "Salman" he believed himself to be and the public "Rushdie" he barely recognised was growing by the day' (131). The *fatwa* begins to destroy his name, both metaphorically and literally, until the police insist that he create an alias, 'sharpish . . . Probably better not to make it an Asian name' (163). So Joseph Anton – Joe to his loyal and efficient protection squad – he becomes: he cites *The Satanic Verses* for himself: 'they have the power of descriptions, and we succumb' (164). This is crucial because, as he explains later to the Nobel Academy, at

> the heart of the dispute over *The Satanic Verses* . . . was a question of profound importance: Who shall have control over the story? Who has, who should have, the power not only to tell the stories with which, and within which, we all lived, but also to say in what manner those stories might be told? (360)

Our names are our stories. 'Salman Rushdie' is destroyed and Salman Rushdie is almost destroyed. And yet, at perhaps one of his lowest ebbs, he cites José Saramago: '"Inside us . . . there is something that has no name. That something is what we are." The something that has no name within him always came to his rescue in the end.' (397). He holds on to his sanity, to himself, to his reputation by the nameless thing within himself. On the penultimate page, one of the protection officers says, 'it's been a privilege Joe, excuse me, Salman' (632) and his name is, as it were, returned. Names of others occur and reoccur through the text: the famous (Thatcher, Clinton, Blair, Major, Pinter, Pynchon) and the not so famous (his protection squad, the other officials he meets). He is persecuted and protected by a network of names.

The choice to write in the name of the third person, indeed to call it after this literary fictional person, however, is the first sign that this book is not, or is not just, a traditional memoir. The opening bravura pages are a stunning account of the early hours and days after the *fatwa* was announced but, after this, the book changes gear. Of course, there is no strict division between a memoir and an autobiography or, more dryly, an account or a history, but traditionally a memoir is a narrative that focuses not on someone's whole life, but on a specific part or moment. The first section proper, 'A Faustian contract in reverse' is a more traditional writer's autobiography, beginning, with the faintest shades of Proust, '[W]hen he was a small boy his father at bedtime told him the great wonder tales of the East, told them and retold them and remade them and reinvented them in his own way' (19). In this section, a Rushdie enthusiast can trace the origins of many people and events from his fiction. His father takes the young Salman to London and from there to Rugby: the same events occur in *The Satanic Verses* as Chamcha is taken to his public school. At Cambridge, Rushdie meets Jan Pilkington-Miksa, who becomes Krysztof Waterford-Wajda (Dubdub) from *Fury*; Robyn Davidson is Allie Cone from *The Satanic Verses* and the Brilliant Café in Southall is the Shaandar Café in the same novel (71). Later in the book, Ambassador Maurice Busby ('a man who didn't officially exist'; 237) is part of Ambassador Maximilian Ophuls from *Shalimar the Clown*. A telephone in the shape of a green plastic frog in Chaggan Bhujbal's office arrives in *The Moor's Last Sigh* (81). Even phrases from his novels interestingly reoccur: how 'newness enters the world' (45) 'how does newness enter the world' (72, 343), a chorus from *The Satanic Verses*; 'Conversation's Dead, man' (38) becomes 'Dialogue's dead' (*The Ground Beneath Her Feet* 284). There are many of these moments, explicit and implicit. However, the book is focussed on the *fatwa*, which is like a black hole which pulls in every part of the author's life and the book's narrative. The section describing his life as a student in Cambridge, for example, pays special attention to retelling the story of 'the Satanic Verses' as young Salman studies it during his history degree. And indeed, the book stops when, 13 years after the *fatwa* was declared its threat has, to a great degree, been diminished, and Rushdie is free from his protection, walks into the street and hails a cab: he escapes from both the book and his near-imprisonment.

If the book is *like* – but *is not exactly* – a memoir, how similar is it to other work by Rushdie? There are occasional comic touches: a special branch officer is called Wilson and his companion, an intelligence officer, is called Wilton: both were called Will (comic in itself and also, surely, an echo of Tintin's Thomson and Thompson). Jokes are occasionally retold. Other familiar Rushdie themes emerge: many of his novels (*The Satanic Verses* and *Fury* especially, and his two books for children) circle around fatherhood and 'sonship': so, too, *Joseph Anton* deals with the relationships with his two sons. Film, too: Hitchcock's *The Birds* is a constant intertextual reference (and, of course, the three 'Goddesses' from *The Satanic Verses* are described as birds as well). And of course, the memoir deals with migrancy:

> [M]igration tore up all the traditional roots of the self. The rooted self flourished in a place it knew well, among people who knew it well, following customs and traditions with which it and its community were familiar, and speaking its own language among others who did the same. Of these four roots, place, community, culture, language, he had lost three. (53)

In addition to this, however, he describes his great theme as 'how the world joined up' (68): not only in terms of East and West meeting ('the impact of globalisation' one might rather dryly put this) but how 'the past shaped the present while the present changed our understanding of the past, and how the imagined world, the location of dreams, art, invention and, yes, belief, leaked across the frontier that separated it from the everyday, "real" place in which human beings mistakenly believed they lived' (69). This 'joining-up' is the work of history. In *Joseph Anton*, po-fa traces a change: not a radical change – his po-fa ideas have antecedents in his *pre-fatwa* work – but a significant one for both his thinking and his art. And this change is most visible in precisely the two issues of migrancy and 'joining up'.

Po-fa and Migrancy

One of the things that the 'mandarin literary discourse' finds most fascinating in Rushdie's fiction is precisely the discussion of the nature of migrancy and its relationship to authenticity. The *locus classicus* of this occurs in *The Satanic Verses*, ventriloquized through a discussion between Lucretius and Ovid. Lucretius is taken to show that change or metamorphosis (or migrancy) means the death of one self and the birth of a new self, while Ovid suggests that under an appearance of change, a real essence remains. (As Salahuddin remarks, this is 'pretty cold comfort . . . Either I accept Lucretius and conclude that some demonic and irreversible mutation is taking place in my inmost depths, or I go with Ovid and concede that everything new emerging is no more than a manifestation of what was already there'; 277). But this thinking through of the issues of migrancy occurs throughout Rushdie's work and, in the fiction, is undecided, an endless argument between the two Romans, with no final, absolute answer. For example, Rachel Trousdale, in her excellent recent book, is typical of many critics when she writes that *The Satanic Verses* destabilizes 'not only its characters representations but also the very notion that there is an absolute truth to represent' (Trousdale 2010: 119). These questions circle around the question of 'authenticity', over what is real, and in much of Rushdie's work this question is rarely resolved. In *The Ground Beneath Her Feet*, the two views occur in the relationship between Vina ('never big . . . on authenticity which she held to be a pernicious notion that needed "deconstruction"'; 338) who becomes a martyr to her opposition to 'authenticity' and the admirable Patangbaz Kalamanja, who angrily points out Vina's many internal contradictions: the 'ayurveda you praise is expressly opposed – diametrically and inalienably opposed – to your brand of debauched activities' (334).

Rushdie raises this in *Joseph Anton*. Although he rightly says that he has been spared many of the terrible problems facing migrants, 'one great problem remained: that of authenticity' (54): 'Was it possible to be – to become good at being – not rootless, but multiply rooted?' (54). Is authenticity – rootedness, whatever this is – possible in our globalized age? Po-fa *Joseph Anton* answers this question. Earlier, I discussed the significance of names, and what Rushdie, citing Saramago, called 'the something that has no name' which is 'what we are': this deep root, this 'deeper self' comes to aid Rushdie:

> [T]here seemed to be a thing in him that woke up and refused that unat-tractive, self-pitying defeat. He instructed himself to remember the most important rules he had made for himself: not to accept the descriptions of reality made by security people, politicians or priests. To insist, instead, on the validity of his own judgements and instincts. (416)

More than aid, however, this something with no name gave him back himself: to 'move towards a rebirth, or at least a renewal. To be reborn as himself, into his own life: that was the goal' (416). Po-fa comes down on the side of Ovid: changes, invented names, are only on the surface. What is essential, real and authentic, eventually emerges and remains. One is 'reborn as oneself'.

Po-fa History

The sense of reality is also crucial to the other aspect of po-fa. Rushdie's fiction, from the moment of the intellectual and aesthetic leap that occurred after *Grimus* and enabled *Midnight's Children*, has always been obsessed by history: indeed, he writes that as 'a historian by train-ing', the point of his fiction was the 'great point of history, which was to understand how individual lives, communities, nations and social classes were shaped by great forces, yet retained, at times, the ability to change the direction of those forces' (55–6). As he suggested, the his-tory he was interested in was the 'joining up' of the past and present, the dream and the waking, the imaginary and the everyday and his fiction inhabits those boundary-lands: alternative realities (where Rock and Roll was invented in Mumbai and Jesse, not Elvis, survived birth), magical powers (the midnight's children) and so on. Yet, po-fa Rushdie moves from those marches to more concrete, 'real' history: like his travel writing (*The Jaguar's Smile*), Joseph Anton is 'real': the 'only reason his story was interesting was that it had actually happened. It wouldn't be interesting if it wasn't true' (340–1). That is, 'true' in the sense of the 'discipline of history': one could check many of the dates, places and conversations (in summary at least) against an archive and find that they match.

This is the core of *Joseph Anton*. It is a work of history: indeed, more than that, it aims to be an *archive*. This in no small part explains the length of the book ('"No more 250,000 word monsters . . . Shorter books more often". For more than a decade he kept that promise . . . Then he got to work on his memoir, and realised that he had fallen off the wagon'; 544). It also explains some of its oddness, the third person, for example: it is an attempt not simply to tell or remember the events but to 'objectively' archive them. It tries to encapsulate the whole history, trying (*pace* Rushdie' speech to the Nobel committee members) to 'control . . . the story'. This explains, of course, the many times when Rushdie corrects people's false impressions of him and his work (for example, he is constantly stressing how grateful he is for police protection, but this message seems never to get out: even the Prime Minister John Major is surprised by his gratitude, so smeared has Rushdie been in the press). This also goes some way to explain the severity of the very many occasions in which Rushdie settles scores. In an archive, perhaps, it's important to 'set the record straight'. Rushdie does this with his ex-wives, with his father ('His parents didn't come to his graduation. His father said they couldn't afford the airfare. This was untrue' (47)), with political opponents and with critics (the critic James Wood is described as 'the malevolent Procrustes of literary criticism, who tormented his victims on the narrow bed of his inflexible literary ideologies, pulling them painfully apart or else cutting them off at the knees' (367): he writes this, incidentally, in the paragraph after he has denounced the 'piranhas of the little pond of the London literary scene' (367)). Indeed, Rushdie is pretty firm with anyone who offers anything other than complete and utter support. Of course, one might speculate that part of the motive for this 'score-settling' is because Rushdie wants to 'settle scores' with the Ayatollah Khomeini and with the form of religion that stole those years from him: if the whole book is an attempt to 'settle a score' it's unsurprising that is repeated over and over again in smaller ways. But more than this Rushdie is aware that as a work of history, an archive, the book will set the case for what happened, for how he reacted and felt: and it's clearly important because, oddly, in history, the archive creates the historical event.

But this desire to 'create an archive' leads to some odd moments. The book is full of imaginary letters to people or concepts, set in italics, indented in the text: The Chief Rabbi (186), Bernie Grant MP (187), Robinson Crusoe (187), Anonymous newspaper profile writer (204), God (282), Harold Pinter (392), Religion (315), Tony Blair (535). Yet there is also an exchange with Harold Pinter: Rushdie describes what he calls 'Pintering', moments in which the Nobel Laureate shouts and bullies people over political issues. After one such incident, he writes (indented, italics) to him to ask him to apologize: Is this a real letter? The form makes the reader expect that it isn't. Pinter replies, contrite. Again, is this real? Can these be seen in an archive? A work of history, of course, footnotes a source. *Joseph Anton* doesn't, leaving this incident hard to understand clearly. Is it how Rushdie would have liked to have *imagined* 'bettering' Pinter (the other letters seem to do this)? Or did it really occur?

An archive is also an intervention. The French philosopher Derrida writes that the 'archive has always been a pledge, and like every pledge, a token of the future' (Derrida 1996: 18). The book is trying to make a case about free speech, about the relationship between Islam and the West. Sometimes, understandably, the book is, for example, very pro-American ('America had made it impossible for Britain to walk away from his defence'; 334). It is trying to stand as a warning.

Po-fa and Rushdie's Work

What then is the impact of po-fa on Rushdie's wider oeuvre? How does *Joseph Anton* change how we read Rushdie or, rather, what changes in his fiction does this non-fiction archive trace? I am going to focus on three areas.

'Inside history'

The first change, I think, lies in Rushdie's view of the power of fiction in relation to the power of events. The earlier Rushdie, before the *fatwa*, found in fiction almost utopian resources to tell and retell, to reshape the past and to 'chutnify' it, preserving but also mixing disparate pasts so that 'the world may taste the pickles of history' (Rushdie 1981: 461) which, despite being 'overpowering' and bringing tears 'possess the authentic taste of truth' and are 'despite everything, acts of love' (461). However, the po-fa Rushdie is very different: in *Fury* he writes of how human

> life was now lived in the moment before the fury, when the anger grew, or in the moment during – the fury's hour, the time of the beast set free – or in the ruined aftermath of great violence, when the fury ebbed and chaos abated. (Rushdie 2001: 129)

And *Shalimar the Clown* is unambiguous about 'tyranny, forced conversions, temple-smashing, iconoclasm, persecution and genocide' (*Shalimar* 239). Here, fiction is limited, weak and unable to face events in the world: in *Shalimar the Clown*, he writes:

> [S]tories were stories and real life was real life, naked, ugly and finally impossible to cosmeticise in the greasepaint of a tale . . . brutality is brutality is brutality and excess is excess and that's all there is to it. There are things that must be looked at indirectly because they would blind you if you looked them in the face, like the fire of the sun.

This is the writing of an author who has seen what he takes to be the limits of fiction and has retreated from his optimistic position. It's almost no surprise, perhaps, that his next novel, *The Enchantress of Florence*, was 'historical', almost in an attempt to avoid facing the present.

The second change is that, as I have suggested, po-fa Rushdie is very different in relation to issues of migrancy and what might be called 'multiculturalism', certainly in its 1980s form. The introduction has already cited an optimistic Rushdie who wrote that his fiction

> celebrates hybridity, impurity, intermingling, the transformation that comes of new an unexpected combinations of human beings, cultures, ideas politics, movies, songs . . . rejoices in mongrelisation and fears the absolutism of the Pure. Melange, hotchpotch, a bit of this and a bit of that is how newness enters the world. It is the great possibility that mass migration gives to the world, and I have tried to embrace it. (Rushdie 1991: 394)

This is the Rushdie whose character, Pyarelal, in the early part of *Shalimar the Clown*, exclaims happily, in a Kashmiri context:

> Who tonight are the Hindus? Who are the Muslims? Here in Kashmir, our stories sit happily side by side on the same double bill, we eat from the same dishes, we laugh at the same jokes. (71)

This Rushdie too (like Vina) was suspicious of authenticity ('the Pure') and liked the transgressive, the questioning. This is almost a 'left' Salman Rushdie ('almost' because as his non-fiction shows, even as early as *The Jaguar Smile*, Rushdie is not unaware of the perils of seduction by the left). Po-fa Rushdie is very different. Indeed, as many commentators have pointed out, it was precisely the Rushdie affair that called time on this positive, rather fluffy sense of multiculturalism. He writes that 'in cultural matters, I am not a relativist, and I do believe in universals . . . [T]he heart is what is it and knows nothing of compass points' (315). In The *Satanic Verses*, the Holocaust survivor Otto Cone suggests that the 'world is incompatible . . . Ghosts, Nazis, saints, all alive at the same time' (295) and that if these lives 'that have no business mingling with one another . . . meet . . . It's uranium and plutonium, each makes the other decompose, boom!' (314). And while this was one position among many in that novel, it seems to be the final position in *Joseph Anton*: a constant sense of struggle. That to live in the 'joined up' world is to live constantly embattled between positions. While Rushdie is clear that he disagrees with the detail of Samuel Huntingdon's controversial 'clash of civilisations' thesis, much of Joseph Anton seems to suggest a parallel line of thought, very unlike his earlier work. Indeed, Pankaj Mishra, in his review of the book makes a similar point, criticizing Rushdie's 'neat oppositions between the secular and the religious, the light and the dark'.

Third, and least surprisingly, is po-fa's view of religion. Rushdie's father was a 'godless man who knew and thought a great deal about god' (23) who passed this fascination to his son, also 'fascinated by gods and prophets' (39), and the idea that, unlike other religions (in his view), 'the story of the birth of Islam was an event inside history' (24). However, Rushdie's view of religion has changed. In relation to *Midnight's Children*, he declares sympathetically that to write about India and Pakistan one must write about 'reality as it is experienced by religious people' (Rushdie 1991: 376), and that, while an atheist, the desire to write is to 'fill up that emptied God-chamber with other dreams' (377). This is what Rushdie means when he writes that the novel offers the 'elevation of the quest for the Grail over the Grail itself' (an Arthurian version of the Simurg myth that underlines *Grimus*): it is a way of 'fulfilling our unaltered spiritual requirements' (422), 'religious pictures for people who have no god' (Rushdie 1995: 220). But, as 'Whisky' Sisoida points out the issue is the use of God: '"Fact is" says Sisodia "religious fafaith, which encodes the highest ass ass aspirations of human race, is now, in our cocountry, the servant of the lowest instincts, and gogo God is the creature of evil"' (Rushdie 1987: 518). This view, of course, hardens post-*fatwa*. In 2002, writing about the massacres in Gujarat, Rushdie declares that "India's problem turns out to be the world's problem. What happened in India, happened in God's name. The problem's name is God' (Rushdie 2003: 403). And *Joseph Anton* is unsparing about all forms of religion.

And yet, it might despite the fact that Rushdie declares himself 'a proudly irreligious man' (314) and throughout *Joseph Anton* derides religion and the religious, there is an odd gap. In his reflections during the worst time of the *fatwa*, he cites a Sufi proverb: "Our lives teach us who we are" (Rushdie 1991: 414). And as I have suggested earlier, it is the 'something with no name' within him – that thing which Saramago discusses – that seems to support him. One does not have to think that there are 'infallible moral Arbiters and irredeemably immoral Tempters above us' (Rushdie 2002: 157) to hear that this language, and his talk of 'rebirth', draws on a religious metaphorical framework. Irreligion and religion seem to draw pretty close together, even in po-fa Rushdie. *Joseph Anton* is the record, the archive, of a man persecuted for his beliefs, and is worthy of a great deal of respect.

Further Reading

There is an enormous amount of material available on Rushdie and on the 'Rushdie Affair' and this does not claim to cover it all: rather, it singles out some useful and key texts.

Introductions

The best introductions to his work are as follows:

> Cundy, Catherine, *Salman Rushdie* (Manchester: Manchester University Press, 1996).

A summary of his work to that date. Good on Rushdie's women, and quite good on Sufism.

> Goonetilleke, D. C. R. A., *Salman Rushdie*, 2nd ed. (Basingstoke: Palgrave Macmillan, 2010).
> Grant, Damian, *Salman Rushdie* (Plymouth: Northcote House, 1999).

A solid account, with a good sense of critical debates and some detail.

> Morton, Stephen, *Salman Rushdie: Fictions of Postcolonial Modernity* (Basingstoke: Palgrave Macmillan, 2007).

This is especially strong on the historical context for Rushdie in India and Pakistan.

> Singh, P. K., *The Novels of Salman Rushdie: A Critical Evaluation* (Jaipur: Book Enclave, 2001).

Good on Indo-English literary context.

> Smale, David (ed.), *Salman Rushdie: Midnight's Children. The Satanic Verses: A Reader's Guide to Essential Criticism* (Cambridge: Icon 2001).

A really good guide to a range of issues, clear and well-organized.

> Teverson, Andrew, *Salman Rushdie* (Manchester: Manchester University Press, 2007).
> Gurnah, Abdulrazak (ed.), *The Cambridge Companion to Salman Rushdie* (Cambridge: Cambridge University Press, 2007).
> Reader, Michael (ed.), *Conversations with Salman Rushdie* (Jackson: University Press of Mississippi, 2000).

Invaluable and a great teaching resource.

Critical Studies on Rushdie

Brennan, Timothy, *Salman Rushdie and the Third World* (London: Macmillan, 1989).

The first book-length study of Rushdie, and well-worth looking at. He's torn between admiring his work and thinking that, as an intellectual speaking to intellectuals, it's not really helping the anti-colonial struggle or suffering billions. Full of interesting insights, very good on 'postcolonial' situation. Also introduces the idea of Rushdie's 'Sufi-ism'.

Clark, Roger Y., *Stranger Gods: Salman Rushdie's Other Worlds* (London: McGill-Queens University Press, 2001).

A book on Rushdie that begins well and becomes superb: one of the very best accounts of *The Satanic Verses* (and the first one that takes really seriously the fact that the narrator is the devil).

Devi, P. Indira, *Salman Rushdie and Magic Realism* (New Delhi: Research India Press, 2011).

Clear and good account of these issues.

Fletcher, D. M. (ed.), *Reading Rushdie* (Amsterdam/Atlanta: Rodopi, 1994).

Excellent, if now rather dated, collection of essays. Especially recommended are the following: Keith Wilson 'MC and Reader Responsibility'; Patricia Merivale, 'Saleem Fathered by Oscar'; Tim Brennan 'S's Holy book'; Inderpal Grewal 'Marginality, Woman and S'; Srinivias Aravamudan 'Being God's Postman Is no Fun, Yaar'; Sara Suleri 'Contraband Histories'; M. Keith Booker 'Beauty and the Beast'

Glage, Lieselotte and Kunow, Ruediger (eds), *The Decolonizing Pen. Cultural Diversity and the Transnational Imaginary in Rushdie's Fiction* (Trier: Wissenschaftlicher Verlag, 2001).

Some good essays here. Especially recommended are Elleke Boehmer 'Neo-Colonialism, Converging Cities and Post-Colonial Critics of Rushdie'; Graham Hugger and Tobias Wachinger 'Can Newness Enter the World?'; and Peter Lange, 'Postcolonial Gothic'

Hassumani, Sabrina, *Salman Rushdie: A Postmodern Reading of His Works* (Madison: Farleigh Dickinson University Press, 2002).

As it says, focussing on the 'enabling power of hybridity'.

Mittapalli, R. and Kuortti, J. (eds), *Salman Rushdie: New Critical Insights* (New Delhi: Atlantic, 2003).

Some new critical insights (e.g. Shaul Bass's excellent essay on *The Satanic Verses* as a bildungsroman) and quite good on newer books.

Parashkevova, Vassilena, *Salman Rushdie's Cities: Reconfigurational Politics and the Contemporary UrbanImagination* (London: Continuum, 2012).

A very up-to-date study of the 'dynamic intersections of colonial, post-colonial and global contexts' in Rushdie's work, using the city as its focus.

Sanga, Jaina C., *Salman Rushdie's Postcolonial Metaphors: Migration, Translation, Hybridity, Blasphemy, and Globalization* (London: Greenwood Press, 2001).

A rather good account of Rushdie's postcolonial metaphors.

Trousdale, Rachel, *Nabokov, Rushdie, and the Transnational Imagination: Novels of Exile and Alternate Worlds* (New York: Palgrave Macmillan 2010).

An excellent study in how 'transnational literature teaches us the ethical necessity of recognizing ourselves in strangers, and strangers in others'.

Books and Chapters on Rushdie

Ahmed, Aljaz, *In Theory* (London: Verso, 1993).

A classic attack on postmodernism and postcolonialism. Rushdie is attacked in an interesting and complex way: his 'aesthetics of despair' mark him not as a migrant but as a vagrant.

Afzal Khan, Fawzia, *Cultural Imperialism and the Indo-English Novel* (Pennsylvania: Pennsylvania University Press, 1993).

Another attack on Rushdie for not offering a 'viable alternative ideology'.

Aldea, Eva, *Magical Realism and Deleuze: The Indiscernibility of Difference in Postcolonial Literature* (London: Continuum, 2011).

An excellent and well-informed account of the Magical Realism, using the thought of the significant French philosopher Gilles Deleuze as a framework.

Bahri, Deepika, *Native Intelligence: Aesthetics, Politics and Post-Colonial Literature* (London: University of Minnesota Press, 2003).

Well-argued book about postcolonial literature with a chapter on Rushdie. The point: to see postcolonial literature as literature, not as the work of 'native informants'.

Ball, John, *Satire and the Postcolonial Novel: V. S. Naipaul, Chinua Achebe, Salman Rushdie* (London: Routledge, 2003).

Banerjee, Mita, *The Chutneyfication of History: Salman Rushdie, Michael Ondaatje, Bharati Mukherjee and the Postcolonial Debate* (Heidelberg: C. Winter, 2002).

Barfoot, C. and D'haen, Theo (eds), *Shades of Empire in Colonial and Post-Colonial Literatures* (Amsterdam: Rodopi, 1993).

Aleid Fokkema's 'Postmodern Fragmentation or Authentic Essence? Character in *The Satanic Verses* is very good.

Bhabha, Homi (ed.), *Nation and Narration* (London: Routledge, 1990).

An influential collection of essays on national identity.

Bhabha, Homi, *The Location of Culture* (London: Routledge, 1994).

Rushdie's most famous literary critic. This celebrated collection of essays is about much more than just Rushdie, but is central for understanding much academic work on his novels.

Bradley, Arthur and Tate, Andrew, *The New Atheist Novel: Fiction, Philosophy and Polemic after 9/11* (London: Continuum, 2010).

Polemical and interesting account of several novelists, with a useful and insightful chapter on Rushdie.

Connor, Steve, *The English Novel in History 1950–1995* (London: Routledge, 1996).

Interesting and well-contextualized in relation to other British fiction on Rushdie.

Gorra, Michael, *After Empire* (Chicago: University of Chicago Press, 1997).

One chapter on Rushdie. Again two attacks on Rushdie (the novel itself as a form has an ideology; Rushdie reduces suffering to entertainment).

Head, Dominic, *Modern British Fiction, 1950–2000* (Cambridge: Cambridge University Press, 2002).

Good account of Rushdie in UK context.

Hutcheon, Linda, *The Politics of Postmodernism*, 2nd ed. (London: Routledge, 2002).

The central account of Rushdie as postmodern.

Israel, Nico, *Outlandish: Writing between Exile and Diaspora* (Stanford: Stanford University Press, 2000).

Reads Rushdie as an exile, draws some interesting parallels.

Moore-Gilbert, Bart (ed.), *Writing India, 1757–1990* (Manchester: Manchester University Press, 1996).
Needham, Anuradha Dingwaney, *Using the Master's Tools. Resistance and the Literature of the African and South-Asian Diasporas* (London: Macmillan, 2000).

One chapter on Rushdie.

Ravi, P. S., *Modern Indian Fiction* (New Delhi: Prestige, 2003).

An account of Rushdie.

Spivak, Gayatri Chakravorty, 'Reading The Satanic Verses', in What Is an Author? Ed. Maurice Biriotti and Nicola Miller (Manchester: Manchester University Press, 1993), 104–34.

Suleri, Sara, *The Rhetoric of English India* (Chicago: Chicago University Press, 1992).

An attempt to offer a new relationship between imperial and postcolonial discourse, paying special attention to the ways in which gender is used. One chapter on Rushdie.

Articles on Rushdie

Ahmed, Aijaz, 'Rushdie's *Shame*: Postmodernism, Migrancy and Representation of Women', *Economic and Political Weekly* 15 (June 1991): 1461–71.

Aji, Aron R., '"All Names Mean Something": Salman Rushdie's *Haroun* and the Legacy of Islam', *Contemporary Literature* 36.1 (Spring 1995): 103–29.

Appiah, Kwame Anthony, 'Is the Post- in Postmodernism the Post- in Post-Colonial?' *Critical Enquiry* 17 (1991): 336–57.

Birch, David, 'Postmodern Chutneys', *Textual Practice* 5.1 (1991): 1–7.

Booker, Keith M., 'Beauty and the Beast: Dualism as Despotism in the Fiction of Salman Rushdie', *ELH* 57.4 (Winter 1990): 977–97.

Brouillette, S., 'Authorship as Crisis in Salman Rushdie's "Fury"', *Journal of Commonwealth Literature* 40.1 (2005): 137–56.

Cook, Rufus, 'Place and Displacement in Salman Rushdie's Work', *World Literature Today* 68.1 (1994): 23–8.

Cundy, Catherine, '"Rehearsing Voices": Salman Rushdie's *Grimus*', *Journal of Commonwealth Literature* 27.12 (1992): 128–38.

Falconer, Rachel, 'Bouncing Down to the Underworld: Classical Katabasis in *The Ground Beneath Her Feet*', *Twentieth Century Literature: A Scholarly and Critical Journal* 47.4 (Winter 2001): 467–509.

Frank, Soren, 'The Aesthetic of Elephantiasis: Rushdie's *Midnight's Children* an encyclopedic novel', *Journal of Postcolonial Writing* 46.2 (2010): 187–98.

Hart, David W., 'Making a Mockery of Mimicry: Salman Rushdie's *Shame*', *Postcolonial Text* 4.4 (2008).

Hima, Raza, 'Unravelling Sharam: Narrativisation as a Political Act in Salman Rushdie's *Shame*', *Wasafiri: The Transnational Journal of International Writing* 39 (2003): 55–61.

Islam, Syed Manzuri, 'Writing the Postcolonial Event: Salman Rushdie's August 15, 1947', *Textual Practice* 13.1 (1999): 119–35.

Ismail, Qadri, 'A Bit of This and a Bit of That: Rushdie's Newness', *Social Text* 29 (1991): 117–24.

Jean Craige, Betty, 'Literature in a Global Society', *PMLA* 106.3 (1991): 395–401.

Jussawalla, Feroza F., 'Rushdie's Dastan-E-Dilruba: "The Satanic Verses" as Rushdie's Love Letter to Islam', *Diacritics* 26.1 (1996): 50–73.

Kane, J., 'Embodied Panic: Revisiting Modernist 'Religion' in the Controversies over 'Ulysses' and "The Satanic Verses"', *Textual Practice* 20.3 (2006): 419.

Kane, Jean, 'The Migrant Intellectual and the Body of History: Salman Rushdie's *Midnight's Children*', *Contemporary Literature* 37.1 (1996): 94–108.

König, Eva, 'Between Cultural Imperialism and the Fatwa: Colonial Echoes and Postcolonial Dialogue in Salman Rushdie's Haroun and the Sea of Stories', *International Fiction Review* 33.1–2 (2006): 52–63.

Kortennar, Neil, 'Postcolonial Ekphrasis: Salman Rusdie Gives the Finger Back to the Empire', *Contemporary Literature* 38.2 (1997): 232–59.

Majid, Anouar, 'Can the Postcolonial Critic speak? Orientalism and the Rushdie Affair', *Cultural Critique* 32 (1995–6): 5–42.

May, Brian, 'Memorials to Modernity: Postcolonialism and Pilgrimage in Naipaul and Rushdie', *ELH* 68.1 (2001): 241–65.

Mishra, Vijay, 'Rushdie-Wushdie: Salman Rushdie's Hobson-Jobson', *New Literary History* 40.2 (Spring 2009): 385–410.

Mondal, Anshuman A., '"Representing the very Ethic He Battled": Secularism, Islam(ism) and Self-Transgression in *The Satanic Verses*', forthcoming in *Textual Practice* (2014).

Mufti, Aamir, 'Reading the Rushdie Affair: An Essay on Islam and Politics', *Social Text* 29 (1991): 95–116.

Mukherjee, Ankhi, 'Fissured Skin, Inner Ear Radio, and a Telepathic Nose: The Senses as Media in Salman Rushdie's *Midnight's Children*', *Paragraph* 29.3 (2007): 55.

Murphy, Neil, 'The Literalisation of Allegory in Salman Rushdie's *Shalimar the Clown*', in *British Asian Fiction: Framing the Contemporary*. Ed. Neil Murphy and Wai-chew Sim. New York: Cambria Press, 351–64.

Newton, K. M., 'Literary Theory and the Rushdie Affair', *English* 41.171 (1992): 235–47.

Sawhney, Simona, 'Satanic Choices: Poetry and Prophecy in Rushdie's Novel', *Twentieth Century Literature* 45.3 (1999): 253–77.

— 'Reading Rushdie after September 11, 2001', *European Journal of English Studies* 5.3 (2001): 367–84.

Schultheis, Alexandra W., 'Postcolonial Lack and Aesthetic Promise in *The Moor's Last Sigh*', *Twentieth Century Literature* 47.4 (Winter 2001): 569–96.

Syed, Mujeebuddin, 'Warped Mythologies, Salman Rushdie's *Grimus*', *Ariel* 25.4 (1994): 135–52.

Teresa Heffernan, Teresa, 'Apocalyptic Narratives: The Nation in Salman Rushdie's "Midnight's Children"', *Twentieth Century Literature* 46.4 (Winter 2000): 470–91.

Teverson, Andrew S., 'Fairy Tale Politics: Free Speech and Multiculturalism in *Haroun and the Sea of Stories*', *Twentieth Century Literature* 47.4 (Winter 2001): 444–66.

Teverson, Andrew, 'Salman Rushdie and Aijaz Ahmad: Satire, ideology and "Shame"', *Journal of Commonwealth Literature* 39.2 (2004): 45–60.

Thompson, Jon, 'Superman and Salman Rushdie: *Midnight's Children* and the Disillusionment of History', *Journal of Commonwealth and Postcolonial Studies* 3.1 (1995): 1–23.

Upstone, S., 'The Fulcrum of Instability: Salman Rushdie's *The Ground Beneath Her Feet* and the Postcolonial Traveller', *WASAFIRI* 21.1 (2006): 34–8.

Ziogas, Ioannis, 'Ovid in Rushdie, Rushdie in Ovid: A Nexus of Artistic Webs', *Arion* 19.1 (Spring/Summer 2011): 23–50.

The 'Rushdie Affair'

With thanks to Dr Nicole Edmondson.

Abdallah, Anouar et al., *For Rushdie: Essays by Arab and Muslim Writers in Defense of Free Speech* (New York: George Braziller, 1994).

Many arguments for free speech, a book praised by Rushdie in *Joseph Anton*.

Ahsan, M. M. and Kidwai, A. R. (eds), *Sacrilege versus Civility: Muslim Perspectives on* The Satanic Verses *Affair* (Leicester: The Islamic Foundation, 1991).

Has an exhaustive catalogue of letters to the editor and other media and personal correspondence from people about *fatwa*.

Akhtar, Shabbir, *Be Careful with Muhammad! The Salman Rushdie Affair* (London: Bellew Publishing, 1989).

Asad, Talal, *Genealogies of Religion: Discipline and Reasons of Power in Christianity and Islam* (Baltimore: The Johns Hopkins University Press, 1993).

The last two chapters give an anthropological view on the Rushdie Affair.

Cohn-Sherbok, Dan, *The Salman Rushdie Controversy in Interreligious Perspective* (Lewiston, NY: The Edwin Mellen Press, 1990).

A collection of essays with varying perspectives.

Kuortti, Joel, *Place of the Sacred: The Rhetoric of the* Satanic Verses *Affair* (Frankfurt: Peter Lang, 1997).

A very informative and interesting examination of (as the title says) the rhetoric each side used to advocate its point of view. 'What is at stake in the *Satanic Verses* affair', Kuortti writes, 'is very much an aspiration to affirm (communal) identity against another, dreaded (communal) identity'.

Malik, Kenan, *From Fatwa to Jihad: The Rushdioe Affair and Its Legacy* (London: Atlantic, 2009).

Up-to-date, polemical, passionate and personal account of the affair.

Ruthven, Malise, *A Satanic Affair: Salman Rushdie and the Wrath of Islam* (London: The Hogath Press, 1991).

Explains the Rushdie Affair with some detail, with an attempt to be impartial.

Sardar, Ziauddin and Davies, Merryl Wyn, *Distorted Imagination: Lessons from the Rushdie Affair* (London: Grey Seal Books, 1990).

References

Works Cited by Contributors

Introduction: Salman Rushdie, Robert Eaglestone

Brooker, Joseph (2010) *Literature of the 1980s: After the Watershed*. Edinburgh: Edinburgh University Press.

Eliot, T. S. (1975) 'Tradition and the Individual Talent', in *Selected Prose of T.S. Eliot*, ed. Frank Kermode. London: Faber and Faber, 37–44.

Jameson, Fredric (1986) 'Third-World Literature in the Era of Multinational Capitalism', *Social Text* 15: 65–88.

Malik, Kenan (2009) *From Fatwa to Jihad: The Rushdie Affair and Its Legacy*. London: Atlantic.

Parashkevova, Vassilena (2012) *Salman Rushdie's Cities: Reconfigurational Politics and the Contemporary Urban Imagination*. London: Continuum.

Chapter One: The Rushdie Canon, Ankhi Mukherjee

Ahmad, Aijaz (1991) 'Rushdie's *Shame*: Postmodernism, Migrancy and Representation of Women', *Economic and Political Weekly* June 15: 1461–71.

Aji, Aron R. (1995) 'All Names Mean Something': Salman Rushdie's *Haroun* and the Legacy of Islam', *Contemporary Literature* 36.1 (Spring): 103–29.

Bhabha, Homi (1994) *The Location of Culture*. London: Routledge.

Brennan, Timothy (1989) *Salman Rushdie and the Third World*. London: Macmillan.

Coetzee, J. M. (2002) *Stranger Shores: Essays 1986–1999*. London: Vintage.

Dalrymple, William (2012) 'Myth and Fiction at the Jaipur Literature Festival', *New York Times* 3 February, http://india.blogs.nytimes.com/2012/02/03/myth-and-fiction-at-the-jaipur-literature- festival/.

Devji, Faisal (2012) 'Does Salman Rushdie Exist?' *Current Intelligence* 30 January, http://www.currentintelligence.net/analysis/2012/1/30/does-salman-rushdie-exist.html.

Freud, Sigmund (1917–1919) "The Uncanny" (1919). *The Standard Edition of the Complete Psychological works of Sigmund Freud*: 17: 217–52.

Gorra, Michael (1997) *After Empire: Scott, Naipaul, Rushdie*. Chicago: University of Chicago Press.

Mufti, Aamir (1991) 'Reading the Rushdie Affair: An Essay on Islam and Politics', *Social Text* 29: 95–116.

Naipaul, V. S. (2004) *Literary Occasions: Essays*. Ed. Pankaj Mishra. London: Picador.

Sangari, Kumkum (2002) *Politics of the Possible: Essays on Gender, History, Narratives, Colonial English*. London: Anthem Press.

Soja, Edward (1989) *Postmodern Geographies: The Reassertion of Space in Critical Social Theory*. London: Verso.

Spivak, Gayatri (1990) *The Post-Colonial Critic: Interviews, Strategies, Dialogues*. Ed. Sarah Harasym. New York: Routledge.

— (1993) *Outside in the Teaching Machine*. New York: Routledge.

Suleri, Sara (1992) *The Rhetoric of English India*. Chicago: University of Chicago Press.

Sutherland, John (2008) 'Of Medicis and Mughals', *Financial Times* 5 April.

Tickell, Alex (2007) *Arundhati Roy's The God of Small Things*. London and New York: Routledge.

Waraich, Omar (2011) 'Would the Real Salman Rushdie Please Tweet Up?' *The Independent* 19 September.

Ziogas, Ioannis (2011) 'Ovid in Rushdie, Rushdie in Ovid: A Nexus of Artistic Webs', *Arion* 19.1 (Spring/Summer): 23–50.

Chapter Two: Salman Rushdie and the Rise of Postcolonial Studies: *Grimus, Midnight's Children* and *Shame*, Eleanor Byrne

Ahmad, Aijaz (1987) 'Jameson's Rhetoric of Otherness and the "National Allegory"', *Social Text* 17 (Autumn): 3–25.

Bhabha, Homi (1994) *The Location of Culture*. London: Routledge.

Cook, Rufus (1994) 'Place and Displacement in Salman Rushdie's Work', *World Literature Today* 68: 1.

Cundy, Catherine (1992) 'Rehearsing Voices': Salman Rushdie's *Grimus, Journal of Commonwealth Literature* 27: 12.

Frank, Soren (2010) 'The Aesthetic of Elephantiasis: Rushdie's *Midnight's Children* an encyclopedic novel', *Journal of Postcolonial Writing* 46: 2.

Grant, Damian (1999) *Salman Rushdie*. Plymouth: Northcote House.

Hart, David W. (2008) 'Making a Mockery of Mimicry: Salman Rushdie's *Shame*', *Postcolonial Text* 4: 4.

Huggan, Graham (2001) *The Postcolonial Exotic: Marketing the Margins*. London: Routledge.

Jameson, Fredric (1986), 'Third-World Literature in the Era of Multinational Capitalism', *Social Text* 15: 65–88, 69.

Kortenaar, Neil Ten (2005) *Self, Nation, Text in Salman Rushdie's "Midnight's Children."* Toronto: McGill-Queen's University Press.

Lazarus, Neil (1994) 'National Consciousness and Intellectualism', in *Colonial Discourse/Postcolonial Theory*. Ed. Frances Barker et al. Manchester: Manchester University Press, 197–220.

Moretti, Franco (1996) *Modern Epic: The World-System From Goethe To García Márquez*. London: Verso.

Nicholls, Brendon (2007) 'Reading "Pakistan" in Salman Rushdie's Shame', *The Cambridge Companion to Salman Rushdie*. Ed. Abdulrazak Gurnah. Cambridge: Cambridge University Press.

Proctor, James (2012) http://literature.britishcouncil.org/salman-rushdie, accessed June 1, 2012.

Slemon, Stephen (1988). 'Magic Realism as Post-Colonial Discourse'. *Canadian Literature* 116: 9–24.

Suleri, Sara (1992) *The Rhetoric of English India*. Chicago: University of Chicago.

Syed, Mujeebuddin (1994) 'Warped Mythologies, Salman Rushdie's *Grimus*', *Ariel* 25: 4.

Chapter Three: Rushdie as an International Writer, Marianne Corrigan

Brennan, Timothy (1989) *Salman Rushdie and the Third World*. New York: St. Martin's Press.

Deleuze, Gilles and Guattari, Felix (1987) *A Thousand Plateaus: Capitalism and Schizophrenia*. London: Continuum.

Faris, Wendy B. (2004) *Ordinary Enchantments: Magical Realism and the Remystification of Narrative*. Nashville: Vanderbilt University Press.

Hamm, Bernd and Smandych, Russell Charles (2005) *Cultural Imperialism: Essays on the Political Economy of Cultural Domination*. University of Toronto Press.

Harvey, David (2011) 'Time-Space Compression and the Postmodern Condition', *Literature and Globalization: A Reader*. Ed. Liam Connell and Nicky Marsh. London: Routledge, 5–17.

Hassumani, Sabrina (2002) *Salman Rushdie: A Postmodern Reading of His Major Works*. Madison: Farleigh Dickinson University Press.

Khatri, Chhote Lal (2006) 'Salman Rushdie's *Fury*: An Exploration of the Self', *Salman Rushdie: Critical Essays, Volume 2*. Ed. Mohit Kumar Ray and Rama Kundu. New Delhi: Atlantic Publishers, 163–77.

Krishnaswamy, Revathi (2005) 'Mythologies of Migrancy: Postcolonialism, Postmodernism and the Politics of (Dis)location', in *Postcolonial Studies in a Globalized World*. Ed. Wendy Faith and Pamela McCallum. Alberta: University of Calgary Press, 91–110.

Morton, Stephen (2008) *Salman Rushdie: Fictions of Postcolonial Modernity*. London: Palgrave MacMillan.

Murphy, Neil (2008) 'The Literalisation of Allegory in Salman Rushdie's *Shalimar the Clown*', *British Asian Fiction: Framing the Contemporary*. Ed. Neil Murphy and Wai-chew Sim. New York: Cambria Press, 351–64.

Sanga, Jaina C. (2001) *Salman Rushdie's Postcolonial Metaphors: Migration, Translation, Hybridity, Blasphemy, and Globalization*. Westport, CT: Greenwood Press.

Tomlinson, John (1999) *Globalization and Culture*. Cambridge: Polity.

Wallhead, Celia M. (2002) 'A Myth for Anger, Migration and Creativity in Salman Rushdie's *Fury*', in *Commonwealth Fiction: Twenty-First Century Readings*. Ed. Rajeshwar Mittapalli and Alessandro Monti. New Delhi: Atlantic Publishers, 168–85.

Chapter Four: Postcolonial Secularism and Literary Form in Salman Rushdie's *The Satanic Verses*, Stephen Morton

Al-Azmeh, Aziz (1993) *Islams and Modernities*. London: Verso.

Asad, Talal (1993) *Genealogies of Religion: Discipline and Reasons of Power in Christianity and Islam*. Baltimore: Johns Hopkins University Press.

Bakhash, Shaul (1988) 'What's Khomeini Up To?', *Contemporary Literary Criticism* 55. Detroit: Gale Research Inc.

Baucom, Ian (1999) *Out of Place: Englishness, Empire, and the Locations of Identity*. Princeton: Princeton University Press.

Bhabha, Homi (1994) *The Location of Culture*. London: Routledge.

Brennan, Timothy (1989) *Salman Rushdie and the Third World: Myths of the Nation*. Basingstoke: Macmillan.

Chakrabarty, Dipesh (2000) *Provincializing Europe: Postcolonial Thought and Historical Difference*. Princeton, NJ: Princeton University Press.

Clark, Roger Y. (2001) *Stranger Gods: Salman Rushdie's Other Worlds*. Montreal: McGill-Queen's University Press.

de Man, Paul (1983) *Blindness and Insight: Essays in the Rhetoric of Contemporary Criticism*. London: Methuen, 1983.

Hai, Ambreen (1999) '"Marching in from the Peripheries": Rushdie's Feminized Artistry and Ambivalent Feminism', in *Critical Essays on Salman Rushdie*. Ed. M. Keith Booker. New York: G.K. Hall.

Hima, Raza (2003) 'Unravelling Sharam: Narrativisation as a Political Act in Salman Rushdie's *Shame*', *Wasafiri: The Transnational Journal of International Writing*: 18.39: 55–61.

Jussawalla, Feroza F. (1999) 'Rushdie's Dastan-E-Dilruba: *The Satanic Verses* as Rushdie's Love Letter to Islam', in *Critical Essays on Salman Rushdie*. Ed. M. Keith Booker. New York: G.K. Hall.

Mahmood, Mamdani (2007) 'The Politics of Culture Talk in the Contemporary War on Terror', Hobhouse Memorial Public Lecture, LSE, 8 March. Transcript available at www.lse.ac.uk/collections/LSEPublicLecturesAndEvents/ events/2007/20061219t1346z001.htm.

Mondal, Anshuman A. (2009) 'An Unfunny Valentine', *Guardian* 16 February, www. guardian.co.uk/commentisfree/2009/feb/10/religion-islam-fatwa-rushdie.

Mufti, Aamir (1999) 'Reading the Rushdie Affair: "Islam", Cultural Politics, Form', in *Critical Essays on Salman Rushdie*. Ed. M. Keith Booker. New York: G.K. Hall.

— (2004) 'Towards a Lyric History of India', *boundary 2* 31.2: 245–74.

Russell, Ralph (2003) 'Getting to Know Ghalib', in *The Oxford India Ghalib*. Ed. Ralph Russell. Delhi: Oxford University Press.

Singh, Sujala (2000) 'Secularist Faith in Salman Rushdie's Midnight's Children' *New Formations* 41: 158–72.

Schimmel, Annemarie (1975) *A History of Indian Literature Volume III: Classical Urdu Literature from the Beginning to Iqbal*. Wiesbaden: Otto Harrassowitz.

Suleri, Sara (1999) *The Rhetoric of English India*. London: University of Chicago Press.

Teverson, Andrew (2007) *Salman Rushdie*. Manchester: Manchester University Press.

Chapter Five: Revisiting *The Satanic Verses*, Anshuman A. Mondal

Ahsan, M. M. and Kidwai, A. R. eds. (1993) *Sacrilege versus Civility: Muslim Perspectives on The Satanic Verses Affair*. Leicester: Islamic Foundation.

Akhtar, Shabbir (1989) *Be Careful with Muhammad!* London: Bellew Publishing.

Amin, Samir (1988) *Eurocentrism*. London: Zed Books.

Anthony, Andrew (2008) *The Fallout: How a Guilty Liberal Lost His Innocence*. London: Vintage.

— (2009) 'How One Book Ignited a Culture War', *The Observer* 11 January 2009, www.guardian.co.uk/books/2009/jan/11/salman-rushdie-satanic-verses.

Appignanesi, Lisa (2009) 'No surrender', *The Guardian: Comment Is Free* 14 February 2009, www.guardian.co.uk/commentisfree/2009/feb/12/religion-islam.

Appignanesi, Lisa and Maitland, Sara eds. (1989) *The Rushdie File*. London: Fourth Estate.

Bhabha, Homi (1994) *The Location of Culture*. London: Routledge.

Bradley, Arthur and Tate, Andrew (2010) *The New Atheist Novel: Fiction, Philosophy and Polemic after 9/11*. London: Continuum.

Bunglawala, Ianayat (2007) 'I used to be a book-burner', *Guardian* 19 June, www.guardian.co.uk/commentisfree/2007/jun/19/notsurprisinglytheawarding.

— (2008) 'Words Can Never Hurt Us', *Guardian* 26 September, www.guardian.co.uk/commentisfree/2008/sep/26/islam.religion.

Caputo, John (2001) *On Religion*. London: Routledge.

Clark, Roger (2001) *Stranger Gods: Salman Rushdie's Other Worlds*. Montreal: MacGill-Queen's University Press.

Derrida, Jacques (2001) 'Structure, Sign and Play in the Discourse of the Human Sciences', in *Writing and Difference*. Trans. Alan Bass. London: Routledge, 2nd ed.

Fabian, Johannes (1983) *Time and the Other: How Anthropology Makes Its Object*. New York: Columbia University Press.

Malik, Kenan (2009) *From Fatwa to Jihad: The Rushdie Affair and Its Legacy*. London: Atlantic Books.

Mondal, Anshuman A. (2008) 'Islam and Multiculturalism: Some Thoughts on a Difficult Relationship', *Moving Worlds: A Journal of Transcultural Writing* 8.1: 77–94.

— (2011) 'The Coalition Government and Muslims: Same Old, Same Old', http://anshumanmondal.wordpress.com/2011/02/05/the-coalition-government-and-muslims-same-old-same-old/.

— (2013) '"Representing the Very Ethic He Battled": Secularism, Islam(ism) and Self-Transgression in *The Satanic Verses*', *Textual Practice* 27:3 (forthcoming).

— (2014) '"Representing the Very Ethic He Battled": Secularism, Islam(ism) and Self-Transgression in *The Satanic Verses*', forthcoming in *Textual Practice*.

Parekh, Bhikhu (1999) 'The Rushdie Affair in the British Press', in Dan Cohn-Sherbrook, ed. *The Salman Rushdie Controversy in Interreligious Perspective.* Lampeter: Edwin Mellen Press.

Sardar, Ziauddin and Wyn-Davies, Merryl (1990) *Distorted Imagination: Lessons from the Rushdie Affair.* London: Grey Seal.

Chapter Six: Salman Rushdie's Post-Nationalist Fairy Tales, Andrew Teverson

Appiah, Kwame Anthony (1991) 'Is the Post- in Postmodernism the Post- in Post-Colonial?' *Critical Enquiry* 17: 336–57.

Bacchilega, Cristina (2004) 'Genre and Gender in the Cultural Reproduction of India as "Wonder" Tale', in *Fairy Tales and Feminism: New Approaches.* Ed. Donald Hasse. Detroit, MI: Wayne State University Press, 179–95.

Barnard, F. M. (1965) *Herder's Social and Political Thought: From Enlightenment to Nationalism.* Oxford: Clarenden.

Brathwaite, Kamau (1984) *The History of the Voice: The Development of Nation Language in Anglophone Caribbean Poetry.* London: New Beacon.

Campbell, Joseph (1993) [1949] *The Hero with a Thousand Faces.* London: Fontana.

Dobie, Madeleine (2008) 'Translation in the Contact Zone: Antoine Galland's *Mille et une nuites: contes arabes*', in *The Arabian Nights in Historical Context: Between East and West.* Ed. Saree Makdisi and Felicity Nussbaum. Oxford: Oxford University Press, 25–49.

Falconer, Rachel (2009) *The Crossover Novel: Contemporary Children's Fiction and Its Adult Readership.* New York: Routledge.

Fanon, Franz (1994) 'On National Culture', in *Colonial Discourse and Post-Colonial Theory.* Ed. Patrick Williams and Laura Chrisman. Trans. Constance Farrington. London: Longman.

Gonzalez, Madalena (2005) *Fiction after the Fatwa: Salman Rushdie and the Charm of Catastrophe.* Amsterdam: Rodopi.

Goopy Gyne Bagha Byne (1968) Dir. Satyajit Ray. Purnima Pictures, India.

Grotzfeld, Heinz (2004) 'The Manuscript Tradition of the Arabian Nights', in *The Arabian Nights Encyclopedia.* Ed. Ulrich Marzolph and Richard Van Leeuwen. Santa Barbara, CA: ABC-CLIO, 17–21.

Haddawy, Husain (ed. and trans.) (1992) *The Arabian Nights.* London: Everyman.

Herder, J. G. (1969) [1772] *Essay on the Origin of Language*, in *Herder on Social and Political Culture: A Selection of Texts*. Ed. and trans. F. M. Barnard. Cambridge: Cambridge University Press, 115–77.

— (1969) [1784–91] *Ideas for a Philosophy of the History of Mankind*, in *Herder on Social and Political Culture: A Selection of Texts*. Ed. and trans. F. M. Barnard. Cambridge: Cambridge University Press, 253–326.

Irwin, Robert (1994) *The Arabian Nights: A Companion*. London: Penguin.

Jani, Pranav (2010) *Decentering Rushdie: Cosmopolitanism and the Indian Novel in English*. Columbus: Ohio State University Press.

Kabbani, Rana (1986) *Europe's Myths of Orient*. Basingstoke: Macmillan.

— (2004) 'The Arabian Nights as an Orientalist Text', in *The Arabian Nights Encyclopedia*. Ed. Ulrich Marzolph and Richard Van Leeuwen. Santa Barbara, CA: ABC-CLIO 25–9.

Kamenetsky, Christa (1992) *The Brothers Grimm and Their Critics*. Athens: Ohio University Press.

Kumar, Thirupathi G. (2007) *Conceptualising Tradition: A Study of Raja Rao, R. K. Narayan and Mulk Raj Anand*. New Delhi: India Research Press.

Lang, Andrew (ed.) (1890) *The Red Fairy Book*. London: Longmans.

Lazarus, Neil (1990) *Resistance in Postcolonial African Fiction*. New Haven: Yale University Press.

Ngugi wa Thiong'o (1993) *Moving the Centre: The Struggle for Cultural Freedoms*. Oxford: James Currey.

Rao, Raja (1989) [1938] *Kanthapura*. Oxford: Oxford University Press.

Reder, Michael (ed.) (2000) *Conversations with Salman Rushdie*. Jackson: University of Mississippi Press.

Robinson, Andrew (1989) *Satyajit Ray: The Inner Eye*. London: Andre Deutsch.

Seifert, Lewis (1996) *Fairy Tales, Sexuality and Gender in France 1690–1715: Nostalgic Utopias*. Cambridge: Cambridge University Press.

Teverson, Andrew (2001) 'Fairy Tale Politics: Issues of Free Speech and Multiculturalism in Salman Rushdie's *Haroun and the Sea of Stories*', *Twentieth Century Literature* 47.4 (Winter): 444–66.

— (2008) 'Migrant Fictions: Salman Rushdie and Fairy Tale', in *The Fairy Tale in Contemporary Literature*. Ed. Stephen Benson. Detroit, MI: Wayne State University Press.

Thompson, Stith and Balys, Jonas (1958) *The Oral Tales of India*. Bloomington: Indiana University Press.

Thompson, Stith and Warren Roberts (1960) *Types of Indic Oral Tales: India, Pakistan and Ceylon*. FF Communications 180. Helsinki: Suomalainen Tiedeakatemia Academia Scientiarum Fennica.

Uther, Hans-Jörg (2004) *The Types of International Folktales*. 3 Parts. FF Communications 284. Helsinki: Suomalainen Tiedeakatemia Academia Scientiarum Fennica.

Zipes, Jack (ed. and trans.) (1989) *Beauties Beasts and Enchantments: Classic French Fairy Tales*. New York: Penguin.

— (ed. and trans.) (1992) *The Complete Fairy Tales of the Brothers Grimm*. New York: Bantam.

Chapter Seven: 'Illuminated by a ray of the sun at midnight', Martin McQuillan

Cixous, Hélène (2006) in Jacques Derrida, *Geneses, Genealogies, Genres and Genius: The Secrets of the Archive*. Trans. Beverley Bie Brahic. Edinburgh: Edinburgh University Press.

Derrida, Jacques (2002) 'The University Without Condition', in *Without Alibi*. Trans. Peggy Kamuf. Stanford: Stanford University Press.

Johnson, Barbara (1987) 'Rigorous Unreliability', in *A World of Difference*. Baltimore, MD: John Hopkins University Press.

Nabokov, Vladimir (1955) *Lolita*. London: Weidenfield & Nicolson.

Chapter Eight: Rushdie's Non-Fiction, Daniel O'Gorman

Ali, Tariq (2002) 'The New Empire Loyalists', *The Guardian*, 16 March, www.guardian.co.uk/world/2002/mar/16/usa.comment.

Appignanesi, L. (2005) *Free Expression Is No Offence*. London: Penguin.

BBC News (2006) 'Full Text: Writers' Statement on Cartoons', 1 March, http://news.bbc.co.uk/1/hi/world/europe/4764730.stm.

Bhabha, H. (1994) *The Location of Culture*. Oxford: Routledge.

Boycott, O. (2011) 'Killing Unarmed Osama bin Laden 'Doesn't Serve Justice' – Rowan Williams', *Guardian*, 6 May, www.guardian.co.uk/world/2011/may/06/osama-bin-laden-killing.

Bradley, A. and Tate, A. (2010) *The New Atheist Novel: Fiction, Philosophy and Polemic After 9/11*. London: Continuum.

Cilano, C. (ed.) (2009) *From Solidarity to Schisms: 9/11 and after in Fiction and Film from Outside the US*. Amsterdam and New York: Rodopi.

Derrida, J. (1994) *Specters of Marx: The State of the Debt, the Work of Mourning, and the New International*. Trans. Peggy Kamuf. London and New York: Routledge.

Donadio, R. (2007) 'Salman Rushdie: Fighting Words on a Knighthood', *New York Times* 3 July, www.nytimes.com/2007/07/04/arts/04iht-15donadio.6482640.html.

Guldberg, H. (2008) 'The Shame of Salman Rushdie's Secular Fatwa', *Spiked* 27 August, www.spiked-online.com/index.php?/site/article/5651/.

Hitchens, C. (2010) BBC Radio interview, www.youtube.com/watch?v=P5G coi0J-DI.

Malik, K. (2009) *From Fatwa to Jihad: The Rushdie Affair and Its Legacy*. London: Atlantic.

Pearsall, J. (ed.) (2001) *The Concise Oxford Dictionary*. New York: Oxford University Press, 10th ed.

Pipes, D. (2004) 'Salman Rushdie, Man of the Left', 10 August, www.daniel-pipes.org/blog/2004/08/salman-rushdie-man-of-the-left.

Sardar, Z. (2006) 'Welcome to Planet Blitcon', *New Statesman* 11 December, www.newstatesman.com/200612110045.

Sawhney, S., and S. Sawhney (2001), 'Reading Rushdie after September 11, 2001 (Introduction)', *Twentieth Century Literature* 47.4: 431+.

Chapter Nine: Po-fa: *Joseph Anton*, Robert Eaglestone

Trousdale, Rachel (2010) *Nabokov, Rushdie, and the Transnational Imagination: Novels of Exile and Alternate Worlds*. New York: Palgrave Macmillan.

Mishra, Pankaj (2012) 'Review of Joseph Anton', *Guardian* 18 September.

Jacques Derrida. Jacques (1996) *Archive Fever*. Trans. Eric Prenowitz. Chicago: University of Chicago Press.

Works by Salman Rushdie Referred to in This Book

Grimus (1975) London: Gollancz.

Midnight's Children (1981) London: Vintage.

Shame (1983) London: Jonathan Cape.

The Satanic Verses (1988) London: Viking.

Desert Island Discs, BBC Radio 4, 8 September 1988.

Haroun and the Sea of Stories (1990) London: Viking.

Imaginary Homelands: Essays and Criticism: 1981–1991 (1991) London: Granta.

Imaginary Homelands: Essays and Criticism: 1981–1991 (1992) London: Granta.

The Moor's Last Sigh (1995) London: Jonathan Cape.

'Salman Rushdie in Conversation with David Tushingham' (1998) Theatre Programme. *Haroun and the Sea of Stories*. Tim Supple (dir.), National Theatre, Cottesloe, 1 October, np.

The Ground Beneath Her Feet (1999) London: Jonathan Cape.

Salman Rushdie Interviews: A Sourcebook of His Ideas (2001) Ed. Pradyumna S. Chahan. Westport, CT: Greenwood Press.

Fury (2001) London: Jonathan Cape.

Shalimar the Clown (2005) London: Jonathan Cape.

Step across this Line: Collected Non-Fiction 1992–2002 (2003) London: Vintage.

The Jaguar Smile: A Nicaraguan Journey ([1987] 2007) London: Vintage.

The Enchantress of Florence (2008) London: Jonathan Cape.

Luka and the Fire of Life (2010) London: Jonathan Cape.

'Pakistan's Deadly Game' (2011) *The Daily Beast*, May 2.

'Salman Rushdie on Luka and the Fire of Life' (2010b) at Amazon.com

Joseph Anton: A Memoir (2012) London: Jonathan Cape.

Index

University of Brighton

C21: Centre for Twenty-First Century Writings

Affiliated with Bloomsbury

*Pioneering approaches to and understandings of
twenty-first century writings*

The first decade of the new millennium witnessed a range of exciting developments in contemporary writings in English. From innovations in recognised forms such as the novel, poem, play and short story to developments in digital writings, creative writings and genres. Alongside these developments, the publishing industry also changed, with technological advances giving rise to the dawn of the eBook and corporate sponsorship igniting debates about the usefulness of literary prizes and festivals. As the first Research Centre dedicated to the study of twenty-first century writings, C21 offers a unique research environment that is a hub for wider networks of research in this emerging field.

For more information visit arts.brighton.ac.uk/research/c21

To find out about the Centre journal *C21 Literature: Journal of 21st-Century Writings*
Visit our blog: c21literature.blogspot.co.uk
🐦 Follow us on Twitter: @C21Literature @Bloomsburylit